Mandela's Children

Growing Up in
Post-Apartheid
South Africa

Mandela's
Children

Oscar A. Barbarin
Linda M. Richter

Routledge
New York • London

Published in 2001 by

Routledge
29 West 35th Street
New York, NY 10001

Published in Great Britain by

Routledge
11 New Fetter Lane
London EC4P 4EE

Routledge is an imprint of the Taylor & Francis Group.

Printed in the United States of America on acid-free
paper.

The passage on p. 123 of chapter 5 is republished with permission of the
Johannesburg-based Saturday Star.

Library of Congress Cataloging-in-Publication Data

Barbarin, Oscar A.
  Mandela's children : growing up in post-apartheid South Africa / Oscar A.
Barbarin, Linda M. Richter.
      p. cm.
  Includes bibliographical references and index.
  ISBN 0-415-92468-5 — ISBN 0-415-92469-3 (pbk.)
    1. Child development—South Africa. 2. Child welfare—South Africa. 3.
Apartheid—South Africa. 4. Children—Crimes against—South Africa. 5.
Family policy—South Africa. 6. South Africa—Social conditions—20th cen-
tury. 7. South Africa—Politics and government—1994– I. Richter, Linda M.
II. Title.

  HQ778.7.S6 B37 2000
  305.231'0968—dc21

                                                        00-031134

To the memory of

Florence Morodi
Born November 30, 1962
Died November 12, 1997

Birth-to-Ten interviewer, courageous and dedicated single mother of 10-year-old Naledi. In her brief but fruitful life, she was an exemplar of the mothers of the children whose stories fill the pages that follow.

Contents

List of Figures

Acknowledgments

The success of a large, complex longitudinal study such as Birth-to-Ten (BTT) is rarely accomplished by a single individual. It requires the teamwork, give-and-take, trust, and dedication of many talented individuals. Birth-to-Ten is no exception. More than thirty investigators have been involved in the development and implementation of BTT. They brought vision, considerable energy, and a high level of research skill to this effort. Included among them are: Noel Cameron, Lucy Wagstaff, Peter Cooper, James McIntyre, Yasmin von Schirnding, Nicky Padayachee, Sharon Fonn, John Pettifor, Derek Yach, Dev Griesel, and George Ellison. Several very dedicated women were the heart, soul, problem-solvers, and face of BTT to parents—Dr. Thea deWet, anthropologist and project manager, and the principal interviewers, Seipati Choene, Mantoa Langa, Meikie Leshomo, Barbara Manapote, Florence Morodi, Thabile Sibiya, and Eliza Tsoeu. They deserve special credit for the success of the project. In addition, Eileen Skuy, April Anderson, and Solly Ntswele were also very important to the day-to-day project administration and data management. Mr. Andries Phake was especially skilled and helpful in the interviews of children at age six and later.

The project has been supported principally by a grant from the Medical Research Council of South Africa and the Centre for Science Development, formerly in the Human Sciences Research Council. The continued support of these government agencies is a testimony to their foresight and concern for the nation's children. Additional support to project investigators has been provided by the University of the Witwatersrand, the Independent Development Trust, the Chairman's Fund for Educational Trust, Liberty Life, Kentucky Fried Chicken, Delmas Milling, Liqui-Fruit, and Anglo-American.

Most of the analysis presented here was performed by Oscar Barbarin during his tenure as Executive Director of the University of Michigan's South Africa Initiative Office. Much appreciation is due to the University for its international vision and its civic responsibility in forging mutually beneficial relations in South Africa. Special thanks are for the able support provided by Linda Russell, administrative associate, who became a lifeline during my long trips to South Africa; to Serena Williams for assistance in compiling the history of racism in South Africa; and to Lester Monts, Associate Provost, and the Office of the Vice President for Research for their generous financial and moral support of this work.

The hands, hearts, and minds of many highly competent people were involved in the production of this book. The debt of gratitude owed to them cannot be easily repaid. Their contributions have made it a much better book than it otherwise would have been. We will single out a few for special mention. Terri Torkko provided very skilled and competent editorial assistance. Her careful reading of the manuscript and thoughtful questions helped us to communicate more clearly. We are also deeply appreciative of Heidi Freund from Routledge, whose early enthusiasm for this book and whose patience in seeing it through to completion will earn a special place for her in publishers' heaven. A word of thanks to Andy Dawes, friend, colleague, and courageous advocate for children, who has taught us so much by word and by deed about true commitment to children.

Finally, we thank our families: the Barbarins and the Richter-Griesels. They tolerated with grace and forbearance the many hours we stole away from family time to do this book. Thanks for the love and acceptance of Isabel, Oscar-David, Olivia, and Andrea in the Barbarin family and of Dev and Stefan in the Richter-Griesel family.

Chapter 1

Social Transformation and Child Development in South Africa

On February 11, 1990, after twenty-eight years of confinement, Nelson Mandela walked from prison to freedom. In doing so, he set into motion a wave of change that was to sweep over South Africa and give hope to millions of blacks who suffered under the yoke of oppression. News of his release became a cause for celebration as South Africans and the world anticipated that peace and justice would return to a land torn apart by the violence of apartheid. The political change signaled by Mandela's release also raised hope that life would be better for future generations of South Africans. Several months later, a group of more than three thousand infants born in Johannesburg-Soweto became known as "Mandela's children" because their births so closely followed upon Mandela's release and the renewal of hope. Appearing on the scene at the dawn of this remarkable period of transformation, they symbolized the beginning of an era in which the nation would cherish its children irrespective of language, culture, or skin color. Because they would never directly know the sting of apartheid, they embodied the unblemished possibilities for the new South Africa. If this grand vision became a reality, they would become the first generation of a rainbow society in which people of all colors might live together in harmony as equals under the law. Under these newly hospitable conditions, it was hoped that Mandela's children would flourish and the nation would prosper. With the passage of time, questions arise about how far they have come toward realizing those optimistic dreams and fulfilling those noble aspirations for its children. Would the promise of freedom lift the living conditions of the oppressed and improve the developmental status of their children? For some, the early answers to these questions are disappointing. Consider the case of Ibrahim and his son, Issak, whose lives were lost as part of the tragic cost of poverty and despair that continue to haunt South Africa in the post-apartheid era.

Ibrahim and Issak

The hope and exuberance following Mandela's release and the joyous demise of apartheid was not enough to salvage the lives of Ibrahim, and his son, Issak.

Little joy could be found in the sight of the father and his little son, whose lives and deaths symbolized the desperation and poverty of so many others. No one who picked up the *Sowetan* newspaper on a winter's morning in September 1999 could help but be moved by what they saw and read. On the front page was a disturbing image of two bodies, a thirty-three-year-old man we will call Ibrahim and his three-year-old son, Issak. Both were hanging lifeless by ropes from the bedroom ceiling of their home. According to his family, Ibrahim had grown increasingly despondent under the pressures of being without work and without the means to provide for even the most basic needs of his son. For a long time, he depended on his extended family for food and a place to live. Ultimately, the pain became too much for Ibrahim to bear. Ibrahim first hung Issak, then took his own life. What must have been running through his mind as he slipped the rope around Issak's neck and tightened the noose? Ibrahim understood clearly that if he were to end his own misery he must end his son's life as well. He must spare Issak the pain that would otherwise come from being an unwanted burden to others who were already destitute. What was Issak thinking as he trustingly allowed his father to lift him up before letting go? Did Issak resist or did he submissively accept the fate Ibrahim had chosen for the two of them? Did Issak cry out to Ibrahim for help as the rope tightened around his neck and choked the life out of his body?

Though many readers may have directly experienced poverty and hardship themselves, it was difficult for most to appreciate how the pain and hopelessness of poverty could become so intense that Ibrahim would be willing to give up his own life and surrender the life of his child. They did understand how the devastating consequence of poverty and a father's despair was symbolized in the two bodies hung side by side, bound together by death because life was too difficult. The haunting image made a stark and powerful statement about how deep the pain and suffering of poverty can become. It is a testament of the hidden psychological costs for parents and the price that children ultimately pay.

Ibrahim and his son were casualties in an unsuccessful struggle against deprivation and poverty. This same battle continues to be waged on many fronts and in many homes throughout South Africa. The challenges faced by the poor in trying to meet their basic needs, sustain life, and promote children's development are daunting. Some people might draw comfort by asserting that the confluence of circumstances and conditions that resulted in the premature deaths of Ibrahim and Issak are unusual and atypical in South Africa. Such an assertion would be falsely reassuring. Although the lives of most poor children fortunately will not end in as dramatic and tragic a manner as Isaak's, many parents and children face very similar conditions of hardship. An intolerable number of South African children live in such dire economic straits that, like Issak, they lack the resources to provide to themselves ready access to such basic necessities as shelter, food, and water. There are more than 3.2 million South African children who are in the age category between zero and three years in which, like Issak, they are most vulnerable to the adverse effects of the social environment. Twelve out of every one hundred South African children die before they reach five years of age, and a quarter of children are stunted because of long-term under nutrition (Wigton et al. 1997). Approximately 42,000 children are in residential or foster care (Kruger and Motala 1997), one in five children in South Africa does not live with either of their parents, and one in three children under the age of sixteen years does not live with their mother (Lund 1996). Between a third and half of all children fail once during their first few years of school (Gordon 1996). Moreover, South Africa has passed on to these children a legacy of racism and inequality that will continue to be a part of their lives for the foreseeable future.

Though many families migrate to urban areas to improve their lives, many observers suspected that the forces of urbanization may have the paradoxical effect of lowering the quality of life of young children. Few data were available to corroborate those suspicions. It is clear that society has a stake in better understanding the dimensions of the strains that affect the lives of urban children and their families. Moreover, there is a societal interest in finding ways to ease children's burdens and provide them with a fighting chance at attaining normal development. Data were needed to develop an accurate picture of the status of children and the scope of the problems that government must address. These conditions and needs provided the motivation for conducting a study of children growing up in urban areas, a project that came to be known as Birth-to-Ten (BTT).

Birth-to-Ten: Tracing the Development of Mandela's Children

The purpose of BTT was to gather systematic observations on the physical growth and developmental status of urban children over time. Earlier work has been done on rural children (e.g. Goduka, Ivy, Pole, and Aotaki-Phenice, 1992). However little systematic work has been done in urban areas. Consequently, BTT was designed as a longitudinal birth cohort study of Mandela's children. The Johannesburg-Soweto metropolitan area in Gauteng province was selected as the site of the study. BTT would attempt to answer questions about the life prospects and developmental outcomes of children whose lives were unfolding in a period of great stress and social change. Thus a principal goal of the BTT study was to track the survival, health, well-being, growth, and psychosocial development of children living in urban settings. As part of its scholarly efforts, it would identify the biological, environmental, economic, and psychological factors that account for developmental differences from their births in 1990 to age ten (Fonn et al. 1991; Yach et al. 1991). The data from those observations would help detect important trends and risks as well as identify which segments of the population experienced suboptimal development. In this way the study could alert policy makers about the extent to which the health and development of children was being compromised, and the role of specific social factors in children's health and well-being. Core support for BTT was provided through the Urbanization and Health Program within the Medical Research Council of South Africa and the Center for Science Development within the Human Sciences Research Council. The study also received supplemental funding from several university and private donors.

In spite of the many positive changes that have occurred in South Africa since their births, the beneficence of the conditions in which Mandela's children live still varies greatly, as do the developmental outcomes they experience. BTT was begun with the belief that knowledge about how variations in the child's social situation are linked to child development would lead to insights about ways to prevent problems among children who would otherwise be at risk of poor developmental outcomes. It was expected that data from this project might lead to creative ways to offset potentially negative developmental outcomes, neutralize the effects of social risks, and promote the full development of every child. In addition, because of its fortuitous timing at the advent of political transformation, it was hoped that BTT would offer a view of the positive and negative impact of social and political change on the development of children.

Variations in family and community life are believed to contribute to children's physical, psychological, and social development. By tracking children from the time of their birth, BTT presents a rare opportunity to interrogate the relationships among social transformation, social environment, and child development. Thus data from studies such as BTT can test the accuracy of assumptions about which of these influences promote resilience and which constitute sources of risk. By its design and scope, BTT can open an unusual window to how children and families deal with the strains and opportunities of change and adjust in ways that help them to develop normally. BTT has made it possible to probe into the key socializing processes impacting the lives of children and has provided information about the possible sources of resilience within children themselves, their families, and their communities. Moreover, it may provide a firmer basis for speculations about whether children continue on a current course of development and what may divert them to a better or less desirable path. In this regard, the study is without peer on the entire continent of Africa. Moreover, few longitudinal studies have been conducted anywhere on so many children of African descent.

Participating Children

The greater Johannesburg-Soweto metropolitan area, the site of BTT, consists of four main, historically determined subdivisions: the commercial inner-city areas of central Johannesburg; the leafy white suburbs with freestanding, individually designed houses; the areas formerly designated for Colored and Indian people, which combine both wealth and poverty in modified township and owner-built houses; and Soweto. The sampling procedure was designed to yield a group of children who would be representative of the universe of children growing up in this metropolitan area. A detailed description of the sampling design and outcome is presented in several previous publications (Richter et al. 1995). Identification of the sample universe of newborns was facilitated by a local government ordinance that requires that the health authorities be informed of all births. These notification records were used initially to identify the cohort and later to assess how closely the final sample came to representing the entire universe of newborns on critical demographic variables (Anderson and Richter 1994). The information extracted from notifications is recorded in official birth registers maintained by local health authorities. The notification forms vary slightly between health authorities and from one health facility to another. However, notification forms used in the Soweto-Johannesburg area include all or most of the following information: mother's name, surname, address, telephone number, parity, age, marital and employment status, and the results of blood tests conducted during the pregnancy. The date, place, time, and type of delivery, and the identity of the health professionals attending the delivery of the child are also recorded, together with the infant's sex, birth weight, estimated gestational age, Apgar scores, and mortality status at birth. Information about the mother's ethnicity[1] is obtained verbally from the mother or copied from preexisting clinic records and identity documents.

Enrollment and Attrition

The study cohort included all children born between April 23 and June 8, 1990. Since many mothers received prenatal care, it was possible to identify and recruit parents as early as six months prior to the child's birth through the local antenatal health clinics. Consequently, enrollment into the study took place over a fifteen-month period, beginning prenatally (at the clinic visit coinciding with a gestational age of twenty-six weeks) and extending up to twelve months after delivery. Mothers or primary caregivers were interviewed and infant assessments made one or more times—antenatally, at delivery, and at six months and one year postnatal. An archival review of the birth notifications for the designated seven-week period from April 23 to June 8, 1990, uncovered more than 5,000 singleton births in the Johannesburg-Soweto area. Many of these births were to women who had permanent addresses outside of the study area. For example, women travel from their residences in rural areas for the superior medical care available in the metropolitan area but return to their homes after delivery. Only 3,275 children were established to have been born to women who actually were residents in the greater Johannesburg metropolitan area for at least the first six months of the child's life. Of these children and their families, 70 percent have been followed for eight years, indicating an average attrition rate of less than 4 percent per annum. Most attrition occurred in the first two years. In 1993, when the BTT cohort was three years old, a major effort was made to ascertain the whereabouts of all cohort members not enrolled to that date. Initial information on nonenrolled cases was available from birth notifications. Comparisons of enrolled and nonenrolled women suggest that in addition to race (or, more properly, population group membership), enrolled mothers were more likely to be younger and to have babies with average birth weights (2500–4000 g) than mothers who were not enrolled in the study (Richter et al. 1995). Nonenrollments occurred for one of the following reasons: stillbirths or early deaths of babies; adoption and abandonment of infants; maternal death; infants being sent to be cared for by relatives in rural areas; untraceable or false addresses; communication problems; and unavailability of the mother for interview because of the nature of her employment. From the more than three thousand families that were approached to participate in the study, only fifty-eight mothers did not consent.

The cohort design intentionally included all segments of the population, particularly with regard to social class and population group. BTT was very successful with respect to social class representation, but less so with regard to population group. The final cohort is more representative of black children formerly classified as African, Colored, and Indian, by virtue of the excellent retention rates of those groups over time. This is somewhat less true of children born to families classified as white. In light of the small number of white children in the population and the difficulty in recruiting and retaining them in the study, the generalizability of these findings to white children in South Africa is questionable. Therefore interpretation of the cohort data with respect to whites must be made with caution. Even with that limitation, the final BTT cohort provides a reasonably accurate representation of the majority of black children born in and growing up in the urban areas surrounding Johannesburg, with findings that are generalizable to other groups of urban children across South Africa.

Interview Methods

Interviews were conducted in person by one of nine African interviewers, seven women and two men. The interviewers were selected because of their multilingualism and their knowledge of the community; they are residents of the black township around which they travel and visit families. Several of the interviewers are active and well-known in their communities; some also have extensive professional experience with young children as teachers or coordinators of preschool or care programs for children. In the main, the same interviewers were involved in the multiple waves of data collection. Over the years, they tended to interview in the same sections of the metropolitan area and consequently became well-known to the mothers, the children, and their families. Interviewers were provided with a conceptual foundation for the content of the interviews and were trained in research interview methods. Quality control was maintained by a field supervisor who reviewed all completed interviews prior to data entry.

Families were notified before each scheduled contact (antenatal, delivery, six months postnatal, and one, two, four, five, and six years to date[2]) first by letters left at their homes requesting them to call to schedule an appointment for the mother and child to come in for personal interviews and a checkup at one of the local health facilities. A follow-up was made via telephone, mail, and a home visit to establish an appointment for them to come into the hospital or clinic. When it was inconvenient for parents to come to the clinic, or when families could not be reached by post or telephone, interviewers went to their homes in the evenings or over weekends. Parents were told that it would take about two hours to complete the interview and to assess the child's physical and psychological development. At the interview, R5 (less than $1) was given to the caregiver to defray the cost of public transportation to the interview site. In addition, food and beverages were provided to caregivers and the children who came into the clinics. More often than not, mothers accompanied their child to the interview; in some cases both parents arrived, or the child was brought by a grandmother if she was the regular caregiver. Interviews with the father alone or other primary caregivers occurred in those instances in which the mother works and was not excused by her employer. At the time of the interview, anthropometric measures were made of the child, and several cognitive tests were administered. Parents were asked to provide information about the family's social and economic status, child-rearing expectations and practices, as well as health experiences, illnesses, and injuries. Ratings of child behavior and adjustment were also obtained through self-report of the parent. At the end of the interviews, small gifts such as special BTT calendars and pencils were given to the parent and child as a token of appreciation. When problems were noted in the interviews, children and parents were referred to medical, educational, and/or social services for follow-up.

Interview Language

In the initial stage of the project, the questionnaires (see Appendix) were designed in English and then translated and rechecked in the three other major languages spoken in South Africa: isiZulu, Sesotho, and Afrikaans. However, because of the proximity and frequent interactions among speakers of the eleven most common languages in South Africa, the vernacular of urban Africans is not a pure form of any single language. In daily usage, words from multiple languages, including English, can be interspersed with one another. For this reason, the wording used in questionnaires and in the interviews was adapted to reflect colloquial speech. The minority of families whose native language was other than one of the four major languages used in the study were interviewed by a native speaker of that language. In these cases, the interviewer worked from a questionnaire in one of the main South African languages and translated the questions for the families. Once they had received training in the purpose of the inter-view and the concepts underlying each question, multilingual inter-viewers reached a consensus about phrasings for the questions for each language group, which they then used consistently.

Measuring Development

Extensive baseline data on physical growth, psychological develop-ment, and family life were collected within the first year of life and in follow-up data waves in 1992, 1994, and 1995. The longitudinal data collected over ten years by the BTT project have made it possible to track and characterize patterns of change and continuity for children in seven domains: (1) health and physical growth; (2) household com-position and family functioning; (3) community environment; (4) externalizing problems; (5) emotional difficulties; (6) academic adjustment; and (7) social competence and maturity. At each point of data collection, a core questionnaire was administered to the parents as part of an interview. The interviews were used to gather information on the health histories of the children and their parents, the family and household composition, the children's development and care, and the caregivers' stresses and social support. Questions were included to characterize the economic well-being and the social status of the family. These items correspond to questions widely used in scales to assess socioeconomic status (SES) and standard of living. They are relevant to the current study in that they provide a gauge of material hardship endured by a family. Additional information on children's health and psychosocial development, family functioning, and community violence was gathered using methods other than inter-views, such as physical examinations, psychological testing, school observation, and archival data. Questions focused on, among other things, the social and economic conditions of families, the stresses and social supports experienced by caregivers, the mortality and morbidity of the children, and their physical growth, as well as their psychologi-cal development and behavioral adjustment (Yach et al., 1991).

Questionnaires were kept short, with questions simply stated and focused to be suitable for studying a multilingual population of respondents with varying educational levels. Exposure to *stressful life events* was assessed antenatally as well as when children were age five years. The stressful events rating scale covered such issues as exposure to violence and injury, standard of living and debt, social maladjust-ment, and family discord. *Social support* was measured, antenatally and at five years, using an eight-item rating scale adapted from the

Inventory of Socially Supportive Behaviors (Barrera and Ainley 1983), to address dimensions of social support relevant to women in South Africa (Bozzolli 1991; Wilson and Ramphele 1989). The rating scale covered material support, emotional support, and affiliation. Mothers completed the twenty-four-item Pitt Depression Inventory (Pitt 1968) to assess *maternal depression* and *emotional distress* when their infants were six months old. *Maternal responsiveness* to the infant was assessed during interviews with the caregiver during the first year, using the framework created by Clarke-Stewart (1973). *Infant temperament* was rated at six months and one year of age, on a ten-item scale based on the Infant Temperament Questionnaire (Carey 1970) and modified as a result of a pilot study of a sample of nine-month-old African infants (Richter 1987). The emphasis in the shortened scale was on the assessment of perceived infant "difficultness" (Bugental and Shennum 1984). *Behavior problems* were rated at two, four, and five years of age on a twelve-item rating scale based on the Behavioral Screening Checklist (Earls and Jung 1987; Richman and Graham 1970). Behaviors covered included bladder and bowel control, speech, appetite, sleep, behavior management, mood, activity level, fears and habits, peer interaction, and aggression. *Developmental level* was assessed at six months, one, two, four, and five years. At six months and one year, the Bayley Scales of Infant Development (Bayley 1969) were administered; at two and four years, the Vineland Social Maturity Scale (Doll 1965); and at five years, the Denver Developmental Scales II (Frankenburg et al. 1990) were completed. Children were interviewed about smoking in their environment and their experience of schooling, particularly with regard to aggression and conduct problems. Anthropometric and developmental measures were administered to the child at each point. Anthropometric measures included weight, height, body fat, and bone density. Blood samples were taken to monitor nutritional and health status.

Table 1.1 presents selected psychosocial and developmental measures from the BTT study that can be tested in longitudinal models of adolescent reproductive health risk. These scales provide important information about the early developmental context of the youth, particularly regarding the quality of the family and the community environments of early child-rearing. Moreover, these data make possible an unusually complete documentation of the developmental trajectories of youth from infancy to preadolescence with respect to social competence, social maturity, externalizing disorders, emotional or internalizing problems, academic adjustment, and physical growth. These measures are described in greater detail in subsequent chapters, where the data from the measures are presented and discussed.

Table 1.1: Measures Used in the Birth-to-Ten Longitudinal Study, Times Administered, and Informants

Development up to Age 10	Data Waves	Informant/Method
Bayley Scales (Infant Development)	6 m, 1 yr	Psychometrician
Carey Infant Temperament	6 m, 1 yr	Parent/Questionnaire
Maternal Responsiveness	1 yr	Observational Rating
Child Care	1, 2, 4, 5 yrs	Parent/Interview
Anthropometric Data	6 m, 1, 2, 4, 5, 7, 10 yrs	Physical Measurement
Hunger, Stunting, Wasting	1, 2, 5, 7, 10 yrs	Physical Measurement
Behavioral Screening Checklist	2, 4, 5 yrs	Parent/Questionnaire
Vineland Social Maturity Scale	2, 4 yrs	Parent/Questionnaire
Denver Developmental Scales	5 yrs	Parent/Questionnaire
Behavior Problem Index	6, 7, 10 yrs	Parent/Questionnaire
SACAS—Competence Scales	6, 7, 10 yrs	Parent/Questionnaire
Connor's Scale (School Adjustment)	7, 10 yrs	Teacher/Questionnaire
Family Relations Scale	6, 10 yrs	Family/Questionnaire
Household Composition, Structure	1, 2, 5, 7, 10 yrs	Parent/Interview
Maternal Distress/ Depression	6 m, 1 yr	Parent/Questionnaire
Social Support	1, 5, 10 yrs	Parent/Questionnaire
Socioeconomic Status	2, 5, 7, 10 yrs	Parent/Questionnaire
Community Violence	1, 5, 10 yrs	Key Informant Rating

Using these measures, the longitudinal information gathered in the BTT will permit us to reach more definitive answers about how well Mandela's children have fared in the early phase of their lives, and the social risks and resources that might account for those outcomes. Thus information gathered about children and their families in the BTT is likely to reveal a great deal about the adequacy of conditions under which children are growing up and the influence of these on children.

Social Change, Political Reform, and Development

The family exerts an important influence over child development. Not an island unto itself, the family exists within a matrix of social forces that shapes family organization, values, and functioning. The political transition that began in 1990 and culminated in the 1994 elections was undoubtedly important, but it was not the only wave of change engulfing the nation, transforming family life and influencing the climate of child development. At play are other secular trends and social transformations that challenge prevailing norms about gender roles and alter family structure and community life. Specifically, family and community life are being reconfigured by a host of demographic and social transformations that include: urbanization; modernity; a weakening of traditional gender roles; the AIDS pandemic; racial inequality; poverty; black political empowerment; and community violence. These trends have resulted in major changes that have left family and community life in South Africa reeling in a period of uncertainty and cultural ambiguity. The issues raise difficult questions about the meaning of family, the utility of time-worn cultural mores and traditions, and the fairness of gender-based prerogatives. In addition, they are profoundly affecting the lives of South African children by altering assumptions about the meaning of childhood, and are sharpening sensitivities to children's developmental rights and needs. These social changes and their relationships to family functioning and child development are depicted in figure 1.1. This figure suggests that they influence family structure and organization, family functioning, and family relationships, which in turn impact outcomes of child development. If the relationships predicted in figure 1.1 are accurate, the prospects for the healthy development of children like Issak will depend greatly on their families' responses to the strains and challenges of social transformation, inequality, violence, and securing material need, and its maintenance of close, nurturing, and stable relationships.

It is also important to weigh how much past adversity has retained its hold on South Africa and maintained an inauspicious climate for development. On one hand, children growing up in South Africa may be exposed to numerous social risks, including apartheid's legacy of social inequality and deprivation. A combination of economic hardship and limited access to supportive services creates lethal conditions in the lives of poor children, and may obstruct their academic progress and emotional development. Associated with economic hardship are varied forms of violence: political, community, and familial. The sequelae of these conditions accumulate across the life span: increased morbidity and mortality, mood disturbances, academic underachievement, aggression, premature sexuality and childbearing, substance abuse, delinquency, underemployment, high rates of divorce, and instability of family life. An understanding of risk and protective factors, as well as of the internal emotionally regulating capacities of the developing child, are important pieces of the puzzle to be solved.

Figure 1.1: Social and Familial Context of Child Development in South Africa

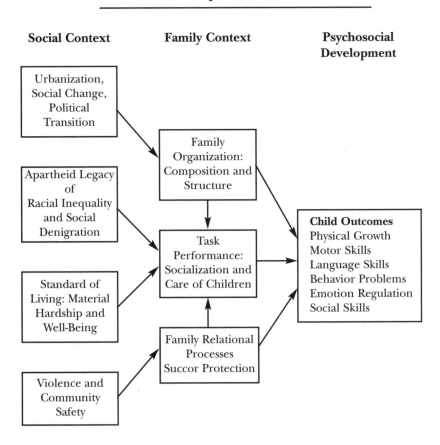

As a balance to this dire view of the conditions faced by South African children, we note the optimism and hope among many South African parents that arises from political empowerment and which is justified by cultural resources within families: tradition, deep spirituality, nurturing family relationships, a favorable African identity, a sense of continuity with the past, and newfound freedom resulting from the transition to a multiracial democracy. To make sense of the future prospects of Mandela's children, it is necessary to analyze how urbanization and the social changes associated with modernity alter the family roles and functioning and impact the lives and development of children. We are uncertain whether these concomitant social changes strengthen hope or constitute ominous clouds on the horizon of South African children. The nature and influence of these social factors must be examined more fully if we are to characterize accurately the prospects facing the children of South Africa. They are described below, with the exception of material disadvantage and community violence, which are addressed fully in subsequent chapters.

Urbanization

South Africa is in the midst of a secular transition from a mostly rural to a predominantly urban society. Already one of the developing world's most urban societies, with over 54 percent of its population resident in metropolitan areas, South Africa's population is moving toward the cities in increasing numbers. As noted earlier, one impetus for BTT was a concern about the consequences for children of the massive influx of black people to urban areas as they seek employment and escape from rural poverty. Families were drawn to urban centers in the hope of improved access to health services, education, decent housing, water, sanitation, and employment. For many people, these hopes have only been partially realized as they encounter new problems of urban crowding, political violence, and crime. Little is known about how the social and cultural dislocation resulting from rapid urbanization impacts families and young children. Community life is second only to family life in shaping children's development. If the hope of the post-apartheid transformation is to become a reality, it must take root in the overpopulated townships and the central-city communities that are home to a large proportion of the nation's black children. In order to understand how risks and hopes balance within the lives of African children, one needs to be acquainted with and understand urban townships as the principal developmental context of black children. While urbanization began in the late nineteenth

century in response to the discovery of gold and diamonds, it accelerated early in the 1980s. At this time the desperation of rural poverty
led many blacks to openly defy the restrictive apartheid influx control
and homeland policies, and to migrate to urban settings in search of a
better way of life for themselves and their children. The possibilities of
employment and improved standards of living, particularly with
respect to health and educational services for children, were powerful
magnets drawing families to urban centers. The new arrivals swelled
the ranks of urban townships,[3] straining their resources and infrastructure.

Living Conditions in Townships
Although the lives they left in the rural areas were exceedingly difficult, few people found life in Soweto much easier. In a story that is
familiar in burgeoning urban areas around the developing world,
most of these new arrivals experienced conditions that can best be
described as infelicitous and harsh. Along with the overwhelming
majority of urban residents who preceded them, they lived under conditions of poverty and extreme material deprivation. Families faced a
variety of stressors seldom anticipated when they first contemplated
new lives in urban areas. Inadequate shelter and health-threatening
environmental conditions presented the most significant challenges to
families. Some of the more fortunate émigrés from rural areas found
a relative to stay with in one of the cramped brick government houses.
For the many others without relatives who could take them in, the
informal settlements or squatter communities in the black townships
were the most likely destinations. The new arrivals showed great
resourcefulness in creating dwellings fashioned out of cardboard, plastic, sticks, and galvanized steel panels. Most of these squatter camps,
which could rise up on vacant land overnight, initially lacked running
water and toilet facilities of any type. Some shacks were colorfully decorated and the dirt floors swept clear of loose dirt. Others were glum
and colorless. No matter how well they were constructed and kept up,
or how creatively appointed and decorated, these informal houses
were makeshift and located in areas with significant problems, not the
least of which was their vulnerability to inclement weather and their
placement near major roads, landfills, and factories. Pollution and
lack of sanitation posed additional health risks to people living in
these shanty or "squatter" settlements. During the rainy season, residents in these settlements often slept in chairs to avoid the water cov-
ering the floors. Urban living brought with it many other threats to
health, including pulmonary diseases from smoke and pollution, and
neurological deficits associated with air polluted by mine dust, coal-

burning stoves, industrial toxins, and lead in gasoline and cheap paint. The lack of water and sanitation and the close living conditions of high-density areas fueled the spread of infectious diseases, including gastroenteritis and tuberculosis.

Living Conditions outside of Townships

Black urban life is not limited to residence in townships created under apartheid. Blacks can also be found living as domestic servants in back-yards, rooms, and garages of affluent homes located in prosperous white suburbs, and in decaying hotels or office buildings converted to apartments close to the center of town. Domestics are often women, sometimes married, sometimes not, with children who live with them in a single room. In the rooms can usually be found water for washing and a hotplate for cooking. These rooms are usually sparsely furnished with a table, a few chairs, and mats on the floor for sleeping. Children who live with their parents in these areas attend schools that are arguably better than those found in the townships. They spend much of their time in restricted areas of the house and yard and out on the streets of the neighborhood. Their poverty is softened by the lushness of the physical space they share with the affluent, but at the same time their destitution is rendered more psychologically stinging by its contrast to the abundance that surrounds them.

Blacks also live in increasing numbers in central areas of the city of Johannesburg. The massive rural-to-urban migration and the dissolution of residential restrictions on blacks have also brought about shifts in the makeup of inner-city areas within Johannesburg that were formerly restricted to whites. Desperate for housing and eager to be closer to their jobs in the town, blacks poured into the inner-city area of Johannesburg into such districts as Joubert Park, the central business district, and nearby areas of the city such as Hillbrow and Yeoville. In a story of white flight and urban decay that is very familiar in many American cities, as the number of blacks in the inner city increased, whites fled to more remote suburbs and businesses soon followed. In their wake was left an inner city whose decline was inevitable under the weight of an influx of a largely poor population forced to live in overcrowded conditions as they lined the pockets of slum landlords determined to extract as much revenue as possible out of properties and to invest little or nothing in their upkeep and repair. Property owners were quite inventive as they squeezed multiple families into apartments designed for many fewer people and into office space carved into multiple living areas as businesses abandoned the inner city. What appear on the outside to be somewhat aging office buildings are in fact slum tenements. Inside are unspeakable conditions of squalor, with multiple families cramped into unsanitary living quarters fashioned from what was a single-room office. Large numbers of families share toilets and taps that are often in disrepair. Only a semblance of privacy for each family is provided by blankets hung from the ceiling. In the absence of safe open spaces on the crowed city streets below, children find ways to play in dark, unkempt halls. The degraded living conditions experienced by these children and their families rival the worst and most unsavory slums in Harlem, Baltimore, Washington, Detroit, and other major U.S. cities.

The changes in life quality that accompany the transition from rural to urban living are not limited to the physical squalor and health hazards encountered, the material deprivation associated with unemployment and poverty, and the experience of living in close quarters. The consequences of urbanization also extend to the quality of community and social relations that arise from transient, bustling life in the townships. In urban settings, social interactions and community life may become strained by a lack of familiarity with, or alienation from, neighbors, and a persistent apprehension regarding victimization. There was a palpable loss of the sense of support, caring, and mutual obligation that at one time characterized much of life in rural communities. The urban social context was further exacerbated by political exploitation of intertribal rivalries, rampant violence, and crime. Many urban dwellers drew the conclusion that they could depend only on members of their own household for protection. They survived through vigilance and precaution in the community and at home.

Ironically, not even the affluent escape the emotional drain of living with chronic worries about crime. Wealthy and middle-class communities were just as vulnerable to the increase of criminal activity as poor communities. If anything, they probably experienced greater distress, because under the former regime they were well-insulated against criminal activities. Under the new regime, surveillance and enforcement resources were shared more equitably among communities, with the result that more affluent communities experienced a net decrease in police protection.

Social Change and the Family

Black families have been at the nexus of social change in South Africa. As a consequence of urbanization, the South African family finds itself at a crossroads, one that it shares with families from areas around the world in which advanced industrial development coexists with severe economic hardship and a marginal, threadbare existence. The contrasts of First World and Third World in South Africa, of industrialization and underdevelopment, of the modern and the traditional, create a distressing social condition of inequality. In these conditions, some citizens experience the best of what modern societies have to offer, while others are shut out, consigned to marginalized lives characterized by extreme material deprivation and sometimes social isolation. Luxury, convenience, and indulgence coexist with extreme deprivation in which there is a lack of even the most basic urban facilities. This creates a core dilemma in South Africa in which the wealthy must decide whether or not to ignore the plight of their less-fortunate countrymen, jealously guarding their own privilege, or to respond generously out of enlightened self-interest. At these crossroads, families are confronted with the conflicting demands and solutions proposed by a modern world—the world of education and work, the world of urbanization and gender equality, and a world with growing sensitivity to the needs and rights of the children.

Family relations also suffer from the alienation of urban life as family members become isolated from the extended kin networks that were such an integral component of their social functioning and a critical source of support in rural areas. As these traditional family ties erode under the force of distance, an unanticipated casualty of urban migration is the cohesiveness that once characterized the extended family structure. The system of apartheid policies amplified the stress associated with urbanization by further distorting family and community life through forced removals and migratory labor practices. Together these resulted in a weakening of traditional family structures and the system of mutual obligations that were critical to survival in traditional African communities.

Modernization of Family Life
Traditional practices in rural communities regulated and gave order to life, particularly the transition of children from one developmental stage to another, such as the initiation of sexual activity, which specified and marked clearly the transition from childhood to adulthood. These traditions invoked principles and practices that are no longer observed in urban environments, such as those that regulated sexual behavior and designated readiness for the responsibilities of marriage. Although these customary practices may not comport fully with modern circumstances, nor reflect current combinations of authoritative and affectionate relationships, in the past they served important regulatory functions. These traditions have few modern replacements, and their functions are unfilled in their absence. When a traditional young

man desired to marry, his family or a representative of his family would contact the family of his intended bride to negotiate an agreement to bring the two families together. This would lead to both material and social agreements upon which the marriage was based. In this way, marriage constituted an institutional arrangement that was built not only from a private contract between two individuals, but on a social contract between extended families. Another major impact on family roles relates to liberated gender roles and the expansion of opportunities for women in the labor force. This, combined with women's ability to compete with men for paid employment and high rates of male unemployment, compromises men's ability to support their families and undermines their traditional authority in the family. Ibrahim was just one of the many casualties of a set of social forces which has undermined the role of men as effective providers for the families. But as in the case of Ibrahim and Issak, the suffering extends beyond men to the entire family.

Urbanization and Family Life

Nowhere is the influence of urbanization more dramatic and telling than on the interior life of the family. Urban migration has wrought significant changes on the formation, composition, and processes of family life. Parents are separated from one another and from their children, leaving schools to fill the void in the transmission of values. Older generations have lost their esteemed positions of wisdom and authority. Women have entered the labor market in increasing numbers to support their families, and financial monetary exchanges have replaced mutual aid and support. Thus, in addition to dealing with the strains of economic inequality, material deprivation, and community violence, South African families are also experiencing the pulls and pressures of modernity that accompany urbanization and reshape relationships within the family and the functions they fulfill. As a consequence, South African families must accommodate to change emanating not only from the welcomed political reforms of their new multiracial democracy, but also to the realignment of cultural values and social mores that frequently accompany and result from urbanization. The strain of these changes is not entirely negative in its effects. Urbanization and modernization have also prompted welcomed shifts in gender roles, altered conceptions of childhood, and increased sensitivity to the rights of children and the obligations of adults toward them. Urban living and the personal and familial adaptations it requires make it at once an important source of innovation and tension, of promise and peril. As countless South Africans have discovered, the journey through change is difficult and demanding.

Strewn along the side of this road are too many casualties who have not been able to cope with the demands of social change. Clearly, Ibrahim and Issak count among those casualties.

Changing Gender Roles in the Family

Even while the political transition augurs favorable improvements in the lives of all, it also represents a source of distress. Political changes put pressures on the family and other institutions to change. As an example, the contemporary rights culture of the South African democracy has begun to question the wide use of physical punishment as a strategy employed to control children for generations. As a consequence of challenges to this and other traditional practices, urban families frequently are caught between the certainty of traditional ways of organizing their lives and the uncertainty of modern values, reflected in egalitarian gender roles, new modes of family formation, and a fundamental restructuring of relationships between individuals and society.

Nowhere is the challenge of modernity to tradition greater than in the domain of gender roles. Labor markets are now open to women, albeit most often in domestic service, at levels with the lowest financial remuneration and status. Women, many of whom have to take on the role of head of household, have greater access to employment in metropolitan areas because they can be offered less-costly and less-secure contracts than men. Mothers of young children are increasingly drawn into the labor market and engaged in work outside of the home; women currently constitute 37 percent of the national labor force (World Bank 1996).

Some tribal rituals continue in urban areas, occasionally altered by the changed circumstances. One of these is the payment of a "bride price"[4] to a woman's family before the marriage is formally sanctioned. Marriages are often delayed in urban areas because the negotiations for marriage and for the settlement of *lobola* (bride price) are difficult when families are widely dispersed across the country, and because young men today seldom receive help from an extended family to assemble sufficient assets to match the young woman's worth. A couple might then decide to have children even when the marriage is not a given. Further, some women feel pressured by men to prove their fertility, a matter of central concern to the identity of African women, while other modern women contend that husbands dominate households and resources but bring few benefits to them and their children. As a consequence, a high proportion of children are born outside of marriage. When marriage does occur, often relatively late in the lives of both the man and the woman, many enter these new relationships with children from other partners. These changes in marriage patterns and women's participation in work away from the home have dramatically altered family relations and functioning.

In many instances this has changed how women have carried out their roles as primary caregivers of children. The expansion in women's work, both outside the home away from the domain of children, as well as inside the home as single parents, raises the burden on women, leaves them with less energy, and makes it increasingly more difficult for them to monitor and nurture their children's development as effectively as was possible when their work permitted them to remain around the home. Families have adapted by accelerating the involvement of older siblings in the care of young children and by relying on grandparents, unemployed female relatives, friends, and paid child care either at home or in centers. This creates strains for children and families despite bringing benefits to those involved; it can provide opportunities for independence and autonomy among children, and a meaningful role for the elderly who might otherwise be unneeded and even unwanted.

AIDS: The Health Crisis Transforming Family Life

Another more ominous threat has emerged for the black family that exacerbates the detrimental effects of the other forces discussed thus far. AIDS is sweeping through southern Africa—over the next ten years it is expected to infect one in four adults, wiping out a generation of economically productive adults responsible for the care of children. The consequences for children and family life are devastating. Mothers and fathers are dying, sometimes after they have passed on the virus to their children. Both healthy and infected children are left to the care of others, including grandmothers and older siblings. Children as young as ten years old are forced to care for two or three younger siblings by begging for food from neighbors and scavenging. While there is great national anxiety about the growing crisis, there are few resources to provide relief.

Consider the following case of children subjected to the irresponsible neglect of a father and the nonresponsiveness of society: A frail eighty-year-old woman has been left to take care of her two small AIDS-infected grandchildren (aged five and three years) after their father abandoned them. The father fled after being summoned to a local clinic for an AIDS test, following his wife's diagnosis of AIDS and subsequent death. The children speak and walk with difficulty as they too have symptoms of advanced AIDS complex. They all depend on the grandmother's meager pension. The grandmother is blind and, given her poor health and low energy, worries about what will happen to these very sick children when she dies. There are no childcare institutions to step into this vacuum, and hospitals refuse to admit children who suffer from AIDS; those children who are diagnosed with AIDS are sent home to die (Molefe 1995). Like the grandmother described above, many worry what will happen to children if they survive the grandparent. The specter looming over the country is that of many homeless orphans who have no one to take care of them until they are able to adequately care for themselves. Many will be forced into adulthood before they are ready for its demands. Since children cannot raise themselves, South Africa must face the question that many other African countries have had to address: Who will care for and raise the many children who will be orphaned by AIDS? Up to now, the default has always been the extended family. However, there are many serious questions about its ability to step into this breach and take on the additional responsibilities without help.

Family formation, the timing of marriage and child-rearing, provider role strain, parental responsibilities, the functions of extended kin, and the effects of social stress related to urbanization are all factors that impact the functioning of the African family. Thus, African families face not only the sequelae of previous government policies, but they are also having to cope with pressures to adapt to modern urban life that require them to forsake traditional practices. In the past, traditional values and customs provided a familiar script for daily living and a clear guide for solving life's conundrums; today, they clash and conflict with democratic values and the exigencies of modern life. For example, traditional practices helped to regulate teen sexuality and childbearing by imposing legal, social, and financial sanctions on the entire families of young men who violated young, unmarried women. Population density and ethnic diversity in urban areas now make these social regulatory practices inoperable; they're not suited to the challenges of urban life, and such practices must be adapted if they are going to continue to be useful approaches to dealing with life's dilemmas. Urban families are giving up the structure of traditional ways of organizing their lives and their relationships, and are finding little to replace them with. They are left in the ambiguity created by urbanization and political transformation. To adjust, they are forced to broker tradeoffs between tradition and modernity, between retaining traditional maternal roles and having sufficient resources on which to live.

Notes

1. Formally an imposed category as part of the population group stratification assembled during apartheid.

2. This book will present data gathered on children and families from birth to age six. Data collected from year seven and beyond will be presented in subsequent publications.

3. "Township" is the colloquial term used for black residential areas, presumably to designate their peripheral labor-pool status in relation to the white towns they abut. No matter how large Soweto grew, it remained *the township*, emblematic of all other townships. (P. Bronner and L. Segal 1998. *Soweto: A history.* [Cape Town: Maskew Miller Longman].)

4. *Lobola*; this entailed the payment of cattle, which, in urban areas, might be cattle and/or money.

Chapter 2

A Brief History of Institutional Racism in South Africa

"FOR WHITES ONLY!"

This phrase was emblematic of white domination and an unmistakable symbol of pervasive racial segregation in South African society. By the time the apartheid regime reached the height of its power in the 1960s, the sentiment the phrase denotes was so fully ingrained in the South African psyche that prohibitive signs were no longer necessary to achieve white privilege and black oppression. Almost no one needed to be reminded that economic advancement was intended for whites and that access to better forms of employment, education, housing, and land was simply out of the question for blacks. Most fundamentally, apartheid was an explicit and comprehensive program of social engineering, the goals of which were to establish and guarantee white supremacy. It was founded on the colonial conviction that whites, by virtue of their presumed superior innate and acquired abilities, had attained a more advanced and morally superior way of living than indigenous people. Privilege was therefore the birthright of whites. Furthermore, white privilege was to be preserved by separation from and subordination of blacks.[1] Extensive laws, both substantial and petty, were instituted both to express this conviction of white racial superiority and to ensure its continuation. Apartheid, or "separate development," implemented a system of selective development through which whites became entitled to all the benefits and protections the state could provide and blacks were tolerated only to the extent that they served the economic interests of the white minority. Job reservations imposed race-based restriction on the jobs individuals could hold, regardless of education and abilities, in much the same way that restrictions were placed on areas of residence. The same result was produced. The choicest, high-status, high-leadership, and highly remunerated positions were reserved for whites, followed by

Indians and Coloreds, with Africans on the very bottom. Accordingly, in employment, for example, blacks were restricted to the unskilled and semiskilled sectors of the labor market and, even here, were systematically paid less than whites. A policy of Bantu Education was adopted with the passage of the Bantu Education Act to prepare black people for the subservient economic role reserved for them. Apartheid touched every aspect of life. To maintain it, whites had to continue to believe and convince everyone that blacks were inferior. Like a self-fulfilling prophecy, apartheid effectively produced and reinforced the very inequalities it used to justify itself. By promoting and sustaining white hegemony and racial separation, apartheid efficiently reproduced racial inequalities in every aspect of life.

By tracing briefly the history of racist policies in South Africa that culminated in the adoption and implementation of apartheid, we seek to demonstrate how these policies set the stage for contemporary social conditions that threaten the development of generations of South Africans to come. Security laws gave legal cover to harsh restrictions of personal freedoms and punitive conditions that made death sentences, brutal torture, and imprisonment for resisting the state possible. Apartheid policies of forced removals of families to separate racial groups into designated areas tore apart and destroyed vibrant communities. Legislative and policy tools used to reinforce separation and white racial hegemony included pass laws and influx control. The residual effects of apartheid can still be seen in the domains of access to land and housing, education, employment, and health and social services.

An Overview of State-Sponsored Racism

Beliefs about racial superiority and the conviction of the necessity of racial separation guided government policy and determined black-white relationships long before the ascendance of the National Party and the creation of the apartheid state in the late 1940s. Table 2.1 lists the principal events in the inexorable march toward apartheid, as well as black efforts to mobilize resistance against it. Racism was the foundation on which white colonial power was built in South Africa. Evidence of racism can be seen as far back as 1652, when Van Riebeek, a representative of the Dutch East India Company, established a supply station at the Cape along the trading route to the East. Racism was formally codified and given the weight of law as soon as black people were incorporated into colonial economic expansion. For example, in 1852, the Glen Gray Act legalized and required territorial segregation

Table 2.1: Timeline of Events in the Development of Apartheid

1832	Slave trade abolished
1852	Glen Gray Act enforces territorial segregation
1876	English and Boers initiate war of conquest against African.
1905	Natal Native Congress formed by Dube, Luthuli, and Msane
1905	White areas created in Natal; Africans not permitted to own land
1905	Poll tax introduced for Africans, forcing them into employment
1910	Unification of Cape, Natal, Free State, and Transvaal into South Africa
1912	African National Congress (ANC) formed
1913	Native Land Act passed, reserving the major fertile areas for whites
1914	Nationalist Party formed
1919	White racism intensifies, Natal Native Policy extended throughout South Africa
1922	Race-differentiated curricula introduced into schools
1923	Urban Influx Control Act instituted to control black access to urban areas
1925	Afrikaans designated as the official second language; English is first
1927	Riotous Assemblies Act introduced to quell African resistance
1934	Last election in the Cape in which nonwhites and whites vote together
1936	Cape blacks lose the vote. Enforcement of the Land Act intensified, depriving blacks of their farms
1944	Homeless Africans create a shantytown that later becomes Soweto
1948	Population Registration Act passed, requiring all citizens to be classified by race stamped in their identity passes. Sexual contact and marriage between whites and blacks declared illegal.
1950	Group Areas Act passed, segregating all residential areas by race
1951	Bantu Authorities Act passed and tribal administration encouraged
1952	ANC launches defiance campaign against unjust laws. Nelson Mandela and others tried under the Suppression of Communism Act for leading the campaign. Their sentences are suspended.

1953 Many ANC leaders, including Luthuli and Mandela, banned under the Suppression of Communism Act even though neither is a communist

1953 Bantu Education Act limits black access to advanced education

1954 Colored voters removed from the Cape common roll

1959 Bantu Self-Government Bill establishes eight fictitious national homelands. University Education Act prohibits black registration at white universities without consent of the internal affairs minister

1961 On May 31, South Africa becomes a republic and leaves the British Commonwealth

1962 Detention without trial; police are allowed to hold suspects for twelve days without charging them or bringing them before a court

1963 Transkei Constitution Act sets up first independent homeland government. Police allowed to hold suspects for 90 days without trial

1966 Home construction for Africans in the Cape halted with the exception of hostels for single men. Police allowed to hold suspects in custody for an unlimited period if authorized by a judge

1975 Minister of Bantu Education issues instruction that math and social studies be taught in Afrikaans. Blacks consider Afrikaans the language of oppression. This policy is protested by teachers, parents, and students

1976 Transkei created as an independent Xhosa state. Police can hold suspects for an unlimited time without any authorization

15,000 students gather at West Junior Secondary School in Soweto to protest the use of Afrikaans as the medium of instruction in schools. The police use tear gas and then open fire. The photograph of Hector Peterson being carried from the confrontation mobilizes the world community. Between August and November there are confrontations, general strikes, school disruptions, and police raids as the government tries to identify the leaders of the revolts. Over 575 people are killed and at least 2,400 wounded. Schools are disrupted for a year. The government eventually drops its order to teach in Afrikaans.

1977 Bophuthatswana receives its independence. 10,000 Africans watch as their shelters are bulldozed on Modderdam Road in Cape Town

1979 Venda receives its independence. Black labor unions legalized because of the pressures of labor shortages

1981 Ciskei becomes an independent homeland

1983 Constitution replaces white parliament with multiracial, tricameral legislature consisting of 178 whites, 85 Coloreds, and 45 Indians

1985 Ban lifted on multiracial political parties. KwaNdebele and Qwaqwa receive independence

1989 Antenatal enrollment begins for Birth-to-Ten Longitudinal Study

1990 Nelson Mandela released from prison

1994 Multiparty, multiracial democratic elections result in victory for the African National Congress and the selection of Mandela as president

2000 South Africa completes its reversal of apartheid policy by banning discrimination entirely. Parliament outlaws all forms of prejudice based on race, gender, sexual preference, disability, and other grounds. It also prohibits hate speech

of the races in South Africa. In 1905 the English in the Natal region set aside separate land areas for whites in a system that subordinated Africans, who were not allowed to purchase land. Blacks were effectively reduced to being laborers and tenants on land owned by whites. In 1910 South Africa was unified into a single country in which the provinces of the Cape, Natal, Orange Free State, and Transvaal were brought together into a single principality. This marked the beginning of a whites-only economy, and the impassable Color Bar, separating whites from other groups, was established. This ultimately gave rise to an aristocracy of color.

In response to this broadening pattern of racial hegemony, efforts were made to bring people together to resist it actively. This resulted first in the establishment of the Communist Party and later in the formation of the African National Congress. The latter was formed in 1912 under the leadership of the Reverend John Dube to resist racial hegemony. Ironically, the National Party, originator of apartheid, was founded in the same year. In 1913 the Native Land Act was passed, to develop a "native policy" in which black South Africans were restricted to 13 percent of the land, while 87 percent was reserved for whites. In 1922, Bantu Education was begun when different, and unequal, curricula were introduced for black and white schools.

In 1923 the Urban Influx Control Act sought to restrict blacks' ability to migrate to urban areas for employment. In 1925 Afrikaans was recognized as an official language, second only to English, thus formally excluding any recognition of indigenous black languages. In 1934 Coloreds in the Cape cast ballots in the last multiracial election until 1994, when the ANC came to power in a Government of National Unity and Nelson Mandela was elected president. With nonwhites final loss of the ballot, white authorities intensified enforcement of the Land Act and evicted blacks from their farmlands and homes in urban areas in an effort to engineer a white South Africa. Thousands of homeless Africans moved to urban areas in search of work and began the process of creating shantytowns outside white areas. Settlements like these ultimately formed such places as Soweto. Although these shanty towns were illegal, black workers were nonetheless needed in the growing economy, and the white authorities contributed modest funds to assist with basic sanitation and other infrastructure, mainly to avoid a public health catastrophe that would affect the white areas.

In 1948 the National Party assumed power and Daniel Francois Malan became prime minister. During the next six years of his term of office, sweeping policies were put into place that sought to entrench the pattern of racial separation and domination that had evolved over time. For example, the government required everyone to register, and everyone was assigned a racial group classification: white, black, Colored, or Indian. Classifications were frequently made through humiliating procedures of personal physical examination, and members of families, even parents and children, could be classified into separate categories and forced to live separately. With a system of racial classification in place, the government made it illegal for whites and nonwhites to have intimate relationships or to marry. Personal identification documents ("passes") were issued on which each person's racial classification was stamped. These passes were required to be carried on one's person at all times. In the heyday of apartheid, huge numbers of black people were imprisoned for either not having a pass or for being in an area to which they had no entitlement under law. The Group Areas Act, promulgated in 1950, prevented black people from entering, living in, or working in restricted white areas. It designated areas for each population group, resulting in a massive upheaval in which blacks were forcibly removed from city areas and farmlands that they had occupied for generations. In effect these lands were appropriated by the government without compensation and made available to whites at rock-bottom prices.

In 1953 the Bantu Education Act was passed, placing even more severe restrictions on blacks' access to higher education. The curriculum was designed for labor and low-level service occupations, and blacks were refused admission to the established universities. By 1959 nonwhite students could not register in white universities without the written consent of the minister of internal affairs. A separate system of higher education was established for blacks that was, by design, inferior both in resources and in curriculum.

Creation of Separate Areas and Fictitious States for Blacks

The Group Areas Act brought about a wrenching expulsion of blacks from towns and suburbs and relocation far enough away for white comfort but close enough to fill low-paying domestic, service, mining, and manufacturing jobs in areas designated for whites only. Few resources were dedicated to basic municipal services for the black and Colored areas. Housing was deliberately limited to discourage the immigration of blacks into the townships at the periphery of white areas. However, the tide of migration was inexorable. Over time, black people would migrate to metropolitan areas in such large numbers that the government would no longer be able to control and contain them. In desperation, the apartheid government expanded black housing areas in areas farther and farther away from the white towns.

In 1963 the first "homelands" (foreign states) were set up, which institutionalized the eviction of blacks from property in South Africa. In effect, tracts of remote, arid land, rationalized as ethnic areas, were designated as homelands for blacks. These rural homelands included Bophuthatswana, Ciskei, Gazankulu, Lebowa, KwaNdebele, QwaQwa, KaNgwane, Transkei, Venda, and KwaZulu. Blacks supposedly held citizenship in these fictitious states of the South African government and were therefore not entitled to South African citizenship. Homeland sovereignty existed in theory only. In truth, the homeland governments were puppet regimes that received their funding and marching orders, from the South African government. The outside world refused to recognize them as sovereign states. Although separate homelands were intended to solve the black (African) problem, there still remained the question of how to create a veneer of democracy for disenfranchised Colored and Indian South Africans, who had no homelands to which they could be consigned. In 1983 the apartheid government struck upon what it considered a ingenious solution for Coloreds and Indians that would hopefully mute the criticism of human rights advocates around the world. It created a tricameral legislature that incorporated separate (and unequal) legislative chambers for whites, Coloreds, and Indians. However, the system lacked fundamental legitimacy, and by 1986 it was beginning to unravel as black resistance grew with the support of the international community. However, by this time much of the damage of apartheid had been done. Black people were left without property, largely uneducated, and unemployed. Moreover their family structures were torn apart by influx control, migrant labor, forced removals, and restrictive housing policies.

Although a brief history of apartheid milestones can document the injustices perpetrated against black people, it cannot portray the daily indignities suffered by individuals as a result of being relegated to an inferior position. It is difficult to acknowledge the pain with which these experiences have afflicted the country, insinuating themselves into every aspect of South Africans' lives. The effects of institutionalized racism have been devastating for blacks both materially and psychologically. Apartheid was fundamentally rooted in a devaluation of blacks that distorted the human capacities of both the oppressor and the oppressed. Many South Africans like Ibrahim were permanently handicapped by sub-standard Bantu education, limitations on access to good jobs, loss of ancestral properties, and being forced to reside on barren desolate lands. Some, though by no means all, were overwhelmed by the hopelessness of their plight.

This formal system has now been dismantled and the population segregation laws repealed. However, the accumulated effects of apartheid will take considerable time to reverse. The social, psychological, and economic effects of apartheid did not end abruptly with the annulment of laws and the transfer of power to a multiracial government. Except for a minority of affluent and well-educated blacks, life has not changed substantially for millions of South Africans. In the first phase of transformation, the separation of groups on the basis of race is being replaced by separation on the basis of socioeconomic status. Thus apartheid's demise does not signal the disappearance of racism and racial inequality in South Africa. Racism takes on new forms, partly related to class and urbanization, and its effects are still evident in the health and well-being of its citizens, particularly children. Moreover, the residue of apartheid continues to generate stress, particularly with respect to urbanization, and to distort family and community life. Apartheid has left an indelible mark on the psyche of the country.

Apart from the wretched social conditions it engineered, apartheid was an unqualified disaster for the South African economy. In the last five years under apartheid rule, the real gross domestic product failed to grow at all and real gross domestic investment and balance of payments capital account were negative.[2] Although state attempts to manage the national economy to preserve white privilege and hegemony were somewhat successful, these efforts proved costly and inefficient in the long run. Vast financial and human resources were squandered in creating and maintaining distinct administrative structures and service systems for each population group. Blacks were further burdened by regressive tax policies that relied principally on a value-added tax (VAT) that placed a 15 percent levy on items purchased and consumed in the country. Through this tax, they returned to the state a substantially larger proportion of their incomes than more affluent whites.

The Making of Soweto: Apartheid in Action

Soweto is difficult to imagine. It occupies a large tract of land located about forty kilometers from the center of Johannesburg, and is connected by light rail and roads to jobs in the city's commercial and industrial zones and in the white suburbs. Soweto developed over a long period, from its informal beginnings in 1904 to the formal declaration of its current boundaries in 1958. It began as a small tract of government-built houses and single-sex hostels for migrant workers. Soweto (Southwest Township) was designed by the government to serve its political and economic ends: to house black workers needed by the gold mines and to accommodate black people forcibly removed from their homes in Johannesburg in areas that were redesignated for whites. All homes were owned by the government, to whom rents were paid. Similar policies and approaches were adopted for other black population groups. Persons classified as Colored or as Indian were each assigned to separate townships designated specifically for them. Within Soweto, ethnic groups were assigned to different sections to create barriers between Africans, presumably to prevent them from uniting against white hegemony in a broad-based political organization. Although townships like Soweto formally date back to the early part of the twentieth century (Bonner and Segal 1998), they experienced massive influxes during the 1970s and 1980s. Soweto is not the only black township in metropolitan Johannesburg, and it has lost its claim to being the largest black township in South Africa. However, it still occupies a unique position in the imagination of South Africans as the seedbed of political resistance and the crucible of urban African culture.

Soweto grew as sections of new housing were added to accommodate families displaced by the Group Areas Act and as squatter settlements arose to accommodate new arrivals from rural areas. Of their own accord, residents of government-built homes contributed to the housing supply by adding to the existing structures in the form of garages, sheds, and extra rooms to accommodate extended family members or offspring with their own children who could not find or afford separate housing. Because blacks were not permitted to own land or purchase the homes in which they lived, through its local housing administrators the government held and often used its power to evict or threaten to evict families suspected of involvement in the liberation movement. In spite of government efforts to divide and conquer, professional, educated, and financially prosperous blacks only had to look out of their windows, down the road, or across a vacant field toward the squatter camps to be reminded of how fragile and vulnerable their own economic status was and how closely aligned their interests were with those of the poor.

Soweto: Life in the Shadow of the City of Gold

Soweto is connected to Johannesburg, also known as "Egoli," the City of Gold, by a major thoroughfare, Potchefstroom Highway, which snakes through the southern third of the township, separating Pimville, Dlamini, and Chiawelo from the rest of Soweto. Today Soweto has a population of close to 1.5 million people that is served by one large public hospital (Chris Hani-Baragwanath) and a series of affiliated primary health clinics located in Soweto's suburbs or subdivisions. Adjacent to the hospital is a busy open-air market in Diepkloof that also serves as the central transportation hub for vans and small buses. The market is a principal place of commerce, with people setting up stands at which they sell fruits, vegetables, school supplies, and small items for the home. Driving south from Johannesburg, along Old Potch Road, as Potchefstroom Highway is called, you reach the crest of a hill just before the Chris Hani-Baragwanath Hospital. From there the township stretches out before you as a seemingly endless mosaic of gray shades veiled by a thick layer of smog. Tin shacks inhabited by the poor and clay tile roofs of more prosperous homes are spread out over a vast expanse that is broken only by the ominously protruding twin silos of the power plant. This large coal-burning, electricity-generating plant is located in the middle of a busy and densely populated section of Soweto. Its twin towers, a landmark to residents and visitors alike, produce the sheets of smoke that cover the area day and night.

In truth, Soweto is not a single city but an amalgam of economically, ethnically, and socially diverse communities. It consists of more than twenty-one separate towns or suburbs composed of formal and informal housing structures and limited commercial areas consisting mostly of small shops, gas stations, fast food outlets, and convenience shops (called *spazas*). The decaying municipal infrastructure of Soweto clearly betrays the flagrant neglect and underdevelopment that occurred under the apartheid regime. Except for two or three main roads, most streets are poorly surfaced or unpaved. Inadequate facilities housing primary and secondary schools are scattered across the township. Few formal recreational facilities exist. Fortunately, things are improving. Community centers are beginning to flourish. The avid interest in and support of soccer in Soweto is evident in its modern sports stadium. Nightlife and tourism are beginning to come alive, with many bars and several good jazz clubs, as well as two hotels. Soweto is a living, dynamic, and changing community, of which only a timebound snapshot can be presented, because even now it is changing rapidly.

In spite of the dynamic life and change taking place, Soweto is still physically challenging. By dusk, on the edge of a winter's evening in Soweto, smog accumulated over the day is so thick that it is inescapable and palpable. A haze hangs over the entire township, and the cloud of smoke envelops the chalky clay earth, choking life out of the treeless, grassless terrain. But social life and the human spirit seem irrepressible. As darkness falls, men and young children appear in the vacant lots and near the edges of the roads. They banter, trade stories, and laugh together as they warm themselves over the flames rising from small fires made by burning tires, trash, or wood. Some men cook a communal meal of meat and a pot of porridge as they talk. Smoke billows from the chimneys of the small brick houses. But there is a price to pay for the warmth of the winter evening fires. Breathing becomes increasingly difficult, and it is apparent why many children develop chronic respiratory diseases under these circumstances.

The housing supply in most townships is so limited that multiple extended families live in cramped dwellings designed for parents and two or three children. Homes were built in a cookie-cutter fashion— small three- or four-room brick houses, semidetached, with little yards around them. The interiors of the brick houses curiously combine artifacts of modern living with uncanny throwbacks to rural society. The houses are sparingly lit, usually by a single low-wattage bulb. Kitchens, when they exist, are small. The space often is dominated by an old wood-burning stove or a fire in the middle of the dirt floor; these are common because electricity is prohibitively expensive and paraffin (kerosene) barely affordable. The salon (living room) may have a small TV or radio. At night, this room becomes the sleeping quarters for up to six people. The chilly bite of winter is sometimes lessened by a small electric space heater. Fortunately the periods of bitter cold last only about two to three weeks in the region, threatening those who sleep out—in empty oil drums, under paper on dumps, in the doorways of small shops, or clustered together in the veld.[3] For many, the routines begin in the early hours, around four or five in the morning, with hand warming in front of small fires, hasty washes, and cups of tea, as workers and children prepare to catch buses, trains, and group taxis to school and work in commutes which take as much as two hours or more to complete.

Family Structure: Effects of Apartheid

By virtue of economic necessity and convention, children continue to live with parents after they become adults and have their own offspring. The underlying rationale of the apartheid population movement and resident policies was to limit the number of black people in the urban areas to those who could be usefully employed (in the case of Soweto, in the gold and other industries of Johannesburg). The plan never envisioned accommodating workers' families. In this, the government was trapped by inherently contradictory goals: to keep black people out of cities and towns, separate from the white population, and yet to ensure a readily accessible source of cheap labor for domestic, service, and manufacturing jobs. One consequence of the artificially restricted supply of housing was that as children reached adulthood, they could not find housing for themselves and their children. The little Soweto houses were not meant for extended families. As a consequence, many families added rooms and sheds to develop new units in which to house newly formed families. Some families had to split up, as young people tried to find rooms or sheds to rent in other parts of the city.

Multiple generations living in the same household had its advantages. The elderly could care for young children while their parents worked. Because the housing supply was so restricted by the government, grown children often had to remain in their parents' homes even after they had their own families. Even those who could afford more generous housing often ended up living in a tin lean-to attached to the main house. Almost all houses had access to running water, some inside, others to a tap outside the back door. Flush toilets, mostly outdoor, were a relatively recent addition, and a majority of families had to go outside to use a long-drop or bucket toilet. These factors significantly impacted families. First, the actual structures in which family groups live dictate an interpersonal dynamic very different from the hierarchically organized rural society. In the tribally organized rural areas, clustered huts are built together to form a kraal to accommodate different age groups, genders, roles, and functions.[4] People had to develop new social relationships to demarcate roles and a different sense of privacy in the very small spaces of the tiny government houses. This, together with the sociality of African culture, led to the use of the street for major aspects of social life. Here children played, youth gathered, men talked, wedding ceremonies were celebrated, and family arguments were enacted.

Bedrooms were too small for the beds needed, even though multiple people would sleep together in a single bed. At night, kitchens, living rooms, porches, and garages became sleeping quarters. One-room shacks were divided by curtains or a piece of furniture moved into place at night, to provide privacy for adults. Children slept together and with adults. This has interesting ramifications of the nighttime socialization and the toilet training of young children, because of the impact of their success or failure on the comfort of others. Apart from the structural imposition of family relationships, the cramped accommodations also affect the sexual relationships of adults. Sometimes privacy is nonexistent and children become aware of sexual behavior at a young age; at other times, privacy is created in the brief temporal and spatial gaps over the day.

Some young families, newly formed with small children, live with their parents or in attached rooms and share a kitchen. This overlapping of boundaries, together with the pooling of income and other resources, plays out in questions about who has the authority to set the rules and expectations about behavior, who makes decisions about family priorities, and so on. The person with the money, education, or access to resources is not always the elder male, which can create tensions in a traditionally patriarchal social order.

Because housing for black people was always located long distances from the white suburbs and cities where they worked, many were required to leave their homes early and not return until late in the evening. Moreover, much of their wages was consumed by transportation costs. The distance of black areas from centers of employment involved long commuting hours by parents to work sites, leaving children unmonitored by parents and in the care of informal or formal caretakers for extended periods of time. Many parents relied on the extended family, older children, and friends to care for young children in their absence. To save on transport costs, some working parents stay at or near their place of work during the week and only return to their families on the weekends. The care structure for children also changes relationships between members of the family, with older children assuming responsibility for the household and care of their younger siblings while their parents are away. Young female family members from rural areas may be brought to a township home to care for children, living in a form of indentured labor to their better-off relatives, and young children may be sent to live, semipermanently, with grandparents and other family members in rural areas where parents hope they will be safer and better supervised than in the town.

Inequality in Access to Medical Care

Lack of access to heathcare resources can be a telling indicator of economic disadvantage. Racism and economic inequality were mirrored in the approach to health care taken under the apartheid regime, which deliberately promoted differential access of blacks and whites. Like most systems constructed under apartheid, there were multiple and duplicated heath systems—separate for blacks, Coloreds, Indians, and whites. Nowhere is the inequality of apartheid more evident than in the black-white differences in access to quality medical care. The striking differences begin with a comparison of two hospitals, one for whites and the other for blacks. The Johannesburg Hospital, originally designed for whites, was a magnificent structure, with the most recent advances in medical technology. In the Baragwanath Hospital in Soweto, blacks were provided a barely adequate physical structure plagued by shortages, understaffing, and a chronic sense of being overwhelmed. In addition to public services, whites and blacks with money could receive services from a large pool of general practitioners and specialists in the private sector who service a largely middle-class group.

The government realized, even if from self-interest, that it needed to provide basic public health services for blacks; infectious diseases and other public health problems do not observe the color line. In Soweto, the first health services were located in a former World War II base, which later became the Chris Hani-Baragwanath Hospital. The facility, which retains many of the original buildings, consists of run-down buildings, poorly suited in design and condition for a hospital. Barracks serve as inpatient wards, and central mess halls are the site of food preparation. Unkempt patients in their surgical gowns move up and down the dirt roads between buildings, with their pole-hung intravenous bags trailing behind them. Medical care is often provided by highly motivated young trainees who tend to get overwhelmed by the inadequacy of resources to service the more than one million residents of Soweto. One doctor said, "We are constantly faced with the challenge of whether we should provide good and adequate services to a few, or mediocre and poor services to the many." Burnout claims many victims, and physicians often seek refuge from the strain in more lucrative and comfortable private practices. There are, however, many notable exceptions who devote their lives to serving the poor. Recently private clinics and a hospital have been built by African physicians to provide an alternative for those who have private medical insurance.

The Costs of Economic Mismanagement under Apartheid Paid for on the Backs of Blacks

The cost of the mismanagement of the economy under apartheid was paid for by a lower living standard for blacks. While whites enjoyed a world-class standard of living regarding health services and quality education, ample pensions, and police protection, the services and infrastructure for the black majority remained poorly developed and woefully inadequate. Blacks endured a lack of electricity and water, as well as poor to nonexistent roads and sewer and sanitation services. Moreover, expectations of white social and economic superiority were not left to chance, as the apartheid government implemented educational, job, and social welfare systems that virtually guaranteed black inferiority. Through a combination of government work programs, remittances, and pensions, apartheid policies created an enviable welfare state that effectively eliminated poverty among whites. All the while, poverty rates soared among blacks. In contrast to the generous economic safety net provided for whites, efforts to buffer blacks against the ravages of poverty were insubstantial and grudging. Largely ignored by the white government, most blacks lived under Third World social conditions. Thus racial inequality was effectively reproduced in most areas of life: health, nutrition, education, housing, employment, and land ownership. In addition to aprtheid's commitment to separate and unequal development, corruption and mismanagement effectively plundered and weakened an economy that might otherwise have been robust in providing a reasonable standard of living for many more citizens than it ultimately did.

Probably as a consequence of these social and economic policies, the South African economy shrunk at an average annual rate of 1.3 percent over the ten-year period from 1985 to 1994 (South African Institute of Race Relations 2000). As a consequence, South Africa has a per capita gross national product of only $3,000 (U.S.) and a median monthly income of only $310. Moreover, it has one of the highest inequality indices in the world. For example, the median annual household income for Africans is less than half the per capita average.

Apartheid left in its wake widespread hardship that continues to compromise the quality of life of black families and communities. Consequently, for a majority of Mandela's children and their families, material hardship and economic disadvantage are lingering reminders of the apartheid era.

Political Reform and Hope

Although pervasive and persistent in its effects, apartheid has been brought to a formal end. Remarkably, the demise of apartheid was to occur early in the lives of Mandela's children. Although the peaceful transition from a racist to a nonracial government may have held little significance at the time for her four-year-old great-grandson, Tumelo, for Maria Khumalo, age seventy, it was an extraordinary event she never expected to see. On April 28, 1994, for the first time in over fifty years, South African citizens of every color were able vote in a national election to decide who would govern the country. The mood of the crowd queuing up to vote was upbeat but solemn as they slowly made their way up to the entrance of the local school. By the time Mrs. Khumalo reached the door of the school, she had been in line for two hours. Nothing would turn her back: not hunger, not fatigue, not the heat of the sun, not even the ache deep in her bones. Her heart raced with anticipation as she approached the table, displayed her frayed identification document, and accepted her ballot. It took just a minute to mark her choices. It was a brief moment, but its memory would last a lifetime. In similar scenes repeated around the country, millions of ordinary citizens like Mrs. Khumalo helped bring an end to a shameful chapter in South Africa's history.

As the world watched and applauded, the open democratic election marked a peaceful transition that has given rise to euphoria and hope for material improvement in the quality of life of ordinary blacks. The optimism is not entirely unwarranted in a place blessed with so many natural and human resources. South Africa occupies a vast area of 1.2 million square kilometers that is well integrated by state-of-the-art transportation and communication networks. Its population, estimated at 40.1 million by the 1996 census, is approximately 75 percent African. In addition, 34 percent of the population was estimated to be children under the age of fifteen (South African Department of National Health and Population Development 1994). Endowed with breathtaking scenic beauty, generous material and human resources, and a modern infrastructure, South Africa is positioned to lead the way in the development of the southern African region.

Although the political transformation has raised hopes about the future, past inequities still weigh heavily on the nation's prospects for social progress. Even though the policies of apartheid no longer carry the force of law, the cancer of racism from which they arose, and which they helped to spread, has penetrated to the marrow of South African society. The policies are still visible in economic inequality, inadequate housing, failing schools, poor nutrition and health, and violence across black communities. Consequently, few South Africans were so swept up by the euphoria to believe that the advent of a nonracial democracy would quickly alter the grim reality of black life or bring about quick improvements in the standard of living of the poor. Once the celebrations of the democratic election were over, few were surprised to find that the dream of social equality and economic progress for many citizens remained as elusive as ever. Understandably, enthusiasm about the future is tempered by the realization that problems of the past will not be resolved easily and might, in fact, block or postpone progress for some time to come. On the other hand, while most adults soberly accept that the trajectory of their own lives will not be altered significantly by recent events, many are sustained by the dream of a more prosperous future for their children. Will this dream become a reality? Will these young children prosper? This is the broad issue we will take up in this book.

Analysis of the BTT data offers a window onto how these competing sources of hope and despair play out in the lives of young children. Although current knowledge about the roles that risk and protective factors have in psychosocial development is substantial, much less is known about the social, community, and familial processes that mediate them. Therefore, it is difficult to predict with any certainty how well Mandela's children will do under the current circumstances in South Africa. Consequently, this book will describe the environment and conditions under which Mandela's children are growing. In particular we will focus on poverty and violence, evaluate the extent to which Mandela's children have access to the resources children need to attain competence and to reach their full potential. In examining the development of children as they move from infancy through early childhood, we will contrast the adjustment of children who live in relatively propitious circumstances with the outcomes of children exposed to significant risks. We will also identify the resources that seem to afford protection to children even when they live under developmentally risky conditions of material deprivation and danger. This analysis begins with a discussion of the living standards of Mandela's children.

Notes

1. The term "black" is used to refer to those not included as whites (e.g. Africans, Indians, and mixed-race or Coloreds).

2. Living standards, socieconomic status (SES), social welfare, and quality of life are broad concepts that have been used to depict the continuum represented by material hardship and well-being. Although these terms differ slightly in emphasis, they refer to a common phenomenon and are often used interchangeably.

3. Veld is open land, usually with longish grass but no trees. Originally it referred to graxing land.

4. A cluster of sleeping and public huts making up a multigenerational household, which is surrounded by a small piece of land for cultivating crops. Cattle are grazed in communal areas between kraals.

Chapter 3

Urban Poverty and Living Standards

Defining Poverty

Of all the potential threats to the development and well-being of children, poverty appears to be the most pervasive and damaging in its effects. In simple terms, poverty is the inability to acquire the materials and services that are essential to maintain life. Poverty and the material hardship associated with it are all too common an experience among South Africans. When poverty is defined in terms of low income, rural poverty is, of course, much deeper and more widespread than urban poverty. Although rural and urban poverty differ in how they present and in prevalence, they have an equally pernicious impact on the development of children. Even within urban areas, families are not all poor in the same way, or for the same reasons. Poverty takes root in different ways in the lives of Mandela's children. Because of its complexity, poverty can be observed alternatively as chronic hunger, inadequate housing, low living standards, low income, low consumption, lack of human capital, low accumulated wealth, and high debt. The purpose of this chapter is to depict the experience of urban poverty in its diverse manifestations by drawing on both national surveys and Birth-to-Ten (BTT) data. Discussion of poverty and living standards begins with a presentation of data on the socioeconomic status of South Africans as a nation, with a goal of understanding the wide population group differences in living standards. The chapter concludes with a demographic analysis of urban poor households based on data obtained from the families of Mandela's children.

Poverty as Low Income
Because we live in a highly monetarized world, poverty is often conceptualized in terms of income so low that one is unable to purchase

life necessities such as adequate food and shelter. On the face of it, the use of monetary income is an elegantly simple and easy-to-implement method for measuring poverty. Therefore it is not surprising that low income has become a widely used approach by which to index poverty and to infer material hardship. But when is income low? Do all uses of a monetary approach agree on the definition of low income? Most monetary approaches to poverty are based on an assessment of total household income for a specified period such as a year, a month, or a day. In fact, several different monetary standards have been adopted to estimate poverty rates. These differences have been a source of confusion for those comparing poverty rates across studies. For example, one of these approaches applies an absolute monetary standard to define poverty. Specifically, a family is classified as poor if its total income is less than $1 per day for each member of the household. This is the minimum amount of money economists estimate is needed to feed one person. At the 1993 exchange rate this is the equivalent of three South African rands. In 2000, that is equal to 7 rands. Table 3.1 presents daily income and other economic status data broken down by population groups. The data reveal an extraordinarily wide gap between what whites earn per day and what is earned by the three other population groups. Whites have the highest daily incomes, earning almost seven times per day what Africans earn. Among the groups designated as blacks, Indians have the highest incomes, followed by Coloreds. Africans fall to the bottom. (Following usage in South Africa, the term black is inclusive of the three nonwhite population groups: Africans, Coloreds, and Indians. Therefore, the label black will be used to refer to all nonwhite groups. African will be used to designate the indigenous population which predated European colonization.)

When the absolute income approach is used as an index of economic well-being, 24 percent of the entire South African population falls below this standard (Klasen 1997). This figure seems small and manageable until one takes a closer look at subgroup differences. Hidden within the figure for the total population are extraordinary differences in poverty rates by population group. As many as 44 percent of Africans but only 2.1 percent of whites are classified as living in poverty by this monetary standard.

The absolute standard is not the only approach that uses income to assess poverty status. An alternative approach employs a relative standard. Societies and communities differ in the effectiveness of the social safety net they provide to protect their citizens against deprivation. Thus a family's relative standing in an income distribution within a country does not tell us enough about the degree of material hardship it might experience. The relative approach addresses to an extent

Table 3.1: Income by Population Group

	African	Colored	Indian	White
Daily household income (rands)	33.5	68.6	133.6	213.1
Daily expenditure (rands)	37.0	61.8	110.2	158.1
Daily per capita income (rands)	10.7	17.9	30.0	85.8
Per capita household expenditure (rands)	11.4	16.5	28.5	61.5
Percent households under 40^{ile} income "the poor"	52.1%	21.5%	6.5%	2.1%
Percent households under 20 mile income "the ultra poor"	26.5%	6.5%	1.6%	1.3%
Percent households spending less than R3/day per capita on food. Poverty as inadequate nutrition	44.0%	28.2%	5.3%	2.1%

the problem of national differences in living standards and the safety net it provides by establishing a poverty line based on the distribution of incomes in a given country. This relative standard approach rests on the assumption that every country or region has people who would be considered poor by local standards. It goes on to reason that these people would be found at the lowest end of the income distribution for that country or region. In South Africa, households whose total monthly income falls below the fortieth percentile (R301) are said to be living in moderate poverty. According to Table 3.1, as many as 52 percent of Africans but only 2.1 percent of whites are moderately poor. This is strikingly similar to the poverty rates produced when the absolute $1 a day standard is used. Sometimes it is helpful to identify rates of extreme or ultrapoverty. A widely accepted standard for extreme poverty is a household income that falls at or below the twentieth percentile of the income distribution for that country. In South

Africa, the ultra poor have incomes lower than R178 per month in 1993. Again, a very high proportion of Africans (26.5 percent) and a very low proportion of whites (1.3 percent) fall into this category.

Although simple and widely used, reports of monetary income used in assessment of poverty may be distorted and inaccurate. In some cases, respondents may not know their actual household income, because they do not have access to the information or do not monitor it fully. A healthy skepticism about the utility of income reports is not limited to questions of accuracy. There are also concerns about the extent to which such reports truly reflect actual variations in the material conditions of the poor. Exclusive reliance on income as an indicator of living standards can also be misleading in places such as South Africa where unemployment is high and money may not be the primary medium for exchange of goods and services. Wage income may be low or nonexistent in some households, but they are able to survive and maintain a reasonable quality of life by working the informal economy. In these cases, the bartering of goods and services may be used as a substitute to acquire necessities that others access through a wage-based cash economy. This point is supported by data presented later which show that African households consume goods whose value exceeds their monetary income. Thus where the informal economy prevails, reports of cash income may not be the most revealing indicator of the resources available to families who rely on bartering and noncash exchanges to acquire the goods and services they need. If other means are used to acquire goods, then monetary income by itself is suspect as an indicator of a family's living standard and quality of life. For this reason, there is increasing concern that income-based poverty indicators are insufficient to represent accurately and fully the material status of many poor families.

Poverty as Food Insecurity

The inherent subjectivity and cultural relativism of basic needs complicates efforts to determine what is essential for sustaining life and human dignity. Universal biological imperatives for food and shelter become the common ground on which agreement can be reached about what constitute basic needs. Thus hunger and the need for food provide another way to represent poverty. Nutritional experts assert that approximately 2,100 calories per day are needed minimally to sustain life. A family is classified as poor if it does not have sufficient resources to provide that number of calories per day for each member of the household. This in fact is the basis for the $1-per-day figure used as the absolute standard for poverty cited above. The ability of a family to provide adequate nutrition can also be assessed through self-reports of hunger experienced by adults and children in a household. This was one of the approaches used in BTT. About one in five mothers reported that their child regularly went to bed hungry. However, the measure of the success or failure of a household to secure food in adequate amounts for its children does not have to rely on self-reporting alone. Such reports can be subject to the same types of distortions that have been described for reports of income. The evidence of a family's ability to feed its children is reflected unambiguously in the physical growth of the child, particularly how it gains and maintains weight and body fat. Interestingly, the subjective self-reported indicators of food sufficiency and hunger are moderately correlated with these anthropometric measures.

Expanding Poverty Indicators beyond Measures of Income and Hunger to Broaden Measures of Living Standards

The cost of food, which is most often reflected in poverty estimates, is not the only requirement for life in a modern society. A strong case can be made that in a modern urban society many other needs emerge, such as housing, clothing, transportation, and medical care, that deserve to be considered *basic life necessities* because they so profoundly determine standard of living and are highly associated with disease morbidity and mortality.

Housing Quality

As we have noted in chapter 2, urban shelter comes in a variety of forms: sumptuous private homes, small government-built houses, apartments, single-sex hostels, rooms in rich estates, add-on rooms or garages and shacks. Differences in shelter reflect financial and social status, ranging from large, well-appointed homes to provisional shelters in informal settlements constructed of materials ranging from cardboard and plastic to sticks and corrugated metal. Shelter also takes the form of a room or extension attached to government-built housing in formal settlements. These extra outside rooms and extended garages are often built to accommodate family, but may also be rented out in an environment of high demand for accommodation. Other living arrangements include apartments, shared housing, and hostels. Beds in hostels or dormitories were originally established for male migrant workers who were later joined by women and children. Population group differences are readily apparent with respect to housing accommodation.

If we consider shelter quality as an indicator of where groups fall along the continuum from poverty to wealth, the data for South Africa reveal how materially disadvantaged the 3 black population groups are in comparison to whites. The apartheid system affected Africans most negatively, followed by Coloreds and then Indians. This pattern is reproduced in just about every indicator of well-being, such that Africans are the worst off, followed by Coloreds, Indians, and then whites. Table 3.2 shows that a much smaller proportion of Africans resides in homes and a much larger proportion dwells in shacks than the other population groups. A similar pattern of inequality is noted when we examine the per capita size of homes. Whites live in homes that have an average of 2.5 rooms per person; Africans and Coloreds live in homes that have an average of 1 room per person. In the Birth-to-Ten study, consumption related to housing is assessed with respect to size, condition, and operating utility costs for cooking and heating. Similar patterns of disadvantage exist with respect to water and sanitation; fewer than one in five Africans have internal piped water, whereas almost all Indians and whites do. Similarly, almost all whites and Indians have electricity, while only slightly more than a third of Africans have access to electricity.

Table 3.2: Housing by Population Group

	African	Colored	Indian	White	Total
Shelter Shack House	14.9% 44.1%	3.7% 82.6%	.8% 71.5%	.2% 81.8%	11.0% 54.7%
Rooms per capita (mean)	.9	1.0	1.2	2.5	1.2
Water Source Flush toilet	34.2%	88.0%	99.6%	99.8%	52.1%

Consumption

Even when wages are the principal source of material resources for a family, self-reported incomes may be inaccurate because they fail to reflect all the resources available to the family. Moreover little is usually known about how secure these resources are and whether they are being deployed to help the child. Male wage earners, for example, may earn high salaries but face income disruptions because of lay-offs. Also, they may spend much of it outside of the home on second families or in ways that do not benefit children or their mothers. High wage earners may also have responsibilities to extended families, whom they support with remittances, thus reducing the base of support for those who reside in the household. These conditions are important for studies that purport to establish a relationship between financial resources, standard of living, economic status, and child development.

If it is difficult to estimate material resources available to a family by the wages and other monies coming into a family, a more revealing assessment of living standard may come from estimating what a family consumes. This approach to overcoming the limitations of self-reported income in essence is a shift from the income side to the expenditure side of the household financial ledger. Assessments of what a family owns, expends, or consumes can provide an alternative view of the standard of living a family enjoys. In addition to providing a fuller picture of resources, it has other advantages. For example, people may be more able and willing to report what they own or purchase than what they earn. Reports of material possessions can be verified through observation. In this way living standards can be indexed by the kinds of goods and resources that a family is able to access, including water, housing, electricity, sanitation, health care, and transportation. This shift in emphasis from income to consumption expands the definition of need or necessity beyond food and shelter to a broader array of goods and services that impact quality of life in urban communities.

Evidence of white economic advantage is made even clearer by this expanded array of household consumption indicators. The pattern of black disadvantage observed in income, hunger, and poverty rates is sustained in the data on the household amenities, durable consumer items, and modes of transportation to which blacks and whites have access. Table 3.3 reveals that while some consumer goods, such as radios, are nearly ubiquitous among South Africans, refrigerators and telephones that are now almost universally present in the homes of whites and Indians are not nearly as common among Africans and Coloreds. Moreover, electricity, the hallmark of modernity and the gateway to many other life enhancements, was available to only slightly more than a third of all Africans in 1993. Other consumer goods such as automobiles are relatively scarce and are found in less than 25 percent of African households.

Table 3.4 provides a revealing portrait of the economic interiors of white, Indian, Colored, and African households by displaying where they expend their economic resources and the materials they have access to. Specifically it shows the percent of total income that is expended on several areas of life's essentials (e.g., food, housing, health care, clothing), discretionary consumption (e.g., jewelry, vacations), and asset accumulation (insurance, savings). In absolute terms, whites have more and spend more money across every category of expenditure, with one exception—remittances, that is, money sent to another household for the support of extended family members. This is the one category where expenditures by Africans exceed those of all other groups. On average, Africans send about R37 per month, as compared to R19 for Coloreds, R20 for Indians, and R24 for whites. Given the low average family income of Africans, this amounts to 3.3 percent of total income. All other groups spend 1 percent or less. In regard to percentage of total income, Africans expend more than half of their income on food, with very little left for other expenses. Coloreds spend 40 percent on food compared to 22 percent for whites. The gap between Africans and whites is startling: What whites spend on food each month per person (R407) is not exceedingly smaller than what Africans spend on an entire household (R588). A very small proportion of income is spent by Africans and Coloreds for child care (.9 percent, 3.1 percent) compared to whites (5.8 percent). This may reflect a somewhat greater reliance on family and friends than on paid care to watch children while parents are at work. A similar pattern exists for health care, where Africans and Coloreds spend

Table 3.3:
Percent of Each Population Group that Has Access to Consumer Durables

	African	Colored	Indian	White	All
Durables Owned					
Gas stove	11.2%	35.3%	23.0%	18.3%	14.7%
Primus cooker	71.9	17.4	6.6	6.1	53.3
Access to electricity	36.5	86.2	100	99.8	53.6
Electric kettle	17.4	70.0	82.9	97.3	38.5
Radio	79.3	77.6	92.2	96.4	82.7
TV	32.6	78.0	94.1	95.5	49.8
Electric stove	20.8	76.0	96.8	93.4	41.0
Refrigerator	23.8	72.7	97.2	96.3	43.4
Geyser	6.1	49.7	85.6	96.5	28.8
Telephone	8.2	48.5	75.21	88.8	28.4
Transport to Work					
Automobile	8.1	25.7	67.7	82.0	29.2
Walk	39.9	27.5	8.9	8.6	30.2
Motor vehicle	9.8	33.2	70.2	91.9	28.8
Bicycle	18.1	26.3	20.1	49.2	23.3
Number	5,744,000	6,413,001	2,265,001	1,541,600	8,153,400

Table 3.4: Household Consumption Expenditure by Population Group[2]

	African	Colored	Indian	White
Total monthly expenditure	R1,111	R1,854	R3,306	R4,742
Per capita expenditure	R342	R495	R854	R1,845
Housing	R110 (9.9%)	R254 (13.7%)	R486 (20.3%)	R962 (20.3%)
Utilities	R88 (7.9%)	R206 (11.1%)	R317 (9.6%)	R390 (7.8%)
Food	R588 (R181 per capita) (52.9%)	R742 (40.0%)	R1,088 (32.9%)	R1,048 (R407 per capita) (22.1%)
Child care	R10 (0.9%)	R58 (3.1%)	R205 (6.2%)	R275 (5.8%)
Transportation	R49 (4.4%)	R74 (4.0%)	R132 (4.0%)	R204 (4.3%)
Household	R9 (0.8%)	R19 (1.0%)	R26 (0.8%)	R28 (0.6%)
Clothing	R46 (4.1%)	R93 (5.0%)	R162 (4.9%)	R152 (3.2%)
Health	R7 (0.6%)	R19 (1.0%)	R66 (2.0%)	R123 (2.6%)
Holiday/ jewelry	R7 (0.6%)	R13 (0.7%)	R76 (2.3%)	R152 (3.2%)
Insurance	R10 (0.9%)	R65 (3.5%)	R192 (5.8%)	R379 (8.0%)
Savings	R22 (2.0%)	R30 (1.6%)	R72 (2.2%)	R166 (3.5%)
Schooling	R24 (2.2%)	R28 (1.5%)	R60 (1.8%)	R147 (3.1%)
Remittances	R37 (3.3%)	R19 (1.0%)	R20 (0.6%)	R24 (0.5%)
Personal expenses[3]	R74 (6.7%)	R171 (9.0%)	R291 (8.8%)	R398 (8.4%)
Other occasional nonfood expenditure[4]	R39 (2.7%)	R72 (3.8%)	R112 (3.4%)	R318 (6.7%)

less than R20 per month, or 1 percent, as opposed to whites (R123 per month, or 2.6 percent). The large proportion of income spent on food and shelter is reflected in the relatively low savings rate among Africans (R22 per month) and Coloreds (R30 per month), and expenditures on insurance to protect assets (R10, R65 respectively vs. R379 for whites). These differences are reflected in the asset as minimal living level for each population group. For example, for a family of four in an urban setting in 1996, the minimum living level was R891 ($197) per month for blacks and R951 ($210) for Coloreds. Overall, about 40 percent of the African population has household incomes below the minimum living level, 32 percent living in urban and 68 percent in rural areas.

Access to Health Services
In ways similar to education and sustained employment, good health is an important resource and a key to quality of life. The absence of good health is often seen as a concomitant to poverty in the form of high maternal and infant mortality, low birth weight, high rates of disability, more extended and serious courses of diseases because they are left untreated, and low life expectancy. While it is clear that high income and wealth cannot guarantee good health, the absence of resources to maintain health and treat illness is a critical component of standard of living because it is so strongly associated with high morbidity and mortality.

Generally, South Africans with money have no difficulty obtaining a level of health care rivaling that provided anywhere in the world. For the poor, the story is entirely different. Publicly subsidized health services, are available on a fee-for-service basis. Even with government support of health care, the starting cost of treatment for an illness could be as much as R8. Together with transport to and from the services and income lost through absence from work, this constitutes a significant expenditure particularly for the most desperately poor. Close to 61 percent of Africans experience financial impediments to seeking health care, whereas only 13.2 percent of whites report such difficulties.

Poverty as Restricted Access to Financial Capital
To conceptualize *household wealth* as integral to an assessment of poverty seems illogical. After all, poverty refers to a chronic lack of resources and wealth to a chronic surplus. Accordingly, household wealth is predicated on the ability to acquire and accumulate assets, to set aside for future use resources that exceed current needs. How can household wealth reveal much about the experience of poverty?

Table 3.5a: Household Debt by Population Group

	African	Colored	Indian	White
Monthly debt repayment (rands)	58.8	104.0	103.2	342.3
Debt repayment as percentage of income	5.8	5.1	2.5	5.3

Table 3.5b: Sources of Household Debt by Race

Type of Debt	African	Colored	Indian	White
Relative/friend	16.2%	6.6%	10.4%	8.2%
Government agency	0.5	1.8	1.7	1.4
Landlord	1.1	2.0	—	3.5
Banks/building society	1.6	5.4	8.4	30.0
Nongovernmental organization (NGO)	0.4	0.3	0.4	0.3
Money lender	2.0	1.0	—	0.4
Stokvel/credit union	1.3	—	—	0.8
Burial services	3.5	1.3	—	1.3
Employer	1.8	2.3	3.7	1.5
Credit purchases	30.7	33.8	42.3	24.4
Shopkeeper credit	37.8	33.4	30.3	22.7
Other	2.9	12.1	2.9	5.5

Accumulated wealth increases certainty regarding a household's ability to meet its future need. This future certainty is a remarkable and important feature in its own right. In truth, notion of wealth helps to highlight a principal source of distress in poverty, namely, the insecurity and unpredictability of deprivation which becomes the hardship of uncertainty. Even poor families vary in the extent to which they manage to put aside resources for a later date. Tracking the capacity of poor families to accumulate even modest wealth will give an important window onto differences among families which are nominally poor.

LOW WEALTH AND HIGH DEBT: Like other indicators of economic status and living standards, accumulated wealth is highly differentiated along population-group lines. For example, if we examine discretionary expenditures for luxury or nonessential items and savings, we note large population-group disparities. For discretionary items such as holidays or jewelry, Africans spend .6 percent and whites 3.2 percent.

The flip side of wealth or accumulated assets is debt. Temporary or short-term debt is frequently not considered a problem. Households often use debt to smooth out temporary cash flow problems related to the timing of receipt of income and making gaps between income and expenditures. In this case, debt is a convenience, and is in fact based on assets. In other cases, debt is incurred because people do not have sufficient income or other resources to meet their basic needs and wants. Debt involves a pledge of anticipated future income to acquire goods or services that one cannot afford to purchase with current cash. The offering of easy credit is often used by merchants and money-lenders as a strategy to entice and enable the poor to consume goods they might ordinarily forgo because they lack money. Tables 3.5a and 3.5b present data on South African families with respect to the amount and sources of debts by population group. The sources of debt reveal striking differences in ways that groups access capital they need when current income is insufficient for consumption. Almost 70 percent of blacks use debt to acquire necessities from small shopkeepers and to purchase household amenities on installment credit instead of paying for them outright. For the most part, Africans are much less likely than other groups to receive loans from the formal financial sector such as banks. Instead their loans are twice as likely as whites to come from family members. On average, Africans have levels of debt repayment that are not very different from Coloreds and whites in terms of monthly income, comprising between 5 and 6 percent of income.

Recently we have come to understand the importance of considering indicators of wealth as part of the focus on the economic status of households. Wealth in this sense refers to access to capital or the capacity to accumulate assets. As such, it relates to the possession of, for example, land and a home, as well as low levels of household debt. Ironically, considerations of wealth indicators may reveal much about the differences that exist even among poor people. Poverty focuses on need, but wealth provides an indicator of the ability of a family to acquire and maintain resources that exceed its minimal needs. Wealth reflects the dynamic aspects of economic status and the value of having resources to protect against vicissitudes in income. In addition individuals and households may be income-poor but asset-rich. This is the situation that people who own livestock may find themselves in. Accordingly analyses of socioeconomic status that expand their focus beyond the lack of resources to include issues of asset accumulation and levels of debt will provide a richer, more informative portrait of the lives of the poor. Importantly, economists have pointed out that the ability of families to possess and accumulate assets, such as in the form of land or savings, is an important indicator of economic well-being. The capacity to accrue savings and to accumulate financial assets over time provides a safeguard against threats to an income stream. In a sense it tells something about a family's ability to meet its needs during unpredictable times of economic distress. Persons who have the capacity to accumulate assets or to acquire wealth have higher levels of food security and security to protect them against periods of economic downturn and other misfortunes. Table 3.1 presents data on daily income and expenditures that make possible comparisons that speak to the relative ability of different population groups to spend less than they make and thus accrue savings. This table shows that in South Africa the financial situation of Africans as a group may be characterized as marginal. In contrast to all the other groups assessed, on average, African families expend more each day than they earn in income. On average, each household earns R33 but expends R37. This situation is akin to living a "hand-to-mouth" existence and suggests that little saving can take place. Although white households expend much more (R158), their significant advantage with respect to income (R213) means that wealth accumulation is possible. The ability to save and accumulate assets is an important indicator of financial status and a basis of financial stability. Material welfare requires an ability to accumulate resources in sufficient quantities to survive inevitable cycles of abundance and scarcity. Africans as a group are significantly disadvantaged.

In South Africa, the ability to bury a deceased family member and feed those attending the funeral is a cultural necessity and a matter of family pride for even the poorest of Africans. Poor families have developed structures to deal with these actual obligations. For example, the heavy expense of burying a family member is handled through borrowing, joining a burial society, or participating in savings schemes, which usually involves making monthly or weekly payments of small amounts to be drawn on in times of need. The burial societies are a form of insurance. Each insured member can count on having money for the cost of a burial and food for mourners who attend the funeral. Savings groups function, in some cases, like cooperatives from which members can take loans in emergencies. In other cases, they are like a Christmas Club in the United States, in which periodic payments are made to a merchant, typically the owner of a grocery and general goods store. Advance payments are made in anticipation of lean months of unemployment or unpaid vacations. Participants receive previously agreed-upon supplies each week for a designated period of time. With respect to savings, blacks, for example, report saving about 2 percent of their income, whereas whites save 3.5 percent. Insurance purchase is another form of savings for families. Here blacks spend less than 1 percent, but whites spend approximately 8 percent.

Human Capital: Education, Occupation, and Social Support

Material resources and financial adequacy, by themselves, are not enough for human development. Although food, shelter, and certain material goods are essential to life and physical growth, much more is needed. Consumption and expenditures are not the only ways to gauge poverty, and other approaches include a focus on individuals' social resources that can be used to acquire, for example, education and occupation. These resources also enhance the quality of life; higher levels of education and the self-esteem associated with high-status occupations give individuals psychological resources needed to solve problems of day-to-day life that might not be available to people with fewer resources.

Coleman (1988) identifies a range of human and social resources necessary for development and coined the term *human capital* to describe nonmaterial resources. The notion of human capital is conceptually related to that of *social status,* a term employed by social scientists to characterize intellectual, nonmaterial resources, as well as worldviews associated with social stratification based on education and income. Building from these notions, *social capital* refers to social and cultural resources available to a family over and above those which are chiefly financial in nature. It also encompasses social support, capacity for modeling coping and problem-solving, provision of intellectual stimulation, and the conditions necessary for the development of healthy ethnic and gender identity conveyed to children by adults, particularly family members.

These additional social resources needed for child development cannot be easily reduced to monetary equivalents and, as such, are difficult to combine with economic indicators into a single index of welfare. Entwistle and Astone (1994) propose a set of guidelines that constitute a plausible approach for capturing social and economic status. Their approach incorporates measures of human capital and family/household structure along with financial resources. In this approach, financial resources are measured in terms of pretax cash income, transfer payments, and subsidies for food or shelter minus housing costs. Human capital refers to personal nonmaterial resources that family members provide to children and is most often indexed by educational attainment. The family dimension refers to the presence of biological parents, stepparents, or grandparents in the household with the indexed child. Hauser (1994) agrees in principle with these recommendations but criticizes the omission of the occupational status of the primary wage earner. Even with disagreements about components to be included under the rubric of social capital, most scholars agree that a family's available social resources cannot be ignored, because they have a demonstrable and palpable impact on material and social quality of life, and that they strongly influence child development outcomes.

Education is important because it is often seen as a means of upward mobility. Better educated individuals typically live in more advantaged material conditions. Several indicators of education pertain in assessments of social status. Typically a distinction is made between literacy and illiteracy, with a Grade 5 education being a widely accepted minimum for literacy. As a whole, South Africa has a literacy rate of 55 percent across the entire population. However, Africans have a lower rate than whites (52 percent vs. 75 percent). Another distinction is whether or not the person graduated from high school, or, the equivalent in South Africa, passed the national matriculation examination at the end of high school. Only about 11 percent of Africans over the age of eighteen had passed this examination in 1993, in contrast to more than 63 percent of whites. Further education includes advanced training beyond high school, and university education or a professional qualification. It is not surprising that very small percentages of Africans enter or complete further education; although they constitute about 79 percent of the South African population, they make up only a fraction of the nation's doctors, engineers, accountants, and lawyers. Only 15 percent of Africans, in comparison to 63 percent of whites, hold high-status professional, administrative, and sales occupations. Interestingly, these rates are similar to those for passing the matriculation exam. (See table 3.6.) For a substantial proportion of the African population, there is no employment other than what they can create for themselves in the informal economy.

Table 3.6: Human Capital Indicators by Population Group

	African	Colored	Indian	White	Total
Percent 18 and older who completed high school	11.0	15.5	40.1	61.0	19.9
High-status occupations (Prof/Admin/Sales)	14.7	27.2	53.7	63.4	18.9

Estimates of unemployment among the black majority are extraordinarily high, with estimates usually exceeding 35 percent (South African Institute of Race Relations 2000). Consequently, many families rely on the informal or microeconomic sector (e.g., hawking goods on the streets, or nonmonetary exchanges such as bartering and trading) to satisfy their basic needs. it is apparent that on all these basic measures of social and economic status income, housing, food, asset accumulation, debt, education and employment, blacks as a group are worse off than whites and among blacks, Africans fare the worst. The poverty prevalences rates differ somewhat depending on the indicator that is used but the pattern is invariant.

Approach Adopted by BTT to Assess Poverty

Concern about family well-being and child development has made the question of poverty and living standards a common focus of academic discussion and policy analyses. These discussions often center on the importance and feasibility of assuring that each person has access to the basic necessities of life. The ubiquity of poverty among blacks and the compelling nature of human suffering often associated with it reinforce the need to consider carefully the impact of poor living standards on family functioning and ultimately child development. However, to engage in serious analysis of the consequences of living standards for child development requires moving from global concepts of poverty on which there is consensus, to more precise formulations with clearly specified indicators. The diversity of views among the parties concerned about these issues, the divergence of their interests, and the lack of a shared language make it difficult to reach consensus on what constitute the most sensible ways to measure notions such as poverty and its associates: living standards, economic status, and hardship. Ironically, we may have greater consensus on the hardship created by poverty and poor living standards than on what they are and how to represent them. The BTT study, with its interest in the impact of living standards and hardship on children's development, attempted to specify indicators to be used in assessing these concepts. Many commonly used indices of poverty lack the specificity needed to differentiate among the extreme levels of poverty that often exist in countries with wide income disparities, such as South Africa.

In BTT we opted for a set of indicators of a family's economic status and living standards that we expected to be especially sensitive in detecting variations in the material hardship experienced by families clustered at the low end of the socioeconomic spectrum. Accordingly, the ideal measure for our purposes would ascertain the success of households in acquiring life necessities such as food, shelter, clothing, and the resources to maintain them. Assessment of a household's *wealth* (i.e., accumulation of financial assets) also seemed critical because of what it might reveal about the degree of stability and security the family experiences with respect to meeting its basic needs. Given the importance that predictability and security of food and shelter have for quality of life, households need to accumulate resources prudently to protect themselves against loss of income or large unexpected expenses. Moreover, material assets alone do not tell the entire story about the child-rearing environment. Other resources (sometimes labeled human and social capital) can significantly impact child outcomes. Accordingly, we decided that human capital in the forms of maternal education and the occupation of the head of household were candidates for inclusion. The outcome of this selection and specification process inevitably involves compromises that may not be entirely satisfactory to all.

The question of what dimensions to include is not the only thorny issue in the assessment of living standards, economic well-being, and social status. For example, whose financial, material, and human assets should be considered as most relevant in efforts to characterize the child's environment: mothers only? the biological parents? the household? the extended family? Are material resources to be defined on the basis of the mother's, or on the parents' joint resources? When the father does not reside in the same household with the mother and children, either because they are not married or because the father is working in another region, should his economic and educational resources be included in estimates of assets available to the child? Should an assessment include the resources of the extended family or household in which the parent and child reside?

The approach adopted by BTT regarding assessment of living standards and economic status assigns a preeminent role to the biological mother or other primary caretaker. The material resources and human capital available to her, whether through a spouse, cohabiting partner, or extended family, are defined as resources available to the child. The justification for this is straightforward. It was driven by an interest in the effects of material hardship on a child's physical, social, and emotional development. This required emphasizing aspects of family structure and organization most relevant to child development. In South Africa, as in the United States, child-rearing environments are diverse in form and can be fluid in membership. Increasingly, children are being raised by their single mothers or other female caregivers in a wide range of household and family structures. For various reasons, fathers may be present only episodically, and may contribute inconsistently, if at all, to the child's maintenance and socialization. For the child, the mother or mother figure is the constant in this dynamic situation. Employment in the formal sector, mostly in personal services, occurs at higher rates for women than men. Consequently, mothers with partners are increasingly the functional if not symbolic heads of household, the primary wage earners, and the primary guardians for children. Male partners may leave, and others may step in to take their places. For this reason, the mother's education and income are pivotal in assigning social status to the family unit that provides the context for children's development.

To assess living standards of mothers and their children, a summary index of socioeconomic status, the Household Economic and Social Status Index (HESSI) was created.[1] The HESSI uses an interview format to gather information, usually from mothers, on material and human capital available to the household. Material or financial capital was indexed by housing quality, adequacy of food supply, material consumption or ownership of consumer goods, and wealth in the form of accumulated financial assets. Human capital was indexed by assets such as education and employment status of the principal wage earner in the household. Specific questions were included in the interview about housing quality, food adequacy, accumulated financial assets and material consumption, and educational and occupational level. *Housing quality* was assessed through questions on: the type of home (shack to single-family home); the number of rooms used for sleeping; the availability of a separate bathroom, separate kitchen, refuse pickup, electricity, water, and a toilet; the presence of household pests (flies, rats, lice, bedbugs, cockroaches); and serious air pollution. *Material Consumption* was indicated by possession of major appliances and modern convenience items. These included: automobiles, refrigerator, stove, washing machine, telephone, radio, television, and children's toys. *Food adequacy* was inferred from questions about household shortages and child hunger. *Wealth,* or asset accumulation, was assessed through questions about savings, insurance, real estate, and other financial assets. Additional information was obtained regarding household composition, cash income, and marital or habitation status. If married or cohabiting, similar information was obtained on the woman's husband or partner. Life insurance, savings, and home ownership are considered important aspects of economic status, because they reflect the ability to garner and store financial assets as a protection against future difficulties or threats to income.

With regard to indicators of human capital, we assessed the educational level of the mother, the biological father, and a cohabiting part-

Table 3.7: Household Characteristics and Living Standards of the African Poor[d]

	Poor (N = 210)	Middle Class (N - 214)	Affluent (N = 201)	F-Value (df = 2,622)
Hollingshead rating	**14.4** (8.5)	**22.0** (8.9)	**31.2** (8.9)	188.5[c]
Housing quality	**2.0** (.5)	**2.3** (.4)	**2.6** (.4)	96.5[c]
Consumer goods	**2.1** (1.0)	**3.1** (1.1)	**4.6** (1.4)	219.7[c]
Income earners per household	**.9** (.7)	**1.3** (.7)	**1.5** (.8)	28.1[c]
Proportion of adults in house-hold employed	**.3** (.3)	**.4** (.3)	**.6** (.3)	45.7[c]
Persons in household	**7.9**	**7.2**	**6.4**	9.6[c]
Per capita rooms	**.3** (.2)	**.4** (.2)	**.4** (.4)	12.3[c]
Monthly utilities cost(R)	**158.50** 64.4	**186.50** 90.4	**228.4** 1 113.1	29.55[c]

[d]Means in bold, and standard deviations in parentheses.
[a]$p < .05$ [b]$p < .01$ [c]$p < .001$

ner if there was one. The second indicator in the human capital category is occupational status or prestige. Occupational status is based on categorizing the job held by the principal wage earner into one of several categories that are organized by prestige and, to some extent, earning power (Nakao and Treas 1992). The Hollingshead Scale of Social and Economic Status is perhaps the most widely cited measure of SES. It uses a seven-point educational attainment scale multiplied by three, added to a nine-point occupational prestige rating multiplied by five for husbands and wives to classify families into one of seven social classes. These social classes are thought to index relative social position, which in turn is strongly related to lifestyle and other outcomes related to health and well-being (Hollingshead 1975). In BTT, a scale related to that of the Hollingshead Scale for occupation was used, but which was extended at the lower end to include employment in the informal sector.

Demographic Profile of Urban Poverty

To answer questions about who the poor are, a series of statistical analyses were computed on the data collected in BTT. Among Africans, what demographic features characterize the groups most likely to experience material hardships associated with poverty? Table 3.7 presents data comparing the economic and material circumstances of families who could be classified according to their socioeconomic status. A family's classification was significantly predictive of its ability to meet basic needs and in its experience of material hardship. Of all the groups, the poorest group has the largest family size, lives in the most crowded households, experiences the lowest adult employment rates, and sustains the highest rates of hunger. Households headed by single mothers with only a primary school education are disproportionately represented among the poor. About half of the families in the poorest group were unable to provide adequate food for their children (about 20 percent of the BTT sample). Children living with mothers and their male partners were more likely to experience hunger than children residing with their single mothers and grandmothers. Our analyses also show that households with higher occupational levels, fewer people, a resident grandmother, and better-educated mothers are more likely to have adequate food and better housing than smaller households without a drandmother or those in which parents are of low educational or occupational status. The presence of grandmothers and partners, along with higher educational and occupational status, is also associated with a higher level of consumer goods in the household. For housing quality, the only significant predictors are education and household size. Overall, the poor often are families with single mothers who did not attend high school, living in households with more than six persons, and who are unemployed or underemployed.

Conclusion

The portrait of poverty and living standards is not altogether negative. The good news in these data is that the majority of South Africans are living well above the subsistence level. Even among Africans, who constitute the most economically disadvantaged group, a majority have resources that are at least minimally adequate. Nevertheless, the importance to children of efforts to address poverty cannot be overestimated: The gap between blacks and whites is great, and the 40 percent who are poor suffer absolute deprivation and the sting of living in conditions in which they are surrounded by affluence. While it is true that material deprivation is a consequence of the inequality spawned by apartheid, differences between blacks and whites in living standards have not receded with the demise of that system's institutional racism. It is a widely held truism in South Africa that in the absence of economic reform to raise the living standards of the poor, peace and democracy will be difficult to sustain. Most importantly, the very low standard of living experienced in some segments of the population is inimical to the health and development of children. This issue is discussed in greater detail in chapter 10, where we also address questions about the relationship of poverty to child development in South Africa.

Notes

1. For additional details regarding the development, psychometric properties, and analysis of the HESSI see Barbarin and Khomo 1997.

2. Sample number = 8,763; Rounding off results in marginal differences in corresponding totals.

3. Personal expenses include: tobacco, alcohol, entertainment. personal care, newspapers, telephone

4. Other expenses include: washing, dues, taxes and household labor.

Chapter 4

The Decline of Political Violence

The Pervasive Experience of Violence in South Africa

Few issues dominate the collective psyche of the South African people as fully or generate as much debate as crime and violence. From newspaper headlines to lead stories on radio and TV news, the nation is inundated with disturbing images of violence in both public spheres and the private domains of family life. Shocking accounts of shootings, stabbings, sexual assaults, murders, muggings, car hijackings, forced entries into homes, and burglaries stoke the fires of public anxiety about personal safety. Concern about peace and safety is not new to South Africa. Throughout much of its history, violence has dominated the social landscape (Sparks 1990). Although some social observers link the current epidemic of crime and violence to the distortions of law and social order that occurred during the apartheid era, historians provide accounts of brutality going as far back as the arrival of European colonizers and even earlier. Although contemporary concerns about safety are not new, the public discourse in South Africa about the nature and motives of violence has shifted considerably over the period from 1980 to the present. In that time, violence in South Africa has taken several forms and served a variety of purposes. Though governments are responsible for the safety of their citizens, under apartheid the South African government abrogated this responsibility in order to preserve white hegemony. It used violence to suppress political dissent and the mobilization of opposition to its separatist policies. During that period, the forms of violence evolved from politically motivated confrontation between blacks and the apartheid government, to secret government campaigns of terror, to economically driven ethnic conflict, to criminal violence, to juvenile gang warfare, and back again to public acts of terror. At the same time, an increased sensitivity and attention to violence and abuse within the family has emerged. Not surprisingly, many South Africans, correctly or incorrectly, have come to believe that violence in both public and private spheres is spiraling out of control. To be sure, the liberation movement responded to government violence with violence of its own. Although few equate violence as an instrument of political oppression with violence as a strategy for resisting oppression, proponents of non-violence such as Gandhi argue that once unleashed, the monster of violence is difficult to contain. To wit, violence in South Africa has persisted beyond the oppressive conditions that gave rise to it. It has survived with new justifications and purposes as a means for redressing perceived inequities, as a strategy for resolving personal and economic disputes, and as a campaign tactic in electoral politics. It is used openly by syndicates to support criminal activity and is justified by citizen vigilante groups to fight crime. It has also become a symptom of psychological alienation by youth who build a code of honor and seek social purpose around warfare with competing gangs.

Most regrettably, within the family, violence has been sanctioned as a principal means of socialization, discipline, and social control, and within educational settings until the recent passage of laws that prohibit corporal punishment in schools (Henderson 1996). Contemporary experience with violence in South Africa is a compelling demonstration that the genie of political violence is more difficult to put back into the bottle after it has been let out. Instead, it reappears under new guises and is energized by new motives such as economic competition, politics, crime, and the territorial wars of youth gangs. The result is a climate of intimidation, fear, and danger that is inimical to the health and development of young children. All the while, the government response to violence is criticized as ineffective, and government supporters in turn dismiss claims about violence as exaggerated, unsubstantiated, and trumpeted solely to embarrass those in power. In the meantime, the poor, particularly those residing in the townships, continue to carry the heaviest burden from crime and violence. For them, nothing else, not even the quest for gainful employment and adequate housing, seems to stir up the same level of passionate yearning for effective collective action as does hope for a peaceful life free of violence.

The roots of South African violence go much deeper than the apartheid era, but the constraints of space and our focus on contemporary child development rule out a thorough social and historical analysis of this issue. Because our discussion of violence is motivated by questions about its influence on Mandela's children, our historical analysis is limited. Accordingly, this treatment of violence is not undertaken to ferret out the historical roots of contemporary violence, to resolve disputes about whether it is worsening, or to draw conclusions about how fully the data justify concerns for public safety. Instead our purpose is to provide information on which to base a later discussion of the impact of political violence, community danger, direct victimization, and family violence on young children. This goal is to be accomplished by reviewing what is known about the forms and prevalence of violence and the perceptions of danger based on evidence from archival accounts, national surveys, and interviews with Birth-to-Ten (BTT) parents. This chapter portrays changes in the sources, functions, motives, and nature of contemporary violence in South Africa. It demonstrates how the dominant modes of violence have evolved from direct confrontation of blacks by the apartheid government, government undercover operations, government condoning of cross-ethnic violence, interethnic competition, crime, juvenile gang warfare, and traditionally controlling relationships between men and women (Straker et al. 1996). The chapter documents changes in the types of violence that have predominated and in the perceptions South Africans have of personal safety at home and in the community. We illustrate these trends using archival accounts of selected incidents, government crime statistics, national surveys, and data collected as part of the BTT project. In this way, we set the stage to interrogate the effects of violence on the development of young children.

Violence and Children

The healthy development of children depends heavily on the confluence of auspicious conditions such as access to material resources adequate to meet basic needs and guarantees of physical safety. For this reason, concerns about public safety in South Africa have direct relevance to our consideration of early child development there and the social factors influencing it.

Children are affected directly and indirectly by violence in South Africa and often pay a heavy price for societal violence. Take, for instance, thirteen-year-old Hector Peterson, who was killed by police during the 1976 school protests in Soweto. The photograph of his shooting was so appalling that it mobilized world opinion against apartheid. In other less-dramatic instances of violence, children living under apartheid saw their parents harassed and beaten by police and insulted by white employers; they waited anxiously for a parent who never returned home, presumed arrested or killed; were thrashed by their parents for what some might call minor wrongdoings; and were forced, with a whip, to work alongside their parents in the fields on white farms. The commonplace nature of violence is reflected in children's own writings. For example, the diaries of preteen children, published by Oswald Mtshali in *Give Us a Break* (1988), are replete with descriptions of violence in the homes and streets of Soweto in the 1980s. Contemporary violence has a new stage and new actors working with new scripts; but children remain unprotected from violence, and are frequently its victims. During 1999, a baby was killed on her mother's back by a white farmer who claimed that they were trespassing; another was raped by her grandfather, causing massive internal damage; and yet another died shortly after birth after being thrown down a drop toilet by a desperate, and perhaps deranged, mother. Children have watched at school while teenage thugs have taken over schools and kept teachers hostage, and while male teachers have compelled young female pupils to have sex with them to avoid trumped-up misdemeanors or failure during the school year. Children have watched their mothers being raped or have been abandoned on highways when their parents were killed in a hijacking. They are the perpetuators and the victims of rampant bullying in schools. For South African children, there seems to be no end to violence and no safety from its effects.

Trends in Political Violence: 1980–1994

In the 1980s, the apartheid government stepped up its use of force, becoming involved in direct confrontations with citizens protesting its racist regime. Government violence accelerated dramatically once black resistance became a credible threat to the continued existence of apartheid rule. Throughout the 1980s, government violence took the form of repressive measures relying on the use of the military, riot police, and surveillance task groups. Its initial tactics were to ban protest marches, rallies, and strikes and enforce these bans with massive police force. It disbanded organizations by making them illegal and banished individuals by a system of detention without trial, house arrests, and forced relocations to remote areas. In implementing this campaign, the government employed overwhelming force that engendered terror and exacted a high price if challenged. Even peaceful demonstrations for political reform were met with government force: In one incident, interracial religious groups from the Johannesburg metropolitan area organized a march of about four thousand people. They were confronted by police and given three minutes to disperse. One of the march leaders appealed to the police commander for the marchers to be given more time to disperse. Many protesters, including clerics and nuns, were still kneeling in prayer when the police charged into the crowd, clubbing protesters with batons. As the apartheid government became increasingly violent in its efforts to repress dissent, the liberation movement responded with violence of its own. Several liberation movements formed military wings to engage in armed struggle against the government. Often this involved guerrilla attacks to destroy strategic targets such as power stations. These were intended to disrupt day-to-day life more than to achieve a military objective such as the overthrow of the government.

Confrontations between blacks and government forces were triggered when blacks resisted government attempts to impose repressive policies on black townships. By the mid-1980s, the apartheid government became increasingly restive in its efforts to quell dissent. Although most demonstrations were initiated as peaceful dissent, violent clashes with the police and the South African Defense Force (SADF) became more and more common. In one case, a vehicle was torched when the apartheid authorities banned a march planned by high school students. Stone-throwing and fire-bombing were frequent tactics, particularly by youth. The government escalated its use of force by placing large police and paramilitary garrisons such as the Internal Stability Units and the SADF in black communities. As parents and children went about their lives at work and school, they were confronted by ubiquitous gun turrets erected on the outskirts of black townships and along roads connecting townships to white areas. Schools were regularly occupied by armed soldiers to suppress dissident activity. Young people viewed the soldiers with great suspicion in spite of occasional efforts to win them over. "These army troops pretend to be our friends while, on the other hand, they are killing us like dogs" (Open School 1986).

The voices of youth are often remarkable for their disarming candor and penetrating insight about the difficulty of life under the oppressive conditions of apartheid. "We can no longer go as free people on our own land. We are always running away from the SADF troops. We are guarded by troops every day as if we are criminals. They cause suffering, hunger, and sorrow to our people" (Open School 1986). Even politically uninvolved youth such as Oupa Sithole came under the widening shadow of suspicion and were drawn unwittingly into violence. One evening, Oupa was walking home from a friend's house. As he reached the corner of his street, he was shot at by white policemen who were hiding behind a fence. Eyewitnesses claimed that when the police caught him, they removed his shoes and shot him again under his feet. Oupa was then arrested. He was not taken to the hospital until the following day. Days later, Oupa's father was allowed to see him. He found that Oupa had more than a hundred birdshot wounds, his left leg was swollen and he had no feeling in it. The inhumanity of events such as these prompted wry comments from children caught in the web of violence. They pose unanswerable questions about human life and the purpose of human existence: "The situation in our townships is so disgusting that you sometimes ask yourself a question which has got no answer and that is 'Why did God create human beings?'" (Open School 1986).

Covert Government Efforts to Instigate Violence

Over time, the apartheid regime recognized that its efforts to contain blacks through police action and occupation were proving to be costly and ineffective. This sober assessment contributed to an escalation of its efforts to intimidate and control the black population through covert means. The government continued repressive police action and overt military occupation of black communities, but combined it with covert operations against the black community that included kidnappings, arrests, torture, assassination, and instigation of violence between ethnic groups (Daniels 1996). Such actions were most often targeted to individuals believed to be active in the anti-apartheid struggle. The state conducted surveillance and raided the homes and offices of persons who expressed opposition to its rule. It used many of its state powers, such as capital punishment, evictions, forced removals, and the destruction of homes and personal property, to victimize and control the black population (Mehlwana 1996). It also resorted to blatantly illegal tactics such as death squads, detention without trials, arson, poisoning, and bombs.

The government also escalated its campaign of violence by promoting and exploiting ethnic differences. For example, it furtively instigated conflict and financially sponsored acts of violence by Zulus against the Xhosas or between Inkatha and African National Congress (ANC) groups. The government's "divide and conquer" strategy took many different forms: recruiting, training, arming, and funding blacks to attack other blacks. Once recruited, armed surrogates of the apartheid regime would engage in indiscriminate massacres, assassinations of politically active figures, intimidation, strikes, attacks on commuter trains, taxi wars, and warlordism, particularly in informal settlements, while the police forces looked the other way. The government played a continuing role in stirring the flames of ethnic tensions by favoring one group over another in enforcing the law, confiscating weapons, and in condoning one group's lawlessness by looking the other way. A frequent theme in narratives about these attacks is that the police revealed a bias in failing to protect one group from the other.

Take, for example, the incident in which three thousand heavily armed Inkatha supporters from hostels around the Gauteng area marched through Diepkloof. They were accompanied by the South African Police. Though both Inkatha and residents from other ethnic groups were involved in incidents, particularly outside Jabulani and Merafe hostels, it was claimed by some observers that police tear-gassed and dispersed residents, while leaving large groups of heavily armed Zulu vigilantes alone. Seventeen people were killed and, according to police, ninety-seven were injured. It is not known how many of the deaths and injuries were caused by police and how many through vigilante actions. In a similar case, residents in one hostel felt that security forces favored competing groups in clamping down on violence.

In a separate incident, residents of Chiawelo have claimed that the police killed three people and injured thirty others when they fired on residents who gathered for selfprotection in anticipation of a possible Inkatha attack. Inkatha members were coming by bus from other areas to Chiawelo to attend a funeral of a member slain in ethnic violence. The police reported that they fired rubber bullets and guns at a group of people attacking the bus of Inkatha supporters on its way to the funeral. They did not know if there were any injuries. The ANC has claimed that the residents, ANC supporters, were not involved in the disruption of the funeral in Chiawelo. Rather, the ANC averred that residents had gathered at a local gas station to defend themselves in the event of an Inkatha attack. Police then shot at the residents.

Sometimes false rumors were spread about attacks supposedly planned by one group against another, in the hope of inflaming passions and precipitating preemptive attacks. In other cases, Zulus posing as ANC supporters would attack their own people to inspire reprisals by Zulus against the ANC. In one incident, a man, who was allegedly Zulu-speaking, was stabbed and beaten to death by a group of about two hundred men. The attackers were described as wearing T-shirts imprinted with the ANC symbol. This was viewed with suspicion by many, since Soweto residents do not usually identify their political affiliation for fear of being attacked by opposing groups. Innocent bystanders suffered most in this secret war waged by the government. Ordinary citizens on their way to work or market simply trying to provide for their families became casualties in a war not of their choosing. Take as an instance the following reported incident taken from the archives of the Human Rights Committee:

> At 3:00 A.M. residents of Chicken Farm squatter camp heard gunshots and saw a number of strange people getting out of mini-buses in an open field not far from the Kliptown train sta-

tion. The men then moved towards the station and boarded the Johannesburg-bound train. The attack took place at 5:45 A.M., a peak train time, between the Kliptown and Nancefield Stations. About 5 gunmen opened fire on commuters indiscriminately when the train left the Kliptown Station. The victims either suffered from gunshot wounds or injuries sustained from jumping out of the train; 3 of the dead were women. Once the train arrived at Nancefield Station the gunmen again opened fire on unsuspecting people waiting on the platform. Two bodies were later found under the railway bridge next to the station. As the train approached Orlando Station additional shots were fired. By the time the train had stopped at the next station the gunmen had disappeared. At least 8 people were killed and 18 injured. One of the injured has claimed that the gunmen called the passengers, "Mandela's dogs."

Even without firm proof, Sotho and Xhosa observers rushed to the conclusion that the violence was perpetrated by Zulus. Many felt compelled by a sense of honor to retaliate. Once started, the brushfires of ethnic conflict were difficult to contain and rarely gave way to reasoned pleas to explore the real sources and motives for the fighting. Even when the government's role in the attack was recognized, the desire for vengeance and the need to avoid appearing so weak as to invite future attacks was difficult to restrain. Thus the violence between Zulus and other ethnic group became a self-perpetuating cycle. As a consequence, well-publicized bloody encounters of Inkatha Freedom Party partisans with members of the African National Congress occurred with increasing frequency in the waning days of the apartheid regime.

It is not at all surprising that the apartheid government routinely denied any role in spreading rumors or in sponsoring such attacks. However, the Human Rights Committee and later the Truth and Reconciliation Commission (TRC) gathered incontrovertible evidence of the role of the government in human rights violations. In an application (No. 2586/96) to the Truth and Reconciliation Commission, Brian Victor Mitchell of the South African Police reports the following: "The African National Congress/United Democratic Front was not looked upon as being anti-government or anti-state, but as the enemy. The Inkatha Freedom Party was regarded as the government's ally and was therefore to be assisted in its fight against the ANC/UDF." Mitchell found the Inkatha leadership in his area to be weak and vulnerable, needing assistance. He considered it his duty to see to it that the ANC/UDF were countered effectively within his area. He discussed the matter with Captain Terreblanche, who decided to make special constables available to render military and offensive assistance to Inkatha.

Testimony offered at TRC hearings demonstrated how extensive government use of violence actually was. Many ordinary citizens came forward to tell personal stories about how they suffered the loss of their homes to arson, as well as poisonings, letter bombs, rapes, maiming, and torture (e.g., having fingernails pulled out). Frank admissions by government agents often corroborated citizen testimony. One amnesty application contained an admission that the Police Riot Unit commonly employed torture to obtain confessions from ANC supporters. If a confession was not forthcoming, police would drive and offload their ANC captives to Inkatha strongholds or would throw them from police vans into rivers. Candor does not characterize all testimony by government officials regarding participation in covert operations. In an appearance before the TRC that is remarkable for its evasiveness, retired police general, J. J. Viktor, founder of Vlakplaas (an internal security force responsible for many atrocities), repeatedly denied that he ordered police in 1986 to fire-bomb the houses of anti-apartheid activists. When confronted with incontrovertible evidence, he replied tersely, "It was only a *suggestion!*" [1]

Black Collaboration with Apartheid

To support white soldiers and police units, blacks were recruited and hurriedly trained as Kits Constables to serve as police. These black police officers committed some of the worst atrocities against blacks and were reviled by their communities as traitors. The disdain was often exhibited in direct attacks. For example, youths in Soweto assaulted a black policeman stuck in a traffic jam they had caused by setting a car on fire. When they noticed that he was wearing a police uniform and driving a police vehicle, his car was stoned, though he managed to escape largely unhurt. Other collaborators targeted for reprisals by blacks were not as fortunate. Moise Khitane (pseudonym), a highly controversial figure in the black community who participated actively in the apartheid civil administration, had refused to accede to exhortations from civic bodies to resign. Mr. Khitane, the Diepkloof mayor, was assassinated after several failed attempts on his life and in spite of extensive police protection surrounding his home and office.

Decline of Political Violence: 1990–1995

The Human Rights Committee in Johannesburg gathered and attempted to corroborate reports on violence using several archival sources, including newspapers, police reports, and reports of other

Table 4.1: Community Violence Indicators for Johannesburg and Soweto

Community	Incidents of political violence, 1990–1994	Households reporting direct victimization (%)	Households reporting some family violence (%)	Ratings of community danger, 1996	Cumulative risk, 1990–1996
Chiawelo	35	19	19	3	1
Diepkloof	812	17	35	4	3
Dlamini	196	18	25	3	2
Dube	135	18	22	1	1
Eldorado Park	5	17	7	3	0
Emdeni	18	17	23	4	1
Jabavu	3	15	17	5	1
Jabulani	726	21	33	5	4
Johannesburg	317	17	29	5	3
Klipspruit	161	20	31	3	3
Lenasia	20	9	7	2	0
Mapetla	10	13	14	2	0
Meadowlands	371	20	27	3	3
Mofolo	51	16	17	2	0
Molapo	5	18	27	4	2

Table 4.1 (Continued)

Community	Incidents of political violence, 1990–1994	Households reporting direct victimization (%)	Households reporting some family violence (%)	Ratings of community danger, 1996	Cumulative risk, 1990–1996
Moletsane	29	35	18	4	2
Moroka	8	14	33	3	1
Naledi	25	23	20	3	0
Noordgesig	8	26	7	3	1
Orlando East	55	18	22	2	0
Orlando West	55	8	28	2	1
Phiri	27	17	40	3	1
Pimville	45	10	21	2	0
Pimville Zone 1	45	27	15	3	0
Protea	138	37	11	1	2
Senaoane	0	20	17	3	1
Tladi	0	7	24	1	1
Westbury	0	29	23	4	2
Zola	16	18	26	5	2
Zondi	50	8	23	4	2
Mean	112	18.4	23	3	1.33

human rights organizations.[2] In particular, they collected data that make it possible to estimate the number of arrests, injuries, and killings occurring in the Johannesburg metropolitan area. Often these data are linked to specific communities or suburbs in a way that permits the identification of communities that have particularly high rates of such violent incidents. Table 4.1 presents political violence data for the thirty-two Johannesburg-area communities in which at least fifteen children from the BTT cohort resided. The political violence data represent the total number of incidents of politically inspired injuries, killings, and arrests recorded for that community during the BTT children's first five years of life. Diepkloof and Jabulani have the largest number of incidents, at 812 and 726 respectively. At the other end of the spectrum, Tladi and Senaoane were free of political violence resulting in injuries, deaths, or arrests.

Over the first five years in the lives of the BTT cohort, a precipitous decline occurred in the level of political violence. Figures 4.1, 4.2, and 4.3 present the total number of recorded incidents of arrests, injuries, and killings that were politically related. Within this period, the year 1990 has the highest frequency of violent incidents. The decrease is particularly striking between 1990 and 1992. The consistent downward trend during this period is broken only by a temporary rise in violence just before the 1994 elections. In the period immediately leading up to the election and transition, state-sponsored violence against black citizens rose to unprecedented levels. Ironically, supporters and beneficiaries of apartheid escalated the use of this violence between the time Mandela was released from prison in February 1990 and the time of multiracial elections on April 27, 1994. Some interpret this as a last-ditch effort by supporters of apartheid to secure political advantage and to preserve a semblance of their former power. This rise is also attributed to the increase of ethnic tensions as groups contested for political advantage, sometimes using physical force and intimidation. Consequently, this period has been described by some observers as the time of the most intense and ferocious political conflict, resulting in the highest number of fatalities. Over 14,000 deaths and 22,000 injuries occurred nationwide, more than at any single period in the apartheid era. Following the election, nationwide, political violence fell to 10 percent of its pre-election level. State-initiated violence against citizens effectively ceased with the change of government, and in 1995 a new or initial experience of some form of violence was reported by only about 10.7 percent of BTT households. Most of the residual violence occurred in a single province, KwaZulu/Natal, which is distant from the BTT study area.

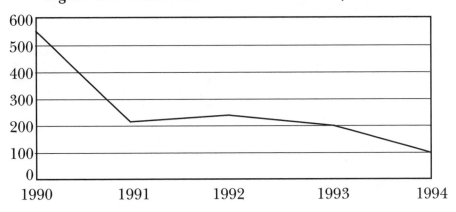

Figure 4.1: Total Number of Persons Killed, 1990–1994

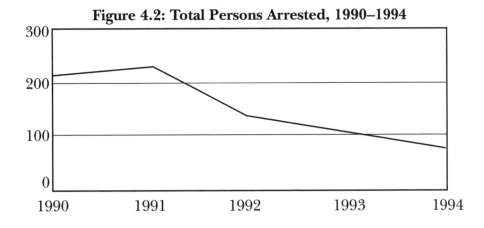

Figure 4.2: Total Persons Arrested, 1990–1994

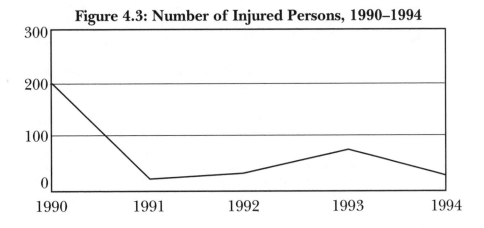

Figure 4.3: Number of Injured Persons, 1990–1994

Table 4.2: Directly Experienced Violence Rates for Types of Violence Reported by the BTT Sample from 1989–1990 to 1995–1996

Type of Violence	5-Year prevalence	Incidence, 1990	Incidence, 1995	Reported at both times
Witness violence	16.4%	9.6%	6.7%	1.3%
Family endangerment	11.7	5.4	6.3	.0
Family injured	5.1	2.3	2.6	.2
Family killed	5.7	2.9	2.8	.1
Family violence	13.0	5.4	7.6	.7

Reports of Violence by BTT Mothers

Table 4.2 presents data for political and family violence obtained from interviews with the primary caretakers of children in the BTT cohort. First, note that the rates are very low, suggesting that very small numbers of families have much direct experience with political violence. The slightly declining trends on two of the four political violence dimensions (witnessing violence and killings) are consistent with the experiences of violence reported during roughly the same period by BTT mothers. For the other two, the risk of being hurt and violence-related injuries to a family member remained low and virtually unchanged between 1990 and 1995.

What lessons can be drawn from this research on the nature and decline of political violence? It is unclear what consequences political violence may have for Mandela's children. After all, much of this violence began before they were born and reached of its peak at about the time they were four years of age. Nevertheless, it is not preposterous to suggest that children's lives might have been affected by the chaos surrounding political violence. After all, disruptions for some parents and youth were quite significant. The loss of life and disturbance of routines were significant. Although it has declined, violence still occupies a strongly symbolic place in the minds and hearts of South Africans. Moreover, as suggested by the testimony presented before the Truth and Reconciliation Commission, the government campaign of political violence against citizens has left deep and lasting scars. Some even argue that this political trauma is a fundamental ingredient and cause of contemporary violence seen in family and community life. Although there remains considerable controversy about its influence on the current climate of violence, political violence is a potent element even today in the highly charged relations between blacks and whites.

Notes

1. (Personal Testimony, Truth and Reconciliation Commission, 1999).

2. Archival data on political violence gathered from police reports, monitoring agencies, and press accounts were obtained from the Human Rights Committee, an independent watchdog group located in Johannesburg. These data are similar to those reported by the South African Institute of Race Relations (see Hudson 1993) and must be interpreted with the same caveats she applied to her use of the data—that is—they are incomplete because many incidents go unreported and unmonitored. Moreover, no claim can be made that these incidents were always reported objectively or adequately corroborated by multiple sources. They are useful because they portray trends in the nature, locus, and prevalence of violence. They include incidents from diverse situations: conflict between political groups; among shack or hostel dwellers and other township residents; between blacks and whites; and in trains, taxis, schools, and mass actions such as strikes and boycotts. Information on incidents was captured in terms of the number of incidents involving arrests, injuries, or deaths separately for each suburb in the BTT study area. Data files on incidents of violence were obtained for the years 1990 through 1994. Correlational analyses reveal that the number of households in the community, as estimated in Daponte (1995), is positively correlated with the frequency of violent incidents ($r = .52$, $p < .05$). Larger suburbs tend to have more violent incidents than smaller suburbs. However, household density is unrelated to such incidents.

Chapter 5

Rising Family and Community Violence

The evidence reviewed in the previous chapter demonstrates that politically motivated violence declined between the birth of the children in 1990 and the time they reached age five. Unfortunately, the demise of political turmoil did not usher in a new era of tranquillity and peace. To the contrary, a pervasive sense of danger persisted, sweeping over many communities as citizens confronted new threats to their safety. The forms of these new threats ranged from fears about the mobilization of Afrikaner resistance to the new government, interethnic conflict motivated by economic competition, widespread criminal activity, and youth-related violence. The impact of these emerging threats to citizens' safety were often not felt as directly as through crime victimization, for example, but they came in the form of subjective and ambient danger fed by worry over coming face-to-face with harm and violence.

Ambient Violence

Often this sense of danger was promoted by the creation of urban legends that take on a life of their own independent of any underlying reality. Across the country, dinnertime conversations are punctuated by the recitation of recent atrocities and flagrant acts of violence. The recollection and elaboration of such events stirs up anger, frustration, and resentment that often takes on racial and class overtones. Such stories about violence are often embellished as they are passed along over the family dinner table, at work, and in social gatherings. Consider, for example, the rumors of attempted robberies surrounding the use of porters in supermarket parking lots. At many supermarkets in South Africa, unemployed persons (usually African or Colored) congregate near store exits to offer assistance to shoppers leaving the store (usually white or middle-class blacks) with the unloading of groceries from carts into the trunks of cars. This courtesy is usually provided with the expectation of a small gratuity. Stories have been circulating about how some people used this as a ruse to set up unsuspecting shoppers for a robbery in their homes. The volunteer porter would load the groceries into the car, slip into the trunk, and then pull it down without the driver knowing what had happened. The shopper would drive home, usually through an electric security gate and into a secured garage, unaware that he or she was carrying an unwelcome passenger in the trunk along with the groceries. When the trunk was opened, the intruder would confront the surprised driver and force him or her at gunpoint to hand over money and other valuables from the home. Whether this has ever actually happened is unclear; however, the story has been widely circulated. As a consequence, many offers of assistance at stores are greeted with suspicion and seen as a potential threat to safety. What began as the creative inventiveness and entrepreneurship of unemployed persons has became another occasion for fear, distrust, and avoidance in the relationships between whites and blacks, between the poor and the affluent.

Another story approaching the status of urban legend has had wide circulation among Africans. It centers on the brazen daytime robbery of shoes right off the feet of a woman walking on the crowded streets of central Johannesburg. The story goes like this: Phelele was enjoying the sunny outdoors as she sauntered slowly down the streets of Joubert Park in inner-city Johannesburg. She was dressed smartly and marveled at the comfort of the elegant new shoes she had just purchased. Just as she turned the corner and headed toward the central taxi stand, two men approached her quickly from the rear. One said to her in a menacing tone, "Climb out of your shoes, sister." She understood fully without any more being said that the men wanted her shoes, perhaps to sell or pawn. Realizing that this was a serious threat and that she must give up the shoes or risk harm from the men, she quickly decided to surrender them before the men became impatient and stabbed or shot her. So, without hesitating, she slipped out of the shoes and continued barefoot, moving on as though nothing had happened. She knew enough not to stop, cry out, or even look back, but inside she deeply mourned the loss of her prized possession.

Like most urban legends, no one can be found to corroborate that they have been personally victimized in this way. Knowledge of the event comes through an acquaintance of one of their friends. Given the level of emotion and rhetoric surrounding crime and violence, it is often difficult to appraise the fundamental dimensions of this problem. Verified or not, these events assume a reality of their own as they exercise powerful sway over the feelings and judgments South Africans have about the deterioration of the quality of life in the public arena. These stories justify public uneasiness as much as they lend credibility that such events actually happen. Realistic or mythical, they say as much about the shared anxiety of a people as they reveal about the reality of crime and violence in South Africa. Not surprisingly, most ordinary citizens, correctly or incorrectly, have become convinced that crime and violence are spiraling out of control. Some citizens' responses to crime sometimes take an unfortunate turn wherein individuals resort to vigilante tactics and compound an already bad situation.

Consider the case of a man who killed another man because he stole his cellular phone. As the story goes, a cell phone thief was chased by his victim and shot seven times, killing him. The victim was taken into police custody. A witness had seen a man running down the road with someone chasing him. The next minute there was a sound like firecrackers and everybody nearby scrambled for cover. A couple of women who were walking past ran into a shop and hid behind the counter. Some thought that the thief had a gun and that this prompted the man to shoot him, twice in the head and five times in the chest. Bystanders were indignant that someone would fire a weapon with such blatant disregard for the safety of others. Few bemoaned the death of the thief. Some may have thought it justified (Greene 2000).

In this case, the chasing and shooting of the assailant appears to have arisen from growing sentiment that crime is so out of hand that citizens have the right to acts of retribution. The shooting is rationalized as a stand not just against the theft of the phone but against the whole rising tide of crime that is the cause of so much alarm.

But communities were not all the same with respect to their ambience of violence. While some communities were perceived as relatively tranquil and safe, others became well-known as locales of violent activities that threatened visitors and residents alike. They were to be avoided if possible, and entered only under conditions of extreme vigilance. Residents of these communities were more likely to stay to themselves, and to protect their children from potential harm by keeping them nearby and supervising them closely.

This aspect of community violence is difficult to index. It is not fully reflected by crime statistics, which are unable to capture the psychological dimension of subjectively perceived community danger. Therefore, rather than rely on police statistics, which may be viewed with skepticism because of underreporting, we turned to community experts to provide assessments of community danger in 1995. To assess differences among BTT communities on these qualities of danger, ratings were made by key informants with considerable cross-community experiences. These informants included persons such as community health workers, taxi drivers, and persons from nongovernmental organizations engaged in cross-community services. These experts employed a Q-sort procedure to rank communities on the dimension of danger-safety. In effect, the ratings are subjective appraisals of the likelihood of being a victim or indirectly experiencing violent events such as: physical threat or intimidation; shooting; stabbing; injury; sexual assault; murder; mugging; car hijacking; forced entry into a home; or robbery. Informants independently sorted communities into five categories from 1 (most safe) to 5 (most dangerous). These ratings of ambient or general community danger proved to be reliable and correlated significantly with other sources of information on violence at the community level: reported incidents of political violence by the Human Rights Committee and the BTT interviews.

Table 4.1 contains information that would be useful to discuss at this juncture. It provides information about three additional measures of violence for communities with large numbers of children from the BTT cohort. These violence indicators are: (1) percent of households experiencing victimization; (2) percent of households reporting family violence; and (3) cumulative risks for violence over the six-year period from 1990 to 1996. The victimization indicator represents the proportion of households from each community in which at least one member of the household was a victim of political violence that resulted in injury, death, or arrest during the previous year. Across the communities, the average proportion of affected families was 18 percent. Moletsane was highest on this dimension, with 35 percent of its households experiencing direct victimization. Otherwise Moletsane was relatively free of violence on the basis of the other indicators. Other communities that were relatively low on other violence indicators had above-average proportions of victimized households. For example, Naledi and Senaoane had 23 and 20 percent, respectively, of their households affected. This suggests that violence may have been a part of children's lives for the first four years of their lives. However, it was unlikely to be prominent feature in their lives after that time. The family violence indicator represents the use by family members of physical coercion strategies such as hitting, slapping, or throwing things as a way of dealing with conflict. These behaviors do not necessarily represent extreme or serious forms of physical abuse that might meet the criteria of criminal abuse. Across all communities, 77 percent on average do not report even minor occurrences of violence within family life.

Economically Motivated Violence

With the decline of overtly political violence, interethnic violence has taken on a different character. It has resurfaced as economic conflict, most commonly in the form of taxi wars and interethnic conflicts over employment in mines. Random passengers at taxi stands or ranks and on buses were shot at and killed. As discussed, the apartheid government exploited ethnic chauvinism, loyalty, and suspicion and successfully accelerated ethnic polarization. Financial support of Inkatha to foment violence against the ANC prior to the elections potentiated dissension among blacks that still arouses passions long after the demise of apartheid. This long-standing "divide and conquer" strategy adopted a more virulent form in the waning days of the apartheid regime. Even though politically supported violence has subsided, the enflaming of ethnic hatred has inserted violence into ongoing political competition between Inkatha and ANC. Once learned, violence is not quickly forgotten. Such conflicts are extensions of earlier ethnic-based conflicts, but the motives are primarily economic.

Taxi vans, or Khombis, are a principal source of transportation (in rivalry with trains and buses) for township residents traveling within the township and to work in the central city and its suburbs. Drivers are organized into associations based on geographical areas. These areas, built under apartheid rule, were deliberately designed to reduce contact and foster cross-ethnic suspicion. Consequently, the taxi associations are organized along ethnic lines, and this becomes an added symbolic layer to contest over routes and passengers. Conflict is predictable when a driver is seen competing unfairly by dropping off or picking up passengers in an area claimed by a rival association. Even public transportation is targeted. For example, a forty-six-year-old woman was killed when a bus careened into her house. The bus driver, who escaped unharmed, had lost control of the bus when shots were fired at the vehicle, apparently by someone from a taxi association serving the area. In another incident, bus commuters escaped uninjured when the bus they were traveling in was stopped by a group of people and set on fire. Each person in the group was carrying what later turned out to be gasoline. They ordered the driver out of the bus, poured gasoline around it, and set it alight. Terrified pensioners were trapped as more agile commuters jumped through windows to safety. These passengers were saved by police who arrived and extinguished the flames. According to police, seven buses were attacked, but only one was completely burnt. It is believed these incidents are related to the taxi conflict.

Even failure to support the political action of a group may be enough to put a person in jeopardy. For example, when a group such as the Zulus calls a strike in which people are asked to stay home from work, intimidation and random violence are used to increase compliance with that strike, including shooting at buses and their passengers.

Criminal Violence

The period of intense political violence between 1980 and 1994 provided no respite from criminal violence. Consequently, blacks were just as susceptible to harm from criminal activity as from political strife. As early as 1985, grave concern was expressed about the escalation of crime, particularly in Johannesburg. Today, with the decline of politically inspired violence, the most significant threat of violence emanates from economically motivated ethnic strife and criminal violence in the form of assaults, muggings, robberies, burglaries, hijackings, and murders. Moreover, some analysts predict that with better reporting and record-keeping, we will see a sharp increase in reported incidents of physical and sexual abuse of women and children. National survey data estimate the incidence of direct experience of robberies in urban households at 7.4 percent. The incidence is 4 percent for assaults, 1.4 percent for murders, and 0.1 percent for reported rapes (Wilson 1994). Some suspect that former combatants from all sides of the armed conflict who have been sidelined by the peace and marginalized by unemployment now apply their coercion skills within their families and communities.

According to Interpol, South Africa is now the fourth most murderous of the eighty countries it surveys. From a high of 69.3 per 100,000 in 1994, the murder rate dropped to 58.5 per 100,000 in 1998. This is still quite high compared to an international average of 5.5 per 100,000. Significant increases occurred in assaults, robberies, and rapes between 1990 and 1994 during the time of the transition. During that same period, reports of rapes are estimated to have tripled; assaults increased 25 percent and robberies 36 percent (Shaw 1995). Between 1994 and 1998, robberies and assaults increased but murders decreased. The poor were more likely to be victim of criminal violence than the affluent. Similarly blacks were more likely to be victims of assaults and whites more likely to experience robbery (South Africa Institute of Race Relations 2000).

Youth Involvement in Violence

An increasingly worrisome source of violence throughout the townships emanates from newly formed youth gangs and vigilante groups such as People Against Gangs and Drugs (PAGAD). Many of these gangs are organized around criminal activity and have become a powerful force of intimidation. The involvement of youth in violent activity is not new. Youth played an unquestionably important role in resisting apartheid through both peaceful and violent protest. Some began their careers of resistance in protest over the imposition of school and exam fees and the use of Afrikaans as the medium of instruction. In many cases, youth led the way in adopting a more militant stance against racial oppression, while their more cautious parents, out of concern for their safety, tried to hold them back. Open conflict with police or the security forces charged with containing student protests became commonplace and resulted in significant injuries, deaths, and arrests. For many students, such incidents became a defining moment of political radicalization.

Youth in the liberation movements responded to government repression and violence with higher levels of aggressive action of their own. Many were pulled headlong into violent interchanges with security forces. Ultimately, parents followed. In time, guerrilla tactics were adopted in the form of sabotage and attacks on selected targets. Schools and government installations were burned and police were attacked. Youth aimed to render the country ungovernable with their limited arsenal of sticks, stones, and fire-bombs. For example, police have reported numerous incidents involving students stoning and setting cars and gasoline tankers on fire. In some cases, they caused extensive damage to nearby homes and cars.

Increasingly, youth have been identified as perpetrators of violent crimes. Many lack skills and are unable to find work. For black youth in urban areas, the unemployment rate reaches 60 percent (World Bank 1994). With time on their hands and no way to earn a living, many turn to crime and drug use. Youth gangs in the townships are a troubling manifestation of this trend. Not infrequently, competition between gangs erupts into violence which spills out into the community. Take as an example this incident involving the loss of life among teen "gangsters" embroiled in a feud whose stakes involved territory and honor.

> As Pimville braces for another funeral this afternoon, that of the ninth and latest victim of a series of pitched gunfights between two groups . . . fearful residents speak about this sense-

less feud in hushed tones . . . a teenage gang has been at war with a rival mob for almost two years in a bloody territorial conflict. The most concerned resident is Queen Malinga, the owner of the house where [the most recent victim] was shot six times. The bullets that missed him found their way through a window of her house. "I feel very unsafe, and so uncomfortable. When I see a car that I don't know I really get scared. I don't care if they want to kill each other as long as they leave us alone." (Madywabe 1997:5)

The toll of violence is high in both human and economic terms. Significant reductions in healthcare costs at major public hospitals could be attained through reductions in violence-related injuries. Studies conducted in major urban centers suggest that over 50 percent of trauma cases admitted to hospitals are violence related. More than half of the trauma-related deaths in one urban area were violence-related, and about 85 percent of these were caused by firearms or sharp objects (Meumann and Peden 1997). Consequently, the public imagination has shifted from concern about political violence to incidents that emerge from the family and from criminal activity. In the post-apartheid era, whites have lost the immunity from harm they once enjoyed as they too express fears about being engulfed by violent crime.

How Pervasive Are Crime and Violence?

The current government and its supporters offer an alternative interpretation to those who proclaim that a wave of violence is sweeping the country. They argue that in spite of rising public alarm about crime and violence, any increases in violence since it took office in 1994 are modest if they have occurred at all. Although some government critics dismiss as self-serving the government characterization of crime and criminal violence as stable, data from independent sources lend credence to their claims. For example, trend data from the South African Institute of Race Relations (SAIRR) for the period between January 1994 and June 1997 show that throughout Gauteng province (in which Johannesburg and Soweto are located) murder declined by 24.7 percent. However, the decline in murders was offset by an increase of 28 percent in assaults (see Corrigan 1997). Burglaries also declined, but rape increased by 20 percent.

Official police figures present a similar if more detailed picture of crime. Crime data provided by the Crime Information Management

Centre (CIMC 1998) in the South African Police Service reveal only slight increases in crime over the period from 1994 to 1997. In Gauteng, the total number of cases reported was 343,854 in 1994 and 354,157 in 1997, representing only a 3 percent increase. A similar increase was found for Soweto, with the exception of public (politically inspired) violence, for which a 75 percent decrease occurred, from seventy-four cases in 1994 to eighteen cases in 1997. In an analysis of specific crime types, the crime statistics for Gauteng province and Soweto from 1994 to 1997 suggest that crimes involving personal violence increased 5 percent in Gauteng and 1.47 percent in Soweto. Rape and sexual crime increased in both areas. Though not always violent, property crimes increased by 6.4 percent in Soweto and only 1.5 percent in Gauteng as a whole. Importantly, the CIMC data also show a 25 percent decrease in murder cases reported in Soweto but a 37 percent increase in assault with the intent to inflict grievous bodily harm, mirroring the South African Institute of Race Relations data. When considering the most serious violent crime categories (murder, rape, and felonious assault) from 1994 to 1997, both Soweto and Gauteng province experienced a negligible increase.

In all, proponents of the "modest change" position can derive comfort from the data above and from the analysis of the BTT data that demonstrate clearly that the experience of violence at the household level is far from universal. Even in the black townships, the likelihood of living in a relatively safe neighborhood free of even minor skirmishes with violence is more common than its opposite. For example, about 60 percent of the BTT sample lived in households that had neither direct nor vicarious experience of family or community violence except for what was seen on television or read in the newspaper. This is similar to estimates from the Living Standards Survey (LSS) taken in 1993, which shows that 57 percent of the African households in Gauteng reported that they were not victimized, did not see anyone victimized, and did not know anyone who was a victim of crime over the previous twelve months (Wilson 1994). Within Gauteng, approximately 12.8 percent of the households in African townships were directly affected by criminal activity. These numbers are high, but they do not exceed estimates of crime in urban areas in the United States, where about 13 percent of the population report exposure to minor violence and 6 percent to severe violence. In the most violent urban areas in the United States, about 50 percent of the residents reported exposure to at least minor incidents of violence and 32 percent to severe violence (Richters and Martinez 1993a, b).

Victimization: The Direct Experience of Violence

Returning to table 4.2, note that it displays the percentages of BTT households that experienced some form of violence in 1990 and in 1995. All other things being equal, the percentage of a population reporting the experience of violence will depend on the length of the time period over which data are collected. The longer the time frame (e.g., five years versus one year or one month), the higher percentage reporting violence. Typically a one-year period is used to report incidents. But incidents occurring as long ago as five years can be remembered vividly and still cause anxiety—for that reason, it can be informative to view five-year prevalence rates rather than one-year rates alone. All one-year incidence rates fall below 10 percent. The highest incidence for witnessing a violent incident (9.6 percent) occurred in 1990. The rates for serious violence such as injury to and killing of a family member are very low for both periods, and in each case is under 3 percent. Over the period from 1990 to 1995, 11.7 percent of respondents in the BTT sample found themselves in situations in which their physical safety was jeopardized.

If we examine the prevalence summed over the entire five-year period from 1990 to 1995 (ranges from 16.3 percent to 5.1 percent), witnessing a violent incident is the most commonly reported experience, and injury to self or a family member is the least commonly reported incident. These are conservative estimates of the total violence experienced because the interview specifically targeted political violence and did not include violence from explicitly criminal incidents such as robberies. Nevertheless, these estimates are consistent with those obtained in larger national studies using probability sampling designs. For example, the prevalence rate for witnessing violence was 16.3 percent in the BTT sample and 16.7 percent in the LSS. Responses of BTT mothers to questions about victimization and family violence reveal slight increases in reports of household and direct violence between 1990 and 1995. Overall, exposure to violence either from residing in a household with direct violent experience or from living in a community with reported incidents of violence declined from 29.4 percent to 14.5 percent in 1995. Interestingly, family use of violence is significantly correlated with community danger and with political violence.

Cumulative Risk for Community Violence, 1990–1996

An analysis of the data on trends for political violence and community danger show that political incidents are high in the first two years of children's lives and subsequently decline, while the level of incidents related to community danger (including criminal activity, interethnic economic competition, and gang problems) increases and is dominant by the time BTT children are four. In effect, the nature of the principal threat of violence has changed over the brief life span of Mandela's children from political violence to community danger. Accordingly, political violence may be a better indicator of risk for children in the early part of their lives, while the community danger rating may be a better indicator for the latter part of their lives.

To characterize the risk of violence over the entire six years of their lives, we developed a cumulative risk indicator by summing up the indicators (political, victimization, family, community danger) on which a given community was high (above average). The cumulative risk indicator ranges from 0 to 4. On the cumulative risk indicator, Jabulani was the most consistently dangerous section of Soweto over the six-year period, followed by Diepkloof, Meadowlands, and inner-city Johannesburg. The safest communities were Lenasia, Eldorado Park, Orlando, Pimville, Naledi, Mapetla, and Mofolo (see table 4.1).

Changes in Perceptions of Personal Safety: A Rising Sense of Danger

Without doubt, vioence is seen as ubiquitous in South Africa. This is so true that violence even against self is becoming a common instrument for resolving problems. Thus the deaths of Ibrahim and Isaak were abhorrent but not surprising. Government assurance to the contrary, appraisals of safety and danger reveal that citizens consider the problem of violence to be worsening and feel less safe in both the home and the community than they did as recently as five years ago. Items on the Living Standards Survey queried respondents separately about safety in and outside of their homes now as compared to five years ago (1988). Table 5.1 presents the proportion of respondents who indicated that they feel more safe, less safe, and the same as five years ago. The data are presented for responses to safety in the home and in the community. These data are disaggregated by area (rural, urban, peri-urban), and population group (Africans, whites, and Colored and Indians combined). The groups are significantly different with respect to ratings on each of these four variables. An overwhelming majority of respondents feel less safe now than they did five years ago. Whites feel significantly less safe than all groups, followed by Africans, then Coloreds and Indians. More than any other group, persons living in peri-urban areas (i.e., in or near the townships) reported feeling less safe now than five years ago. Persons who were recently victimized understandably felt less safe than those who were not recent victims of violence. There were no significant differences in the responses of men and women. Remarkably, the decline in the sense of personal safety is as marked within the home as it is in the community.

Interestingly, data from this study suggest that proximal or direct exposure to violence in the home or community may not be increas-

Table 5.1: Changes in Percentage in Perception of Safety in and outside of the Home between 1988 and 1993 among South Africans

	Urban Areas			Peri-urban Areas		
	African	Colored	White	African	Colored	White
(Number of Households)	(1,162)	(427)	(459)	(1,150)	(476)	(1,058)
Out of Home						
More safe	13.8%	7.3%	2.8%	3.7%	1.7%	1.8%
The same	26.2	27.1	24.0	13.6	19.3	16.0
Less safe	60.0	65.6	73.2	82.8	79.0	82.2
At Home						
More safe	18.9	12.7	4.8	3.4	5.7	5.3
The same	23.4	29.5	30.1	17.6	27.7	29.5
Less safe	57.6	57.8	65.1	79.0	66.6	65.2

ing at all. If victimization from criminal violence were on the rise, it would be reflected in increased reports either in the 1995 BTT follow-up or in the LSS data, but this is not the case. These self-reported data admittedly depend on respondents' definition of crime, their interpretation of crime victimization, and the salience of acts that constitute violent crimes. Moreover, the frequency of violence in these reports would probably be higher if youth were the primary informants rather than their mothers. Nevertheless, patterns in the data are striking enough to contradict the view that violence is spiraling out of control. The prevalence of reported crime in our samples of South Africans is no higher than rates reported for urban areas in other countries such as the United States. These trend data from police records during the post-apartheid era show that criminal activity has increased moderately, offsetting the postelection declines in political violence. Though criminal violence may have supplanted political violence as a threat to public welfare, the data suggest that the net level of violence is remarkably stable and not unreasonably high in comparison to major U.S. cities. Even with these slight increases, violence may not be as ubiquitous as media representations imply. When we control for increases in the population size, the differences are even smaller.

Even with these data, the extent to which these modest increases in violence constitute a valid phenomenon continues to be matter of great debate in South Africa. One interpretation is that the changes are negligible because they may be due to data reporting and recording errors. Moreover it is problematic to compare data trends over periods that include the apartheid and the ANC governments.

There is a risk of attributing responsibility for all of contemporary South Africa's problems to apartheid. Nevertheless, the current epidemic of violence must be understood within the context of the systematic violence condoned or actively carried out by the apartheid government against its people. Moreover, as suggested in chapter 3, apartheid laws and social policies engineered the current state of economic and social inequality that has created a spawning ground for violence. Apartheid is also recognized as a period in which government winked at cronyism and white-collar corruption, which siphoned off resources that might otherwise have been applied to social and economic development. Lacking opportunities for gainful employment, physical aggression and rage have become hallmark expressions of social alienation by youthful gangs. Moreover, without a voice in local and national politics, blacks have had few effective means by which to stem the rising tide of crime themselves or to influence law enforcement to address it assertively on their behalf. Most importantly, the apartheid policies of forced removals and relocations disrupted families and destabilized communities. Along with key social forces, apartheid accelerated social change such as transformations of family, urbanization, the erosion of community life, and the growing irrelevance of culturally sanctioned means of social control. All contribute to an ethos of violence in South Africa. These policies established the conditions for community anomie and family distress that encourage crime and permit family violence to flourish unchecked.

Apartheid has directly and indirectly played a significant role in the climate of violence in South Africa. But it has not done so alone. Violence is a consequence of disparate forces, some of which are exacerbated by the moral climate and social conditions that existed under the apartheid regime. Urbanization, with its population density, lack of community cohesion, anonymity, and indifference is also accorded a central role in the concerns about violence. The increasing sense of danger from ambient community violence felt by many people may be accelerated by the erosion of protections previously afforded by family and community life. Consequently, vulnerability to crime is heightened by a diminished community spirit and increasing alienation from neighbors who once served as a backup source of protection and support. With full awareness of the risks and uncertainty about who might come to their aid, many citizens live in a state of continuous alert. Striking urban and rural disparities in material conditions have accelerated the migration from rural communities, exacerbating the density and alienation of people from one another in urban metropolitan areas. Blacks with the financial resources have attempted to reduce some risks by moving from the black townships to former all-white suburbs, while whites seek refuge in more remote gated-communities. This movement is like a game of musical chairs in which each group attempts to improve its situation by landing in an environment that is perceived as less risky than the one it occupied previously. A very similar process of white flight has occurred in major cities in the United States. In a larger sense, this does not and cannot solve the underlying problems of inequality and racial divisions.

A most important lesson to take from these data is that violence, like economic hardship, is by no means a universal or ubiquitous experience in South Africa. On the contrary, the majority of South Africans in our sample experience no violence or danger on a day-to-day basis—direct or vicarious. Moreover, they live in communities that are considered relatively safe. Although data reviewed here will not end the debate over whether violence is leveling off or spinning out of control, they unquestionably demonstrate how the nature of violence has changed over the period from 1980 through 1996. For the majority of South Africans in urban areas, violence is not a tangible part of life; but for the minority who do experience it, the effects are likely to be detrimental. Political violence peaked in 1993 and has continued to decline since then. In its place have arisen other forms of community violence that have social, economic, and criminal overtones.

Contemporary violence in South Africa is more often economic, criminal, and familial in nature. The violence faced by children in the BTT cohort is no longer from soldiers, police, or agents attempting to suppress legitimate aspirations for freedom and equality. The new faces of violence for these children are taxi drivers fighting to protect their economic interests, thieves and hijackers, overly conscientious private security guards, armed youth gangs, drug dealers, and vigilante groups. These new threats to public safety are often subtle and psychological in nature. They create a climate of danger that may in itself have undesirable consequences for children.

It should come as no surprise that black and white South Africans bring different perspectives that shape their understanding of contemporary threats to public safety. For blacks, the escalating gangsterism, rape, robbery, assault, theft, and murder in South Africa are viewed as sequelae of the violent tactics and social policies of apartheid; its policies have helped perpetuate the ethos of violence that permeates South African society (Daniels 1996). For whites, concerns about violence carry with them an undertone of mistrust and suspicion about the government's ability and commitment to protect them. These fears are confirmed by occasional random acts that may touch their lives. At the same time, it hardly escapes anyone's notice that violence occurs within the context of unimaginable material hardship that can best be described as inhumane. Moreover, no one questions that such conditions began with apartheid and found their fullest expression in a brutally violent campaign of political violence. The continuing suffering of many blacks cries out for redemption, alleviation, and some fear that it may lead to calls for retribution. Subconsciously at least, the rising concerns about violence may be linked to fears about the rising tide of black political power and possible retribution against whites for the oppression experienced under apartheid. The slow pace of change and the lack of improvement in the lives of the poor lead those who are materially comfortable to become psychologically vulnerable, and this vulnerability is expressed in terms of fear of violent crime. Many recognize that this fear is a by-product of economic inequality and results from having so much when others have so little. The fear of crime and violence comes from an understanding that severe material deprivation may suppress the human qualities and humanity of the poor and suffocate their human spirit. With this loss of humanity among the poor come dire consequences. For the rich, the poor pose an ominous threat.

For children, the dynamic of violence operates at a different level and comes from unsuspecting sources within their homes, communities, and schools. Growing up in communities regarded as dangerous presents Mandela's children with conditions that are no less ominous and adverse than those experienced by their older siblings who faced soldiers, rifles, and tanks. For them, the consequences of violence may be even more severe. In chapter 11, we will summarize the findings from BTT regarding the impact of political, family, and community violence on Mandela's children.

Chapter 6

Physical Growth and Social Development

In the previous chapters, we portrayed the historical forces and conditions of racial inequality, poverty, and community violence which we argue have significalntly shaped the environments in which Mandela's children are being raised. Though rooted in the past, these forces continue to exert powerful influences in children's lives. In later chapters, we will address how each one specifically affects children's physical and psychosocial development in contemporary South Africa. In addition, we have highlighted several secular trends such as modernization, urbanization, and political transformation which constitute significant challenges for family and community life and which reverberate throughout efforts to raise and socialize children today in South Africa. Child development can refer to children's growth and change across many diverse domains. Most often discussions of child development attempt to identify, describe, and predict patterns in children's cognitive, linguistic, motor, social, behavioral, and emotional functioning and in their physical growth over time. Our treatment of child development will depict children's physical growth and health and emphasize continuities and changes in their socioemotional functioning from birth to age six. We begin by describing the principal assumptions of and issues surrounding contemporary examinations of child development. Then we initiate discussion of the developmental status of Mandela's children by presenting what we have learned about their early physical development and health.

Assumptions about Development

Notions of development fundamentally rest on a number of shared assumptions about the nature and process of stability and change in children's lives (for example, see Shaffer 1999). The most important of these assumptions include the following:

1. Development is assumed to be holistic in the sense that physical development, cognitive development, emotional development, and social development are interrelated with one another in such a way that reciprocal influence occurs between these domains of study. If children have poor growth, for example, we make the assumption that other aspects of development will be affected to a greater or lesser degree and there is a need to understand the factors that exacerbate and alleviate these effects.

2. Development is also assumed to be a continual and cumulative process and that early developmental attainments lay the foundation for later ones. The first ten to twelve years of life are thought to be strongly determining of later psychological functioning. Children who have poor beginnings and whose development falters in its early stages are at a considerable disadvantage in facing the challenges of later stages and may not have the capacities necessary to do so adequately, particularly if the difficulties they face compound over time.

3. Despite the assertion above about continuity of development, development is also characterized by considerable plasticity. That is, an enormous margin of adaptation and adjustment to both positive and negative life experiences can occur during the development of children. Infants who begin life precariously sometimes show amazing recovery and compensation if afforded opportunities to catch up. Similarly, children with many resources may flounder in their development when faced with hardships for which they have little preparation.

4. Development cannot be fully understood outside of a historical and cultural context. What is encouraged and endorsed in children's development differs from one cultural context to another, and what may be considered to be satisfactory development differs from one child to another, at different ages, and in different circumstances.

Related to these assumptions are a number of questions that require investigation in studies of children's development. These include: the conditions under which development proceeds sequentially or sporadically; the likelihood of functional deficits persisting over time, and the relative importance on later development of early-appearing delays or difficulties; the potential for recovery and the possibility of deterioration from earlier states of poor or defective functioning; and the spillover from developmental difficulties or delays in one functional domain into other functional domains.

Essentially such questions are best answered by longitudinal investigations of children's development, in which change itself, the very essence of development, is the subject of study. Generally, longitudinal studies aim to, among others: describe both the pattern and magnitude of intraindividual changes in children over time, as well as differences that occur between children; describe the observed changes in terms of available explanatory frameworks at the individual and social levels; and lastly, predict the direction of future changes in children based on knowledge of their early or current developmental status, their history, and their current conditions. For these reasons, despite the difficulty of collecting longitudinal data, studies over time are an invaluable resource for understanding children's development (Young et al. 1991). Birth-to-Ten is the only study of South African children's development of substantial duration, and it is unique in that its historical view into the lives of children is during an immensely dramatic and important phase in South Africa's development.

With this understanding of child development as a background, let us proceed to a discussion of the early development of Mandela's children through pregnancy and birth, their physical growth and maturation, and the emergence of behavioral and emotional self-regulation and social competence. We are convinced that both physical and social risk factors associated with violence, poverty, and racism impact conspicuously on children's development during the first few years of life, and important connections can be drawn between developments in the early years and later competence and adjustment.

Pregnancy and Birth

Central nervous system development occurs early in fetal development and has been shown to be vulnerable to the influences of a number of teratogens, including drugs; environmental hazards; and maternal age, nutrition, emotional well-being, and disease. These factors are particularly important in developing countries because they are more prevalent than in resource-rich countries, and their effects may remain unmitigated during pregnancy because of women's poor access to antenatal care, particularly to care of high quality. For example, in Birth-to-Ten, more than a third of women did not attend antenatal care until well into the third trimester of their pregnancy, and close to a tenth of mothers received no antenatal care despite giving birth to their babies in an urban environment. The reasons for the lack of antenatal care are complex, and include the cost of health visits (which became free to pregnant women only in 1994) and transport, and the fact that a large number of women, approximately a fifth of the cohort, come into urban areas from close and distant rural areas to deliver at urban health facilities.

The migration of women between rural and urban areas during pregnancy and the early years of their children's lives stems from migrant labor practices that separated families, so that visits and temporary sojourns in one or the other environment occur as part of the maintenance of family life. Women may go to deliver their babies close to where their husbands work to solidify family ties and to remind the father of his financial responsibility to support the child through increased remittance to his rural family. Urban women often travel to the rural homes of their families to present their children to the clan for recognition of his or her membership of this important social network. In addition, families, and especially women, made huge sacrifices to deliver their babies in Johannesburg or Soweto, even by falsifying their addresses, in order that their children could be recorded as residents of the city—a requirement under apartheid laws aimed at restricting movement and inhibiting urbanization—to obtain work in the city.

Maternal emotional well-being during pregnancy is recognized as contributing to children's development, and prolonged and severe stress is associated with stunted prenatal growth, premature delivery, low birth weight, and other birth complications (Lobel 1994). These effects are thought to occur through the operation of stress, which can reduce the flow of oxygen to the fetus, weaken the mother's immune system, and affect her eating patterns and substance use.

A pregnancy that is not wanted can be a considerable stressor for a woman. In many developing countries women have poor access to contraceptives. (In South Africa, women became suspicious of family planning services and their potential implication in efforts by the apartheid government to limit black population growth. Evidence submitted to the Truth and Reconciliation Commission gave some substance to these fears.) Moreover, an additional child can bring economic hardship to a family where no one is employed. Forty-two percent of BTT women, interviewed during the last trimester of their pregnancy, said they definitely had *not* wanted to be pregnant with this child, 41 percent said they had longed for this child, and 17 percent said they were not sure, as the joy associated with the impending birth of their baby hinged very much on the continued love and support of the man with whom they were currently involved.

Most BTT women (about 80 percent) reported feeling supported, emotionally and materially, during their pregnancy; however, about a fifth of women felt largely abandoned and had neither plans nor hopes about how they were going to manage to support and rear their child. In earlier chapters we outlined the stresses that pertained in Soweto-Johannesburg in early 1990, particularly relating to unemployment and poverty, but also to political, criminal, and family violence, the latter frequently associated with substance abuse. As in many other parts of the world, personal desire for a pregnancy and the wider social circumstances in which a birth occurs have been found to be related to postnatal depression, which may also have additional causes. About 20 percent of BTT women were classified as depressed when their babies were six months old on the basis of their responses to the Pitt Depression Inventory (Pitt 1968). About a third of women felt at that time, that looking back, having a baby at this time was definitely not the right thing to do in terms of the emotional and financial burdens they were currently experiencing.

Maternal age is a significant risk factor in pregnancy, and both very young primiparous and older pregnancies with prior multiple births contribute disproportionately to perinatal mortality. In South Africa as a whole, about a third of all pregnancies occur to teenagers and 5 percent to mothers sixteen years old and younger (Bult and Cunningham 1992; Zille 1986). The age of BTT mothers ranged from fourteen to forty-eight years, and gravidity from 0 to 12, with a mean of 2.4 years per woman. About 130 mothers in the sample were sixteen years old or younger, and about the same amount were forty years or older at the time they delivered their babies. Nearly a fifth of pregnancies were in women nineteen years and younger. Poor children grow up quickly, and need to take responsibility for some part of household duties early in life, and in rural South Africa in the early part of the century women were considered to be ready for marriage by the time they were sixteen years old. However, modern urban life is different, and teen pregnancies in South Africa significantly disrupt the education of young mothers, leaving them vulnerable to unemployment or employment limited to the unskilled domestic sector. Looking back on these young mothers, fewer than a third have been able to return to school and continue their studies. Studies in many other parts of the world, including the United States, show that unless teen mothers can return to school and delay having more children, they are likely to become socioeconomically disadvantaged compared to teens who delay parenting (Furstenburg et al. 1989).

The vast majority of all births in Soweto-Johannesburg take place in public facilities, with only about 16 percent of deliveries occurring in private health facilities. Nearly two-thirds of the public hospital deliveries take place at the Baragwanath Hospital in Soweto (now the Chris Hani-Baragwanath Hospital), which handles about 30,000 births annually. Of these, approximately 3,000 low birth weight babies are looked after in the high-care facilities for newborns. In most public hospitals in South Africa that catered for black women at that time, mothers were required to be discharged about six hours after delivery, unless the birth took place in the late afternoon or evening. Women were seen leaving Bara, as it is called, walking home or taking public transport, carrying their bag and their carefully wrapped newborn baby.

In our discussion of inequality in access to medical care in chapter 2, we alluded to the inequity of services in apartheid South Africa, where the best facilities in the world were available to the rich whites, while black people, even those with some money, had to make use of the worst facilities in the country. This fact is starkly illustrated by cesarean section (CS) rate data taken from Birth-to-Ten. While only 9 percent of CS delivers occurred to black women attending public hospitals, 17 percent of white women at public hospitals had CS. The rate was 35 percent among white women who delivered their babies in private hospitals. These figures can be interpreted to indicate distortions of under- and overservicing of sectors of the population, based largely on race and, secondarily, on socioeconomic status.

The conditions outlined above are some of the factors that start to form what has been called a "funnel of causality" affecting the outcomes of poor and disadvantaged children. Each of these disadvantages alone exerts negative influence that can be compensated for by advantages experienced in other spheres. But their effects are cumulative. When these factors are compounded, they develop a strong pressure on the developmental potential, one that can be inexorable if no conditions exist for counterbalancing positive forces.

Birth weight is one outcome of pregnancy and is regarded as a sensitive indicator of the conditions of the pregnancy, both endogenous and exogenous. In BTT, 13 percent of children were born with low birth weight (2500 g or less) and 2 percent (105 babies) with birth weights of 1500 g or less, or very low birth weight. In the United States, the corresponding figure for low birth weight is 7 percent. About 22 percent of BTT children were born before the thirty-seventh week of pregnancy and therefore could be classified as prematurely born. As noted before, developmental effects tend to cluster together so that, for example, in BTT teen mothers had the highest rates of low birth weight and prematurely born babies. Developmental effects are also cumulative, and the implications of low birth weight and prematurity for a child's development depend critically on the quality of the postnatal environment in which they are raised.

Official figures of infant mortality in Soweto about five years before the start of BTT were estimated at about 25 per 1,000 births, considerably lower than in some rural areas in South Africa, where it is as high as 150 per 1,000 (Yach 1988). However, the direct figures obtained from BTT were higher than expected, 38 per 1,000, indicating the severe pressure on life conditions and health services associated with the very rapid, unplanned increase in urbanization that began in the 1980s. In BTT, we tracked the sadness of these losses in the day-to-day lives of people—106 deliveries ended in stillbirths, 58 babies died immediately after delivery, and a further 80 children died during their first month of life.

Growth and Health in the Early Years of Life

Emphasis in the earliest stages of child development is often given to physical growth and maturation. The emergence of complex neural networks that occur with brain development early in life make possible the acquisition of motor, communicative, and social skills that are the essential building blocks of psychosocial development. In this regard, physical growth is the foundation of development in infancy and early childhood, and it sets the scene for critical developmental processes related to the emergence of biological, behavioral, and emotional self-regulation. The evolving capacity for self-regulation can be traced in several spheres of functioning, including neuromuscular, behavioral, emotional, and social regulation. In turn, these forms of self-regulation are precursors to, and provide a foundation for, psychomotor skills, language, social competence, and academic adjustment in later childhood, as well as psychosocial maturity in adolescence and adulthood.

For these reasons, fetal growth, birth weight, infant feeding behavior, illnesses, and postnatal increases in body mass and height are carefully monitored during pregnancy and early infancy. This surveillance is indicative of these factors, known importance in influencing psychomotor skills, language, social competence, psychological adjustment, and, in time, also academic achievement. Consequently, most analyses of development proceed from a focus on physical growth and self-regulation of biological functioning to the acquisition by the child of a capacity to regulate and express a newly emerging sense of self through language, behavior, and emotions. Early physical growth and development provides an essential foundation for later development and, consequently, deserve special attention. Growth during the first two years occurs at a more rapid pace than at any other time in life. Normal physical growth during these early years is essential to concurrent cognitive and emotional development, but also to long-term health and well-being. At the most basic level, an adequate body mass and length is important to a young infant's prospects for survival. It signals that the infant's genetic potential for growth is being supported by a nurturing environment and that the child's immune system is in place to respond to infections and disease. It indicates that the basic organ structures and functions are sufficiently developed to sustain life and to thrive. All other things being equal, normal growth affords the developing infant a level of protection against opportunistic infections and acute or chronic stress that might threaten life and well-being. Low birth weight and poor infant growth, on the other hand, signal potential problems in physical and even cognitive development. This is because they render the infant vulnerable to an array of diseases and dysfunctions, and create disadvantages that are difficult to overcome.

While there are marked individual differences in growth, as well as differences in the growth rates and eventual sizes of people in different regions of the world, there is an expected broad band of growth rates during childhood and adolescence. This is illustrated by the photograph of the three children born within weeks of one another. Apart from rare genetic conditions, marked deviations from this broad band of expected growth occur in response to inadequate physical and social environments. Insufficient nutrition, chronic infections, and nonsupportive social conditions explain the poor growth of children in Africa, Southeast Asia, and parts of South America. Nonetheless, even among children growing up in generally similar environments, marked individual differences in growth occur that need to be explained at the proximal level of the household and personal experience.

Nutrition is one of the most important environmental determinants of growth. At the very least, a child needs to consume food rich in proteins and calories. However, other nutrients have assumed significance in light of the discoveries of the importance of a range of micronutrients to health, growth, and development, including iron, zinc, and vitamin A. Nutritional, including micronutrient, deficiencies early in life create problems for later cognitive development that cannot be overcome once the critical window for neurological development has closed. Two broad indicators, stunting and wasting, are most often used to assess the nutritional adequacy of children's environments for physical development. Stunting refers to a child's height-for-age and is associated with long-term hunger and undernutrition. Wasting refers to weight-for-age and is associated with acute malnutrition.

Indicators of nutritional status are derived from growth curves such as the NCHS Growth Curves for Children Birth to 18 Years, developed by U.S. government agencies from information collected on a large group of American children (Hamel et al. 1979). The use of such growth charts outside of the United States is based on the assumption that, with adequate food and a balanced diet, the rates of growth should be about the same for all children with only minor variations. This is a principle most child advocates uphold, because poor growth is sometimes attributed to racial or cultural factors in ways that absolve authorities from responsibility. This is what happened in South Africa, when energy and debate was taken up in the 1970s and 1980s, not with the fact that many rural black children were starving, but with questions about the appropriateness of the standard against which children's growth was being assessed.

Table 6.1: Mean Height by Age for South African and American Children

Height (cm)	Age					
	2 months	6 months	2 years	3 years	4 years	5 years
African children	57.6	68.7	78.1	86.4	93.4	100.6
American children[1]	58.1	67.8	87.6	95.1	102.6	108.8

Nevertheless we concede that the use of universal growth charts do have problems. One problem with the current charts is that the infant information was collected from babies who were, by and large, formula-fed, and who were generally larger than breast-fed babies. The World Health Organization is preparing new charts based on breast-fed infants' growth, which will be more appropriate, particularly for children from developing countries where breast-feeding continues to be normative, in much of southern Africa.

Growth charts can be used to draw conclusions about the nutritional status and history of possible deprivation of both individual children and of populations of children. For example, whether a child has experienced chronic or acute hunger and malnutrition can be determined by comparing a child's height-for-age, weight-for-age, or weight-for-height to the group norms represented in the growth charts. Similarly, the proportion of children in a particular weight-for-age group—for example, African children in South Africa below the third percentile (which is an accepted criterion of malnutrition)—can be used as an indicator of the level of poverty and nutritional need in a country or among a particular population group. Data related to both wasting and stunting permit comparisons by population groups on these indicators of material deprivation.

In table 6.1 height data for urban African children, much like the children we have studied in Soweto, are compared to white American children from urban areas. Similar comparisons have been made between the heights of normally growing European and American children as compared to populations exposed to food shortages and famines during and following the Second World War. South Africans as a group are very similar to Americans until about age 2 when South Africans evidence lower height-for-age.

Children who are very low relative to other children with respect to the ratio of their height-for-age are described as stunted, and this is attributed to long-term nutritional inadequacy. Figure 6.1 presents the mean height-for-age differences by population groups in South Africa:

African, Colored, Indian, and white. To facilitate comparisons across population groups, the fiftieth percentile for each group is displayed (the optimal or normal range is between the twenty-fifth and seventy-fifth percentile). The figure makes it clear that the African group at birth is close to the normal range, but the accumulated effects of later nutritional inadequacies and infections become increasingly manifest among older children. This graph shows that the typical African child is mildly to moderately undernourished. The progression toward increasing undernutrition with age is similar for Coloreds although not as markedly negative in its effect. The most optimal pattern occurs among whites and Indians, who are close to normally expected ratios of height-to-age.

Figure 6.1: Stunting—Standard Scores for Height by Age by Population Group, from the Living Standards Survey

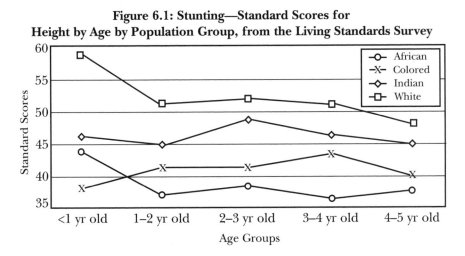

Figure 6.2: Percent of Children Malnourished by Age and Population Group, from the Living Standards Survey

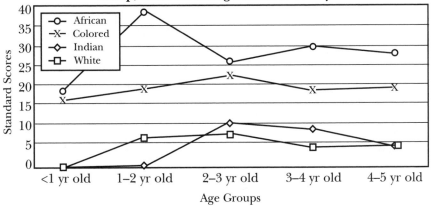

In South Africa, it is estimated that about a third of African, Colored, and Indian children below the age of fourteen years are underweight and stunted for their age (Molteno et al. 1986). See figure 6.2. In some areas, the figure is as high as 60 percent. Severe forms of protein-calorie malnutrition (marasmus and kwashiorkor) occur in up to 3 percent of the preschool population, which is associated with a high admission rate to hospital and considerable morbidity. In BTT, 22 percent of two-year-olds were stunted and 7 percent were wasted. Some catch-up growth occurred and these figures were reduced to 5 percent and 1 percent respectively by age five years. Differences in growth between children from different socioeconomic status groups are apparent throughout childhood, but in BTT these differences in height and weight reached statistical significance only after four years of age (Cameron et al. 1998). That is, early childhood growth is undermined for the majority of black children in South Africa, and the most vulnerable period affecting growth is between birth and four to five years of age. The effect of poor growth on children's development is pervasive and extends to health status, psychological development, and social capacity (Richter and Griesel 1994).

Health of Young Children

South Africa is classified among countries with a high infant mortality rate (the number of deaths that occur in the first year of life per 1,000 live births), the figure being about 90 per 1,000 depending on the area. In general, perinatal mortality (stillbirths and deaths during the first week of life) tends to reflect the extent and standard of available health care, while deaths after that period are generally attributed to social and material conditions associated with poverty (Molteno et al. 1986). Typical causes of death in developing countries are diarrhea, measles, malaria, acute respiratory infection, and malnutrition; malnutrition plays a strong causal role in more than 50 percent of deaths associated with these conditions (Richter and Griesel 1994).

BTT children showed patterns of illness in their early years typical of children in developing countries. A very high percentage (more than 50 percent) in the first two years of life suffer from coryza, and close to 30 percent from diarrhea. Infant illness is a significant source of stress and concern to parents, and is often associated also with worries about financial support for children. Health care during the infancy period of BTT costs families money for transport and services, as well as lost income in daily paid jobs when parents take children to a clinic.

Neuromuscular Development

As newborn babies adapt to the external environment, a number of vegetative processes need to be adapted to human conditions and lifestyle. Infant sleep-wake cycles slowly come to coincide with the diurnal rhythm of the night and day; besides feeding, the sucking reflex will aid the baby to soothe its states of distress, and crying will increasingly become part of the complex communication that becomes established between infants and their adult caregivers in the early months of life. However, these developments occur within a cultural context that gives them meaning and determines their form and appropriateness (Nsamenang and Dawes 1998).

Studies in Africa, including in South Africa, of the ages at which children attain certain behavioral milestones indicate that African children generally develop at a faster rate than American children. African children sit, pull themselves up to stand, and walk at younger ages than children in Europe and the United States. This "African precocity" has been speculated to be the result of care practices in early infancy that are common in southern Africa, including close physical and continuous social contact with the mother and other adults, infant carrying in an upright position, and the deliberate stimulation by

Table 6.2: Percentage of BTT Children Rated by Their Parents or Caregivers as Having Behavior Problems

Behavior (%)	2 years (N=1,805)	4 years (N=1,606)	5 years (N=1,535)
Not toilet trained	20	—	—
Sleep problems	17	—	—
Wet bed	41	25	25
Tempers/management	48	17	23
Passive/daydream	24	7	16
Miserable/irritable	29	11	20
Poor peer relations	4	—	19
A loner	—	8	7
Bully/aggressive	—	18	26
Fearful	26	48	45
Poor appetite	23	16	16
Clumsy	13	3	5
Speech difficulty	17	8	8
Immature	—	6	4
Stutter	—	10	13
Habits	—	25	26

adults of motor development. On the Bayley Scales of Infant Development, South African infants have been shown to have significantly higher psychomotor and mental development indices than American children during the first year of life (Richter and Griesel 1988).

At age two, Mandela's children seem quite mature and capable. The majority of children in Birth-to-Ten were reported to be able to get along with other children in a play situation (99 percent); to get a mug of water without help (82 percent); to narrate simple things that had happened to them (81 percent); and to take off their clothes except for the buttons and zippers. In the main, independence at a young age is encouraged among African children, and even two-year-old children are given responsibilities to do things around the house, carry messages to neighbors, and buy things from the local market. Moreover, they show early signs of accommodating to social circumstances and as a group are able to get along well with others.

As might be expected with increasing maturity, poor appetite decreases among all the children over time. See figure 6.3. Like children all over the world, African children exposed to poor physical and social conditions show delays and disturbances in development, including, for example, in the acquisition of fluent speech, and in bladder and bowel control. Birth-to-Ten caregivers reported, when their children were two years old, that 41 percent wet their beds and 17 percent had speech delays. By the age of four, these figures had dropped to 25 percent and 10 percent respectively, as late-developing children catch up with their peers. However, a substantial number of children at four years of age show unexpected delays in these milestones, indicating the influence of both biological and social constraints on their developmental potential. See table 6.2.

Agnes, a Birth-to-Ten mother, left school after completing Standard 5 (seven years of schooling). She is now an unemployed single mother who had a baby boy when she was eighteen years old. She lives, together with her mentally retarded mother on whose disability grant she and her child depend, in the home of her uncle and aunt, with six other adults and two children. Agnes's son, Boetie, was hospitalized four times between birth and twenty months with a primary diagnosis of malnutrition and dehydration. At twenty-one months, the baby was burnt by boiling water, but Agnes could not afford treatment for the child. Currently, at two years of age, Boetie's convulsions are being investigated.

Imagine what young Boetie, in this account of one Birth-to-Ten boy, needs to recover from the physical challenges to development he has faced during his first two years. Yet shadowing the story is the knowledge that few, if any, resources are available to the child to assist with his recovery and catch-up in growth and development.

As indicated in the first part of this chapter, concern in the first few months of life is appropriated directly to how well the infant grows, since physical growth at this stage is a sign of continued health and development. In the toddler phase, from roughly one to three years, attention shifts to the development of physical functions that emerge

Table 6.3: Transience of Problems of Toddlers

Behaviors Appearing . . .	At 2 *but not* 4–5 "Transient"	At 2 *and* 4–5 "Persistent"	At 4–5 *but not* 2 "Late Onset"
Wet bed (41% of 2-yr-olds; 25% of 4–5-yr-olds)	58.2%	41.8%	51.9%
Tempers/difficult (48% of 2-yr-olds; 23% of 4–5-yr-olds)	58.3	41.7	37.8
Passive/daydreams (24% of 2-yr-olds; 16% of 4–5-yr-olds)	76.3	23.8	70.5
Miserable/irritable (29% of 2-yr-olds; 20% of 4–5-yr-olds)	65.1	34.9	62.8
Poor peer relations (4% of 2-yr-olds; 19% of 4–5-yr-olds)	65.5	34.5	93.0
Fearful (26% of 2-yr-olds; 45% of 4–5-yr-olds)	29.1	70.9	73.5
Poor appetite (23% of 2-yr-olds; 16% of 4–5-yr-olds)	63.9	36.1	67.7
Clumsy (13% of 2-yr-olds; 5% of 4–5-yr-olds)	89.3	10.7	76.8
Speech difficulty (17% of 2-yr-olds; 8% of 4–5-yr-olds)	80.3	19.7	61.5

from increasing maturation and coordination. Though continued growth in weight and height are good barometers of overall development, the focus expands to include the attainment of gross and fine motor skills, the maturity of physical functions reflected in eating, sleeping, and bladder and bowel control, and the emergence of socially appropriate behavior that increasingly comes under the control of environmental expectations and demands. Following this, the preschool child, between three and five years of age, is expected to increase her ability to regulate her behavior and emotions in a way that facilitates adaptation to the social environment and promotes strong social ties with others. To accomplish this, the child needs to strike a balance between the demands of her own egocentricity and the needs of others.

Gender and Social Development

Overall rates of behavior problems among children mask important sex differences in their rates and patterns of occurrence and persistence. Gender is a widely recognized risk factor for psychological problems and therefore one that must be analyzed in discussions of behavioral and emotional development. Compared to girls, boys are more likely to exhibit delays in development, and deficits in their regulation of behavior and attention (Offord et al. 1989). They are more often found to be conduct-disordered, undercontrolled, and aggressive than girls. In contrast, girls are more likely than boys to exhibit problems of emotional regulation, including irritability, unstable mood, depression, and anxiety. These gender-related behavioral and emotional risks identified in broadly representative samples of American, Canadian, and British children appear to operate in similar ways within specific subgroups. For example, Barbarin and Soler observed, in a nationally representative sample of African-American children, that young boys under twelve were more likely than same-aged girls to act impulsively, exhibit anger, break things, be withdrawn, feel worthless, have difficulties concentrating, be disobedient, and have problems getting along with adults (Barbarin and Soeller 1993).

Similar patterns of gender differences were observed among very young South African children. Table 6.3 shows the prevalence of common behavior problems among Soweto children at ages two, four, and five years. This table shows which differences between boys and girls are significant.

Interestingly boys and girls did not differ in reported sleep problems, daydreaming, passivity, and being miserable and irritable.

However, from an early age boys are more likely to show developmental delays in bladder control, motor coordination, and speech development than girls. By the age of four or five years, they are also more likely to exhibit temper tantrums as well as aggression toward others and bullying. In contrast, girls show a higher prevalence of internalizing problems, including poor appetite and fearfulness.

BTT's Advantage in Ability to Examine Behavior over Time

An important facet of the longitudinal design of BTT is the capability it provides of observing whether and how children's behavioral and emotional functioning changes over time. We can track when problems arise, how they evolve, and if and how they resolve. In addition to looking for problems, we can also search for evolving competencies. For example, we can pose questions about the timing of behavioral and emotional responses that may be antecedents of either psychosocial competencies (self-esteem, self-efficacy, delay of gratification, empathy, academic effort) on the one hand, or chronic behavioral and emotional disorders on the other hand.

In considering the impact of earlier forms of adaptation on later behavior, it is helpful to pose a number of questions, including:

Do problems in the first two years of life lead to similar or different kinds of problems at age four and five years?

Are there detectable precursors of later maladjustment? Do biological, behavioral or emotional dysregulations predict specific problems?

Do competencies in the motor, cognitive, linguistic, or social arena or in self-regulation act as protective mechanisms for children who are at high risk for behavioral and emotional problems by virtue of biological predisposition, poverty, or disordered family life?

Persistence and Resolution of Early Behavior Problems among BTT Children

In table 6.3, the percentage of children who were rated as showing a problem behavior only at two years of age, or only at four to five years of age, is given in comparison to children who were rated as showing that problematic behavior at both two and at four to five years. For example, of the children who wet their bed at two years (41 percent of all two-year-olds), more than half (58 percent) were not wetting their bed at four to five years; and of the children who wet their beds at four to five years (25 percent of all four- to-five-year-olds), more than half (52 percent) were dry at two years. That is, the table indicates what proportion of problems evident at two years resolve by age four to five years, and what proportion of problems arise at four to five without occurring earlier. From this point of view, the table indicates the following:

• More than half of all children who are rated as showing particular problematic behaviors at two years appear to have transient problems. That is, the behaviors do not persist to age four to five years. This is especially true of clumsiness and speech difficulties, which are likely to have a strong developmental component. Thus early manifestations of these difficulties should not be cause for alarm in that they often resolve on their own.

• Similarly, more than half of all children who are rated as showing particular problematic behaviors at four to five years do so without any previous history. That is, the behaviors appear without earlier indications of the problem. This is especially true of fearfulness, clumsiness, poor peer relations, and passive daydreaming. Thus for these behaviors, development is discontinuous. This suggests that the ages of four and five may be the critical period for long-term problem development.

• Some problem behaviors, appearing early, are more likely to persist into the preschool period. For example, fearfulness persisted in 70 percent of the children who were fearful at two years of age. Similarly, bed-wetting, temper and management problems, miserable and irritable mood, poor peer relations, and poor appetite persisted to age four or five years in more than a third of the children who showed these problems at two years of age.

• Management problems, including tempers, at four or five years of age are the least likely of all behaviors examined to arise without antecedent signs at two years of age. This suggests a higher degree of continuity for oppositional and defiant behaviors.

Summary and Conclusion

In regard to the physical growth of Mandela's children, the picture of early development of South African children is mixed. One of every five children was premature, placing them at risk for a range of health and psychosocial difficulties. In addition, one of ten children was born at low birth weight. Nevertheless, from the beginning of life through age one, the growth curves of African children, who constitute the most disadvantaged of South Africa's children are reassuringly similar to the growth rates reported for American infants, who are among the most advantaged children in the world. Thus, in spite of the high rates of premature births and low birth weights, the early physical growth of Mandela's children could be considered normal and typical. Note that normal growth permits wide variations in children's height and weight as attested by the photograph in this chapter. Nevertheless this mostly rosy picture changes for the worse by the time the children are two years old. Between ages two and five, the average height-for-age of African children is much less than it is for American children. Recall that low height-for-age is used as an indicator of stunting which presumably is caused by chronic malnutrition. This suggests the unhappy situation of high malnutrition among African children. Under the age of one, food supply for infants may be assured by the breast-feeding which traditionally has occurred at high rates among African women. From age two and on, when breast-feeding is less common, young children may suffer from the inadequate and inconsistent supply of food that affects the rest of the family.

Evidence regarding social development yields a similarly mixed picture. Some problem behaviors such as clumsiness and speech difficulties did not stir up much concern in parents. These were viewed either as difficulties that resolve on their own or as normative behaviors which constitute steps on the way to competent functioning. Because such symptons occur commonly in early childhood and because they are often transient and of relative brief duration, they need not be precursors to chronic impairment. For the majority of children, isolated delays and disturbances are often just a passing phase of development. Even behavior problems such as tantrums, excessive crying, and enuresis which may be bothersome in the short run are prognostically unimportant in the long run for the majority of children. Delays in the attainment of developmental milestones can be overcome by sudden, unexpected leaps or growth spurts, and leave no enduring adverse consequences. Even emotional disturbances which may be a source of grave concern to parents often resolve themselves, leaving behind few traces of maladjustment.

However, for some behaviors, there is growing evidence that early onset is cause for concern. For example, excessive irritability, aggression, fearfulness, and opposition in very young children seem to be predictive of later difficulties. Although early onset problem (that is, those occurring among toddlers, for example, before age three are possibly transient and their appearance dismissed as insignificant), we cannot treat them as cavalierly when they occur later, for example, by age four and five years. An alarming situation exists for Mandela's children among whom behavior problems such as irritability, temper tantrums, aggression, and fears occur at a comparatively high rate by the age of five. In addition, by the time they were five years old, other developmental delays and behavioral problems occurring in about a fifth of Mandela's children had coalesced to form a perception in the minds of their parents and caregivers that they were "problem" children. Such persistence in problem behaviors seem to be associated with social risks. An examination of the social and familial characteristics of children with persistent problem behaviors emphasized the strong relationship that such problems have to biological precursors expressed in low birth weight, developmental competence as assessed by development scales, and features of the social enviornment indexed by marital status, exposure to stressful life events, and attenuated levels of social support. These will be explored more fully in subsequent chapters.

Notes

1. These figures are from the fiftieth percentile off the nchs curves.

Chapter 7

Self-Regulation of Attention, Behavior, and Emotions

Self-Regulation as the Foundation of Socioemotional Development

It must be by design that the heavens have blessed infants with adorable features that endear them to their families and caregivers. Fortuitously, it takes considerable time before families realize that these cuddly bundles of joy do not come fully equipped at birth with a capacity to control themselves and direct their feelings in ways that respond to anyone's needs but their own. By the time children are in their third year of life, many families have more than once contemplated returning their little "angels"—if not permanently, for a long-term respite. By the time most families reach the brink of despair and lose all hope that their two-and-a-half-year-old will ever resemble anything that is close to being human, nature happily intercedes to reveal to families glimpses of each child's budding capacity for regulating his behavior and emotions and with it the hope that he will ultimately be able to accommodate to the needs and demands of the world in which he lives.

Over time and in interaction with their physical and social environments, children do gradually discover that the world does not revolve around them and that for the sake of their well-being, if not their very survival, they must learn a reciprocal dance to a rhythm of give-and-take. This lesson is not an easy one to teach or to grasp. However, it constitutes one of the most important outcomes of development between birth and age six. This is the most fundamental achievement in early socioemotional development and it is a principal basis of later adjustment. It specifically includes the capacity to regulate attention, behavior, and emotional arousal. These are, of course, interrelated rather than completely distinct capacities. Regulation of attention is important because it speaks to the ability of children to marshal their cognitive resources, to learn to make sense of their world and the people around them. Through attentional regulation, children come to perceive order in a world that otherwise seems chaotic and unpredictable. Regulation of emotion is important because of the critical role that emotions play in personal motivation and communication. The experience, recognition, and display of emotions can have strong survival value. Like emotions, the regulation of behavior can significantly shape our interactions with others and how we are perceived by the world. The ability to control behavior and channel it in a prosocial manner facilitates social relationship and is among the most powerful indicators of early child adjustment.

As we shall see later, early-onset difficulties in the area of behavior regulation may also foreshadow a lifelong difficulty. In infancy, difficulties in regulation can be manifested as physiological, sensory, attentional, and motor difficulties, as well as deficits in organizing a calm, alert, or affectively positive state. Many children with problems in this area are described in infancy as having difficult temperaments and are overresponsive to even neutral stimuli (Campbell et al. 1991). Infants with regulatory difficulties display hypersensitive, underreactive, aggressive responses, sleeping and often eating difficulties (Greenspan and Wieder 1993). These symptoms are remarkably similar to the features South African parents identified as troublesome in their characterizations of children with problems. These infants are later described as noisy, disruptive of other children, and peripatetic wanderers as toddlers. These regulatory disorders in toddlers can be predictive of a range of developmental, sensory-motor, behavioral, and emotional problems by age four (DeGranges et al. 1993). Moreover, while there is considerable debate about how much control anyone has over the experience of emotions, the ability to regulate the expression of those emotions is not contested. Ability to regulate the expression of positive or negative affective states can have strong survival value and shape one's place in the world. For example, inability to regulate affect and impulses may make a child difficult to be around and place the child at risk for sanctions and social rejection.

Although these basic competencies in self-regulation are important in their own right early in life, their significance is magnified by their association with important outcomes of later development. The capacity for self-regulation lays a foundation on which much of later social competence and emotional development is built. In the short term, the principal goals of development center around self-regulation of impulses, behavior, affect, and attention, in themselves. In the long-term, attainment of these skills have implications for development of a much broader range of competencies. Thus attainment of emotional self-regulation is just a first step on the way to other favorable outcomes in adolescence and adulthood that include the capacity for intimate reciprocal relationships, a favorable view of self and the world, the ability to derive satisfaction from one's achievements, and the ability to cope with life's expected and unexpected stresses. Self-regulation is a fundamental building block for these favorable outcomes.

A major benefit of longitudinal research on children's socioemotional development is the insight these studies have provided about the multiple processes involved in the acquisition of the capacity for self-regulation and the diverse ways normal development is exemplified. Such development requires the contributions of biological and genetic factors, neurodevelopment, socialization experiences, and a measure of luck. However, multiple other forces unrelated to these particular processes may also define and shape the prospects of children and the outcomes of their early psychosocial development. A range of scenarios in normal socioemotional development is possible, and the expression of healthy social development is quite varied. The following description of Patrick, one of the BTT children, shows just one of the scenarios that might characterize normal and favorable development.

By all accounts, Patrick was a lovely but unremarkable child. He weighed about 3500 grams in an uneventful vaginal delivery after a brief period of labor. He cried a great deal when he was teething, but otherwise he was a contented infant. He gained weight as expected, and by the time he was six years old he weighed 25 kilograms—just about right for his height and age. He learned basic isiZulu words quickly and was very talkative. He was toilet trained and walking by his first birthday. At two, he would pout and grow sad when he was reprimanded, but he did not take long to bounce back. His parents would smack his hand when he did things he shouldn't. They shouted at him and spanked him when he misbehaved. He did not need very many trials to figure out what was acceptable and unacceptable behavior for his parents.

His fine and gross motor skills seemed to develop rapidly. He fed, dressed, and washed himself without difficulty. He was easygoing and well-liked by other children. He was able to throw a ball, to button and unbutton clothes, and to tie his shoes; he enjoyed playing soccer and appeared to have good reflexes in kicking and passing the ball. At age four, he was very afraid of the dark and did not like to be left in a room by himself at night. To help him adjust to going to bed earlier than everyone else in the house, his mother and sometimes his father would tell him stories. He would listen intently, and after a while he learned the stories well enough to tell them himself. When he first encountered the neighbor's dog, he was very fearful and ran away. Fortunately the dog was gentle, and over time Patrick recognized that it would not hurt him. By age five, he was described as affable, quite independent, and able to take care of himself.

Most of the time, he seemed cheerful. When denied something he really wanted, he became quiet and sulked for a bit, but he rarely displayed temper tantrums. When told to do something, he did not always respond immediately but usually complied after a reminder or two. He was very, very talkative. Although he would express disagreements openly, he would comply and follow rules set by his parents. He got along well with his peers, and although they would fight and argue occasionally, he was never bossy and did not pick fights or deliberately hurt others. He adapted quickly, shared easily, and knew how to take turns when playing and working with others. He could be generous and was careful not to hurt anyone's feelings. As a result, he was well-liked by his peers, who found him to be an agreeable person. Although a bit shy around new people, he generally warmed over time and was able to hold a conversation when asked questions by adults. He seemed to cope with disappointments and did not appear to be overly anxious or worried. Although he enjoyed being with other children, he seemed content to be alone to watch TV or play quietly. By age six, he started school and was learning to read. His teacher described him as a polite and attentive child who waited his turn and shared with other children. The teacher said he was clever and highly motivated in school. He wanted to become a teacher himself when he grew up. In most ways, Patrick seemed like the typical well-balanced child in South Africa.

All these early signs suggest that Patrick is developing well in each of these domains related to self-regulation. However, not all of Mandela's children are as fortunate as Patrick. Very early in life, some are starting down a road that worries those concerned about the future of children. The difficulties they are exhibiting now are reflected in measures of behavioral and emotional development used here. These measures give a general reading of the evolving capacity of young children for self-regulation of emotions, behavior, and attention that are the central tasks of social development at this age. Table 7.1 presents a list of the constructs which are the basis for our discussion of self-regulation among Mandela's children. They include maternal-reported measures of withdrawn behavior, somatic complaints, anxious-depressed emotions, attention problems, and aggressive behavior.

Cross-Cultural Relevance of Self-Regulation

It is impossible to avoid questions about the appropriateness of concepts of self-regulation developed principally from Western formulations of psychological health and social adaptation. To what extent are notions of self-regualtion applicable and useful in cultural contexts such as South Africa? Challenges to traditional Western frameworks for understanding children and their development have arisen around the world, most especially from Africa (Aderibigbe and Pandurangi 1995). Cultural and social conditions in Africa are sufficiently unique to give rise to alternative conceptualizations of the self, of personal agency, of illness, and of personal competence. Accordingly these notions are not only different in themselves from Western views but also in the relationship they presumably have to health and adjustment. Consequently the goals of child socialization and deisable outcomes of child development may differ (Ogbu 1981; Robertson and Kottler 1993). As a consequence, doubts have been

**Table 7.1: List of Child Behavior
Checklist Scales Used with BTT Children at Age 6**

Withdrawal	Social attractiveness, which includes qualities such as being affectionate and lovable, and having a sense of humor
Somatic complaints	Symptoms such as dizziness, upset stomach, headaches, and other pains for which there is not apparent physical cause
Anxious depressed	Unusual level of fear, worry, and tearfulness, excessive sadness, irritability, and loneliness
Attention problems	Impairment in concentration, inability to focus and pay attention, forgetfulness, impulsivity
Aggressive behavior	Repetitive and excessive arguing, bragging, destruction, cruelty, teasing, bullying, threatening, fighting, destruction, severe temper tantrums, and uncontrolled rage

expressed about the usefulness of notions of dysregulation developed for children growing up in Western societies.

Thus assertions of cultural variation in social adaptation do not constitute new challenges to Western notions of mental health and adjustment. "The forms which adjustment difficulties assume differ slightly under different cultural, economic, and religious conditions . . . each has its specific hurdles; and those who leap over one most easily may be least adapted to leap another of a different type" (R. Catell 1938, *Crooked Personalities in Childhood and After*, p. 70, as cited in Mash and Barkely 1996). Cultural demands, values, and worldviews determine how children's social behaviors are expressed and interpreted. Behavioral and emotional responses promoted as adaptive in one setting may be judged problematic in other cultural milieu. Partially as a consequence of environmental demands and social conditions, families differ in socialization goals and practices that might be reflected, for example, in beliefs about how independent children should be and how early in life independence should be encouraged (Lambert and Weisz 1992; Weisz and Sigman 1993). Similarly differences in cultural conceptualizations of social relations may shape expectations of how children should behave or express their emotions.

Culture, subsistence lifestyles, traditional wisdom, and experience clearly influence what any group of people construes as aberrant, disordered, or unhealthy. Western views are infused with etiological notions that can be at odds with African cosmology. For example, in some African countries disturbed behavior is often considered a moral failure or a form of social disturbance rather than a mental illness. Etiologically, problems of emotional development are frequently thought to arise from a failure to meet familial or societal expectations rather than hormonal imbalances, neurodevelopmental anomalies, or flawed cognitive processing.

The persistent diarrhea and poor growth of Nonhlanhla, a child in BTT, was attributed by her caregivers not to poor nutrition and exposure to waterborne pathogens due to the family's lack of access to clean water, but to their failure to present the child to her father's family. Once this was done, even if the physical symptoms did not remit, it was believed that she would be less likely to fall prey to similar difficulties. At this ceremony, Nonhlanhla would be named and recognized by her father's family, rituals would be performed around her to invoke the protection of her ancestors, and a feast would be held to celebrate the child and welcome her to the community. In this way, Nonhlanhla would be accepted into a network of care in addition to that provided by her mother's family. Such extensions of care are critical for young children, as they bring additional financial and social resources to bear on a child and, for this reason, are frequently critical in maintaining healthy development.

Others argue that Western conceptions of children's disorders may be relevant to African children, but skewed in their emphasis toward difficulties that occur in the developing world. In other words, the commonly used notions of mental health and disorders reflect problems that are central to and attributes valued within a Western context. These may not be the same attributes that are valued in South Africa and thus fail to give sufficient attention to problems of greatest concern and highest prevalence in Africa. For some cohorts of children, pervasive malnutrition and resulting neurological damage result in high rates of suboptimal brain development. Mental retardation and neurodevelopmental disabilities are more prevalent in poor countries and countries at war. Not surprisingly, mental retardation, physical disabilities, and behavioral disorders associated with both retardation and disability make up a high proportion of reported mental and behavioral disorders in the developing countries of Africa. Close behind, in order of prevalence, are sleep disturbances, speech disturbances, frequent headaches, depression, and anxiety. Familial or societal expectations and the inability to meet them or a failure to honor one's ancestors are accorded a much greater etiological significance in developmental anomalies and adjustment problems by Africans than occurs in the Western world. In Swaziland, for example, a somatoform illness, the "brain fag syndrome," is a widely reported disorder resulting from an individual's failure to meet the extraordinary pressure to achieve academic success and to provide economic security for one's family.

South African Conceptions of Child Adjustment

Cultural critiques of Western frameworks and nosologies of behavioral and emotional adjustment are compelling and cannot be ignored. They require that we clarify whether there is sufficient justification for applying Western notions of child development in South Africa, and if so, that the problems selected for focus be those that are most relevant to the views and concerns of South African families. To test whether African cultural perspectives of childhood lead parents to hold distinctive views of what constitutes disordered behavioral and emotional processes in children, we set about the task of constructing prototypes of childhood dysregulation from parental descriptions of problem children. We explored conceptions of dysregulation in childhood by asking parents to describe specific children they judged to have problems that might seriously interfere with their development over time. Information for the prototypes of childhood dysregulation was collected in focus group discussions with parents from Soweto. Parents in the focus groups came from diverse ethnic backgrounds: Zulu, Sotho, Tswana, Xhosa, and Colored. All had at least some high school education, but not all had graduated from high school. The answers they provided were surprisingly consonant with Western views of self-regulation, but as expected their responses reflected local emphases and nuances. Four prototypes of dysregulated children emerged from these discussions with parents. These prototypes included (1) the disobedient child, (2) the impulsive/aggressive child, (3) the emotionally fragile/withdrawn child, and (4) the immature child. These types apparently reflected the values of parents regarding an ideal or desirable level of behavioral and emotional regulation. Interestingly, the impulsive and the emotionally fragile types incorporated both emotional and behavioral features suggesting that the distinction between emotional and behavioral functioning may not be as clear-cut or salient in parental conceptions are they appear in Western formulations.

1. *The Disobedient Child.* Disobedience represents a deficit in behavioral self-regulation. The disobedient child basically fails to comply with the directions and admonitions of adults. Discussions with parents about the meaning of disobedience revealed a core value attached to compliant, quiet, and self-controlled children. BTT parents considered opposition and loudness to be a breach of decorum, and it is unambiguously judged to be serious violation of norms. A child who does not listen and who needs to be scolded is unquestionably a tribulation to most parents. As a result, defiance, loudness, or acting out are universally frowned upon and are strictly sanctioned behaviors. In addition to the shame of violating cultural expectations, noncompliance was also viewed as a problem by parents because it could place children at risk, such as when against the admonitions of parents, children play in dangerous areas of traffic, on rubbish dumps filled with broken glass and rusted tins, and near paraffin bottles or stoves. The environments of poor children in developing countries are clearly more hazardous and, in parents' minds, justify unquestioning compliance with parental injunctions, particularly at an age when children may not yet fully appreciate the jeopardy they face from some places and activities proscribed by parents.

Evidence of the value parents attach to unquestioning child obedience and self-control is clearly visible in the waiting-room behavior of parents and children who come to the Chris Hani-Baragwanath Hospital for the BTT interviews. Parents admonish their children to be quiet, and to not disturb others, or draw attention to themselves. Severe sanctions are imposed on children who fail to comply. By American standards, the BTT waiting room is a remarkably quiet and serene place where conversations occur in hushed tones and children sit quietly next to their parents occupying themselves for hours with paper and pencils. The children, as a group, appear calm and self-contained, and they do not display typical signs of restlessness despite the long wait to be interviewed. Nevertheless, among Mandela's children at age five, this prototype was the most common childhood disorder identified by parents. More than one out of every ten children was rated by parents as frequently oppositional. Essentially, these children are described as out of control because of their persistent opposition to parental authority, noncompliance, and disobedience. This disorder is akin to the oppositional defiant disorder as described in the American Psychiatric Association's *Diagnostic and Statistical Manual of Mental Disorders* (*DSM*). Moreover its prevalence seems comparable to that reported for oppositional behavior among U.S. children.

2. *The Impulsive/Aggressive Child.* Another common problem type involved children's difficulties in regulating emotions and social exchanges. For children fitting this prototype, the core deficit is the loss of control that often resulted in angry outbursts, temper tantrums, and aggression toward others. The impulsive aggressive child is often irritable, short-tempered, and explosive. These children became frustrated easily and frustration can turn into anger with minimal provocation. For adults, impulsive aggressive children are not only difficult to manage but their disruptive behavior has a flavor of minimally provoked and thoughtless. In comparing this to Western formulations, this prototype combines elements of attention deficit hyperactivity disorder and conduct disorder from the *DSM*. Among BTT children, this was the second most common of the child problem prototypes identified in the parent focus group discussion. By age five, about one of every five BTT children exhibited aggression and one of twenty exhibited the combination of impulsivity and aggressive behavior matching this prototype. This is about half the rate for the children who fit into the disobedient prototype.

Illustrative of an impulsive aggressive child is Thabo, a six-year-old boy growing up in Soweto. As an infant, Thabo was very spirited and a joy to his family. Even though a few weeks premature, he was active and seemed determined. During infancy, he was described as fussy and easily startled. As a toddler, he was highly active and quickly learned to do things for himself. He was always on the move, running, climbing, and jumping. He had a mind of his own, and would throw tantrums when he was not permitted to have his way. As a toddler, Thabo pouted often and didn't play well with other children. Easily frustrated, he often blew up unexpectedly like a storm that was followed by high emotionality and even crying. At age four, he had few friends. He did not like to share and would hit other children and take their toys. In return, he often was teased and got into fights with other children. By age six, he was described as a bully. Thabo was stubborn and volatile. He displayed frequent temper tantrums with adults and bursts of aggression with peers. He often acted without thinking and seemed unable to control his anger. Because he did not have many friends his own age, he played with the older boys from whom he learned to curse and smoke. His family tried to be strict with him but it did not work. The effects of warnings, threats, and reprimands by adults were not long-lasting. He blamed others for his problems, and showed little remorse for his misbehavior. Moreover, he seemed oblivious to their disapproval and was continually in trouble.

3. *The Emotionally Fragile/Withdrawn Child.* The principal self-regulatory deficit in this prototype is an inability to control emotions. The emotionally fragile child is very unsure of self and reacts to minor demands and challenges with excessive emotionally. He lacks self-confidence, is hypersensitive to criticism, seems uncomfortable in the presence of persons with whom he is not familiar, and whines or cries easily. She is uncomfortable in drawing attention to herself and also has difficulty fitting in with her peers. Instead of reaching out to others as socially gregarious peers do, she isolates herself from other children and often feels inferior. Parents' descriptions of children fitting this prototype include the following: "The child needs to be hugged and constantly reassured." "The child that will not even smile when you try to make her laugh." One could infer that the emotional state underlying the social withdrawal is anxiety or sadness but parents were not explicit in drawing such conclusions. However they did make comments such as: "She will always show a sad face and never trust other people that she does not know well." "The child, I am thinking of is unsure of herself and continually seeks reassurance by asking her mother if she loves her." One father described his child as follows: "I have a son that is very self-conscious, quiet and unsure of himself. He does not like to be scolded. He is emotionally crushed even if he is reprimanded for his misbehavior. If you detect a sign of sickness on him, as soon as you ask him about it, he starts to cry. At first tears would well up in his eyes and then a serious cry would arise. He will suffer a headache without saying anything about it; he would rather go lie down and avoid attention." Another BTT parent described her son as a child who is afraid to ask for food, even when he is very hungry and food is available. The child would spend the day in fear without eating and would not eat unless food was offered directly to him. This proto-

type was reported infrequently. Less than one in fifty of Mandela's children fit the description of this prototype of dysregulation.

4. The Immature Child. This prototype is very different from the others. Its core deficit is a biological or a neuropsychological deficit. It involves delayed development, particularly with respect to communication, motor skills, or social functioning. The children in this group often displayed deficits in language use or gross motor skills, or lacked the degree of bowel control and bladder control expected of children of the same age. This included, for example, children who wet or soiled themselves, children who couldn't do the chores that children of their age were commonly expected to perform, children who were recognized as being intellectually slow, and children with speech delays. The term "lag" is used because these are most often issues related to maturation and might be construed as neurodevelopmental or neuromuscular in nature. This type of problem was of low frequency. It occurred in about 4 percent of Mandela's children at age five.

The Multiproblem Child. Overlap among categories of behavioral and emotional problems is commonplace. For example, moodiness, impulsivity, opposition, temper tantrums, and aggression often occur together in young children. The children in our study are no exception. Thus when young children experienced difficulties in the regulation of behavior or emotions, they often manifested difficulties across both behavioral and emotional domains. As a result, a number of children fit into more than one of the four basic prototypes. These children can be called multiproblem. About 8 percent of Mandela's children fit the combined or multiproblem prototype. Comorbidity of problems can occur at any age. This multiproblem prototype for young children is also consistent with observations that problems of psychosocial adjustment may be even less differentiated and focused among preschool children than older children. It is important to underscore that some combinations of problems, though common, are especially lethal with respect to long term socioemotional adjustment. For example, children who displayed shy, oppositional, and aggressive behavior in the preschool years were more likely than other children to engage in smoking, abuse of substances, and delinquent behavior (Kellam, et. al., 1975). They were also more likely to terminate schooling prematurely.

These four problem prototypes and their combinations generated by South African parents can clearly be accommodated within Western nosologies of children's problem behavior. By asserting that these notions are compatible with Western notions of child development, we do not deny differences in how South African parents think about these notions and how they are treated in the West. Although there is considerable overlap with Western views, the childhood problem types proposed by South Africans derive more fully from and are supported more by their own indigenous cultural views than the Western conceptions of these symptoms.

It is interesting to note that self-regulation of behavior weighs more heavily than emotional regulation in parents' appraisal of disorders in young children. Behavioral self-regulation is clearly an important issue for South African parents. Prominent in descriptions of problematic behavior are disobedience, impulsivity, aggression, shy-withdrawn behavior, and immaturity. Concern about emotional regulation was expressed in terms of children who cry frequently, show anger, and are overlysensitive. Not unlike parents in the West, South African parents tended to underemphasize control of emotions which are less salient and less easy to detect, such as anxiety and sadness, but which are central to Western formulations of child problems. This may also reflect a greater effort expended by adults in managing the naughty behavior of undercontrolled children. Less attention is given explicitly to the regulation of emotions, even though discussions with parents suggest that they give strong implicit messages about the value of reserve and caution in emotional expression. Perhaps they gave less attention to emotions in the focus groups because they experience fewer difficulties in the arena.

Changes in Emotional and Behavioral Regulation, Ages Two to Six

As we have noted in chapter 6, many of the problem behaviors exhibited by children early in life wax and wane over time, principally in relation to maturational and environmental challenges. To examine changes over time in the behavior of Mandela's children, we graphed the reports made by parents in regard to behavioral and emotional self-regulation when children were two, four, five and six years old. These graphs present the percent of parents who reported that their child had attained one of several developmental milestones, or was exhibiting a problem of behavioral, social, or emotional regulation that often triggers referral to child mental health services (Richman and Graham 1971). These problems included excessive fearfulness, loneliness, opposional behavior, fighting, and crying. See figures 7.1 and 7.2.

Figure 7.1 depicts data for fearfulness, crying, and loneliness. These indicators are very interesting from a developmental standpoint because they represent behaviors that are influx during this stage of life. Between ages two and six, children proceed from being fearless to being fearful. Does this mean that the capacity for emotional regulation weakens with age? Hardly! New fears do arise in response to stimuli such as furry animals and snakes which were not present prior to age three. Figure 7.1 demonstrates that the proportion of BTT children with fears increased from about 30 percent at age two to almost 50 percent at age four. However by the time the children were six years old, the proportion dropped back to its earlier level of around 30 percent. This pattern is highly consistent with other reports of childhood fears. Although fears of being abandoned, lost, or left alone are common at this age, the symptom of loneliness is not often reported by parents. Few children were rated as lonely. Moreover this number decreases to close to 1 percent by the time children reached age six. Thus at this stage in life, loneliness and social isolation are very uncommon experiences for Mandela's children. Rates of crying conform to a pretty typical pattern of decrease between the ages of two and six. About 30 percent of the BTT children at age two cry often, but this number decreases to 10 percent at age six. These data provide convincing evidence that Mandela's children considerably increase their capacity for emotional regulation as expected. Thus with repect to development of socioemotional competence, they are on target in development of skills needed for the regulation of emotions. The outcome is not as favorable with regard to development of behavioral self-regulation.

Figure 7.2 presents changes in the proportion of children with deficits of behavioral regulation shown in two areas, namely opposition and fighting. The line for oppositional behavior shows a surprising drop in the proportion of children rated as having difficulty in that domain. At age two, over 50 percent of the children are described as oppositional. Perhaps this finding is a result of the "terrible twos" in which a family's efforts to socialize and direct the behavior of young toddlers meet with little success as defiance, temper tantrums, and passive resistance become common features of parent-child interactions. By the time children are six, these normative issues have been resolved and the number exhibiting this pattern of behavior drops to below 20 percent. Fighting is the only indicator of self-regulation that increases between ages four and six. This is a highly atypical pattern that does not augur well for Mandela's children. Other studies of young children would lead to the prediction that the frequency of fighting would decrease as children get older. By age six, over 30 percent of the children are described by the parents as often fighting.

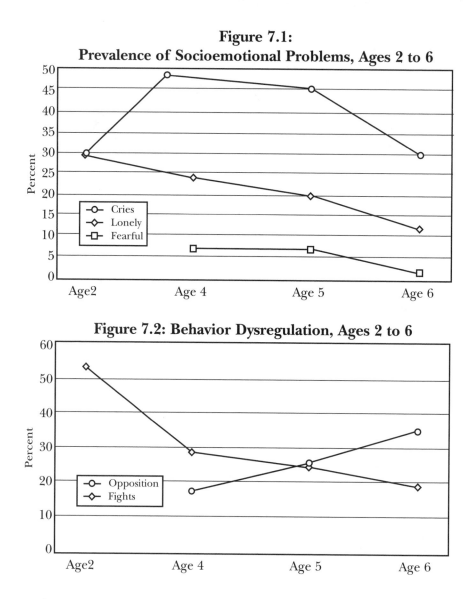

Figure 7.1:
Prevalence of Socioemotional Problems, Ages 2 to 6

Legend:
- Cries
- Lonely
- Fearful

Figure 7.2: Behavior Dysregulation, Ages 2 to 6

Legend:
- Opposition
- Fights

Stability of Disorders in Young Children

In spite of the generally diffuse and mercurial nature of behavioral and emotional symptoms, clinically significant and serious problems in young children are relatively stable across the preschool years and are characterized by heterotypic continuity. Available evidence suggests a degree of persistence over time such that early-onset problems of self-regulation and temperamental difficulty are associated with delinquency, substance abuse, and diagnoses of conduct disorders later in life (Campbell 1990; McGee et al. 1991). Moreover generalized anxiety in very young children seems to be a precondition for depressive and anxiety disorders later in life. Four dimensions of early-onset symptoms appear to predict the stability of behavioral problems in children: the frequency,the generalizability of disruptive behavior across multiple settings, the variety of maladaptive behaviors, and the age of onset (Loeber 1982). Research on the stability of behavior problems from age two to five suggests that behavioral aggression emerges in the first two years of life and has the capacity for stability throughout preschool (Keenan and Shaw 1994). Patterson, Debaryshe, and Ramsey (1989) use the term "early starter" to characterize a pattern of problem behaviors, where the behaviors of children at one stage lead to predictable reactions from the child's social environment at the following stage in an action-reaction sequence that puts the child at risk for long-term maladjustment and antisocial behavior. This pattern, thought to manifest very early in life, is characterized by excessive levels of child noncompliance, aggression, and oppositional behavior in parent-child interactions during the preschool years (Dishion, French, and Patterson 1995; Patterson 1982). Specifically psychological difficulties are more likely to be stable and of long duration when problem behavior is high in frequency, occurs in more than one setting, takes varies forms, and manifests early in life.

Scores on Child Behavior Checklist (CBCL) Clinical Scales

CBCL scores for Mandela's children point strongly to the conclusion that Mandela's children have difficulty as a group with self-regulation. Figure 7.3 presents the proportion of children who scored above the clinical cutoff points for scales measuring shy-withdrawn behavior, somatic complaints, anxious-depressed emotions, attention problems, and aggressive behavior. On three of the five scales, Mandela's children exceeded the expected proportion of children. These scales are: withdrawn, anxious-depressed, and aggressive behavior. Table 7.1 gives a brief description of the scales. The significance of the clinical cutoffs is that these cutpoints represent a threshold for scores above which children are thought to be in need of clinical and therapeutic interventions. In groups consisting primarily of a nonclinical community sample such as this one, it would be expected that not more than 10 to 12 percent of the children would attain scores above the clinical threshold on any of the scales. In light of our earlier discussion of the

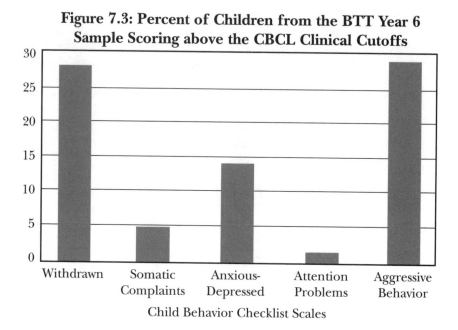

Figure 7.3: Percent of Children from the BTT Year 6 Sample Scoring above the CBCL Clinical Cutoffs

Child Behavior Checklist Scales

self-regulation of attention, behavior, and emotions, several conclusions are possible. First, BTT children are developing about as expected with respect to the regulation of attention. However, more children than expected are experiencing difficulty with regard to the regulation of behavior and emotions. These CBCL data on higher than expected difficulty with behavioral regulation are consistent with the results presented in the previous graphs.

Social Risks and Developmental Deviations

The contrasting images of the behavioral and emotional regulation displayed by Thabo and Patrick convey in a small way the widely divergent outcomes we observed among Mandela's children between birth and age six. It is difficult to explain why Patrick and Thabo have taken such different paths. It is conceivable that both children may ultimately end up in a good place psychologically, and Thabo may recover from his fitful start. It is also possible that he might deviate further and that Patrick too might veer off the normal path and end up with a problem-filled adulthood.

How can we account for the possibility that the directions of their development may reverse or remain stable? A determinist view of development is attractive for its simplicity but is dead wrong for that very reason. Genetic predisposition and anomalous neurodevelopment provide partial but not full explanations of the current differences between chidren like Patrick and Thabo. Social and familial conditions over the course of childhood will also make significant contributions to children's outcomes. Longitudinal data that examine a variety of social risks for the development of young children provide a picture of the factors that lead children to deviate from patterns of development that are typical for most children of the same age and living under the same general life circumstances. Research in developmental epidemiology has uncovered a wide range of factors that may be implicated etiologically in the development of behavioral and emotional disorders of childhood. These include:

1. Genetic predisposition, physiological influences, and neuropsychological dysfunctions reflected in overreactive and underresponsive infant dispositions, impulsivity, and inattention.

2. Socioeconomic circumstances and social context, including poverty and unstable community environments and family victimization (Nelson 1994).

3. Parenting and caregiving processes, including family instability, insecure child-parent attachment, maladaptive patterns of parenting (for example, detached, intrusive, anxious, nonresponsive, or punitive parenting), deficits in social learning and social reasoning, and impaired emotion regulation and impulse control.

The adverse effects of these factors on children are cumulative seem to magnify when risk factors appear in all three domains and simultaneously exert influence over children's growth and development. Temperament, material deprivation, and parental social status seem to be particularly significant in the etiology of early-onset behavior problems (Campbell 1995).

How Important Is the Early Onset of Problems in Regulation of Behaviors and Emotions to Later Development?

To date, suitable levels of self-regulation have been attained by most but not all of Mandela's children. A sizable minority, like Thabo, evidence difficulties in the regulation of affect and behavior. What are the implications for his later development and those of Mandela's children like him? Will these problems impede further development? The most important concern is whether children are on an trajectory that will eventuate in the acquisition of basic competencies needed to function as adults in South African society. Will they ultimately exhibit the maturity, mutual respect, academic skills, empathy, independence, and maturity expected of adults? Can these desirable developmental outcomes still be achieved in spite of a poor start? We have made good progress in understanding the connections between the early presentations of psychological disturbances and later adjustment. This has largely been the result of programs of longitudinal study that have assessed behavioral and emotional functioning from infancy through adolescence and even into adulthood. On the basis of such studies, we have developed estimates of the continuity and stability of internalizing disorders, externalizing disorders, and problems of academic achievement.

Developmental Course: Self-Regulation of Behavior

With respect to the early onset of difficulties in the self-regulation of behavior as exemplified in aggression and opposition, the evidence for continuity over time is striking. The developmental course of serious conduct problems is characterized by heterotypic continuity. While there is stability of disordered conduct, the manifestation of problem behavior changes with age. Several features surfacing during infancy and toddlerhood stand out as precursors of later conduct problems, including characteristics associated with a difficult temperament, such as irritability, overactivity, and fussiness. As early as age three years, what appear as isolated behavior problems form a discernible pattern that can be predictive of serious conduct problems later in life (Ruth-Lyons 1996). At this time, defiance and noncompliance are common in the child's interaction with adults (Sampson and Lamb 1994). In the preschool years, these problems can be expressed in argumentative, defiant behavior and physical aggression. Stealing may emerge in middle and late childhood. By the time the conduct-disordered child reaches adolescence, he or she may exhibit sexually aggressive behavior, substance abuse, and property destruction. Under certain circumstances, this syndrome can evolve into an adult pattern characterized by psychopathy, interpersonal callousness, and chronic criminality.

Self-Regulation of Emotions: Developmental Course

With respect to emotion regulation, Mandela's children are doing well. Research suggests that anxiety and fearfulness have an early onset. If serious, they are relatively enduring, and often worsen with age. Fearfulness is initially expressed in the form of dependent behavior, excessive crying, and clinging. Common precursors include irritability in infancy, and shyness and fearfulness as toddlers. By the time children begin school, those with anxiety difficulties are described as introverted, quiet, cautious, or behaviorally inhibited. In addition, they exhibit a low threshold for arousal, suggestive of a diminished capacity for emotion regulation. Serious bouts of sadness associated with early internalizing symptoms tend to occur in later childhood and, until recently, were thought to be rare among children. Fortunately this does not loom as a major issue among the children in our study. It should be noted, however, that anxiety and depression may arise in the future as a consequence of difficulties in behavioral regulation.

The Persistence of Behavior Problems Justifies Concern

Early onset and persistence of deficits related to regulation of behavior justify early detection and prevention efforts. The continuity of problems is striking for both early-onset behavioral and emotional problems. The lesson here is simple and unavoidable. By age five, substantial numbers of Mandela's children exhibit behavioral problems that they will not simply outgrow. If we ignore them, they are likely to worsen and contribute to additional problems before they improve.

The provision of preventive services can make a difference in altering the trajectory of children with high-risk behavioral profiles. Moreover the significance of early intervention in preventing the long-term deleterious effects of these early-onset problems among children with similar or identical patterns of behavior and risk cannot be underestimated (Ramey and Ramey 1998). In addition, it has become clear that certain social and biological risk factors may interfere with the development of self-regulation. Understanding the factors that constitute the most significant risks and learning about the process by which adverse outcomes materialize gives us an advantage in targeting scarce preventive resources.

To balance this somewhat pessimistic view, it may be helpful to recall the optimistic note on which the previous chapter concluded, namely childhood is a time of great change and adaptation. Not all of the difficulties with self-regulation will worsen. Some symptoms commonly occurring in early childhood may be unstable and of relatively brief duration, they are of uncertain significance and do not necessarily act as precursors to chronic impairment. In other words, we cannot say with complete certainty how the attainment of normal developmental milestones, the failure to maintain "on-time" development, or the onset of psychological symptoms early in life are related to maladjustment in later life. But given the potential dangers of long-term adjustment problems arising from behavioral and emotion dysregulation in childhood, it seems unwise and even foolhardy to justify inaction in the hope that things will just work themselves out without the intervention of caring adults and supportive communities.

Conclusion: Exploring Resilience and Its Sources

The mechanisms by which adaptive behaviors and the capacity for emotional regulation are strengthen remain unclear. Aspects of ethnic culture and family life are possible sources. In addition Sameroff and colleagues have identified socioeconomic status, maternal education, and maternal competence as protective factors in child development (Sameroff et al. 1993; Sameroff and Chandler 1975). Other aspects of family life may also play a role in moderating the impact of risk: for example, the number and availability of caregivers, the number and spacing of siblings, and the marital status of the biological mother (Werner and Smith 1989). Family life can play a significant positive role in nurturing the development of self-regulation in children. In addition, the impact of social risks such as violence and poverty on children's socioemotional adjustment and development must be considered. These issues we take up in subsequent chapters.

Chapter 8

Urban Households and Family Relationships

Conceptualizing Households as Organizations

The word "family" evokes deep, rich, and diverse reactions. Its meaning is at once universal and personal. It is experienced in some way by almost everyone, yet it resists definition. It is a commonly uttered word, but two people rarely mean exactly the same thing by it. In form, its composition and tasks vary considerably within and across cultures. No two families are cut from the same mold. Yet some would argue that happy families tend to have much in common. Others would disagree and claim that it is dysfunctional families that have much in common, while happy families are as different as the stars are numerous. Family can refer exclusively to a nuclear unit composed of a couple and their offspring, or broadly to persons related by blood with a shared ancestor and a common identity. To complicate matters even more, the term "family" is often applied to persons who do not live in the same place yet retain symbolic obligations to one another. It can also include fictive kin who are not related by blood or marriage. To function effectively, members of a family organize themselves into structures that are adapted to match the social conditions they live in, as they give life to and honor the cultural values passed on to them by their ancestors. In Western and industrializing societies, the nuclear family consisting of biological parents and children is suited to a highly transient and autonomous society. Extended family structures may be more suited to land-dependent rural societies whose principal protection against the vagaries of weather and nature is the mutuality and sharing among a network of family members.

Interest in understanding and predicting variations in child development has led to a decision to focus more narrowly on the proximal setting in which children are raised, the household. The term "household" is used in this chapter to convey a slightly more restricted notion than family, one limited to persons coming together under the same roof to share food, finances, and material resources, and who are likely to be in regular contact with and influence child development. Accordingly, households can be family living units composed of individuals who dwell in a common place, share food, and who are bound together by a system of mutual dependence and commitment. Households may be almost as varied as families. They take many shapes and forms: from the parent-and-child nuclear family unit to clans and kinship networks that are traditional in African societies. Very common in black townships are multi-adult, multi-generation living units that are the urbanized version of the rural extended family. Such was the arrangement in which Ibrahim and Issak lived prior to their deaths. The extended family structure was motivated and driven perhaps by a sense of responsibility and obligation to share their home and food with Ibrahim and his son. It sucessfully provided for them materially but could not fill the psychological void Ibrahim experienced and could not provide safety for Issak.

Although black households are influential and successful in safeguarding the welfare of their children, adverse social conditions have placed them under duress and have increased the difficulty of fulfill-

Table 8.1: Dimensions of Families as Organizations

Household Configuration and Composition
Mother's marital status
Paternal or partner presence
Household type and size
Grandmother presence
Dependence ratio (adults per child)

Relationship Quality
Satisfying family life
Cohesion and emotional closeness
Amicable conflict resolution and problem-solving
Balancing family privacy vs. isolation

Tasks Related to Socialization and Care of Children
Obtaining financial support to maintain children
Securing adequate food
Protecting children from harm
Socialization of values and transmission of cultural legacies

ing the protective and nurturing roles they once held. If social adversity and modernization profoundly affect child development in South Africa, they most likely do so through their impact on family life, particularly on the way families are structured and function. In *Childhood in Crossroads* (1989), Pamela Reynolds wrote, "The South African economic and political realities create turmoil within families, forcing adults to fight for the right to live with whom and where they choose and children's rights to uninterrupted schooling, access to books and lights, need for privacy are all subsumed under these." (p. 22) This analysis seems just as apt today as when it was proposed over a decade ago. Family functioning and its relationship to child development and welfare can be more easily analyzed if the families are conceptualized as organizations. They can be thought of as a particular type of organization composed of members arranged in one of several configurations for economic survival, for a common or joint "life-project" (Glanz and Spiegel 1996), and for performing specific tasks such as the socialization and care of children. By viewing families as organizations, attention is drawn to key features such as composition, relationship quality, and effectiveness of task performance. (See table 8.1)

Household composition refers to the persons identified as making up the family unit. At the minimum, a family can be composed of one or more adults and their dependent children. For example, for financial reasons or custom, a family may be composed of multiple other adults and children in what is termed an extended family structure. Alternatively, childbearing outside of marriage, as well as divorce and separation, may lead to units composed of one man or woman and one or more children in what is called a single-parent or single-adult household.

Relationship quality among family members is quite important to its effectiveness with children. The quality of family relations can be indexed by its ability to maintain an environment that is cohesive, emotionally satisfying, and amicable in dealing with inevitable problems and conflicts. High-quality relationships among members are a sine qua non condition of effectiveness in carrying out family functions and responsibilities. The importance of high-quality relationships extends beyond immediate family members to relationships with the community. Because no family can be completely independent or meet all of its own needs, it must cultivate relationships that demand reciprocity in the sharing of material resources, support, and information with the outside world. Therefore the quality of family life can also be gauged by the degree to which the boundary between the family and the outside world is clear but permeable. With clear boundaries between itself and the world, a family can be firmly rooted in and confident of its own identity but at the same time receptive, trusting in its relationships with persons outside of the immediate family or household.

Family tasks refer to the functions for which the family assumes responsibility or for which it is assigned responsibility by society. Although families have many functions, this discussion will center on some primary tasks associated with the socialization and care of children. To fulfill their child-raising tasks, family members often must acquire and deploy resources to provide for the basic needs children have with regard to food, shelter, and succor. In addition to supervision and meeting tangible needs, the family also contributes to children's ability to cope with stress through supportive relationships, directive guidance, and instrumental assistance.

This chapter presents details of the South African households that form the principal contexts for the early development of BTT children. This chapter also reviews BTT data on family composition and on the quality of family relationships, principally in black households. It addresses questions about the nature and composition of urban households and considers the implications of different household configurations for the quality of relationships among family members. Discussion of the family task performance component of the model will be taken up in chapter 9. In addition, chapter 9 will examine the consequences of each model parameter—household composition, family relationships, and task performance—for the early development of children.

Household Configurations

Household Formation and Membership

In urbanized and Western societies, households are formed as offspring mature and become capable of living as independent adults. A common litmus test of readiness for such independence is financial self-sufficiency and the ability to set up a home away from parents and extended family. In traditional African family life, the process can be more complicated. Negotiations must take place between the families of the prospective partners regarding a monetary or material offering to the woman's family as a first step in the arrangement of a marriage. This payment or offering is called *lobola* (Zulu) or *Bhohadi* (Sesotho). Some couples, particularly those that are financially marginal, must save to make such a payment, and the prospective wife, if she is working, sometimes contributes to the payment of *lobola*. Often a down payment is acceptable and the remainder is paid to the wife's family after the marriage has occurred. Only 51.8 percent of mothers of BTT children ever reached the stage of getting married. However approximately one of six (or 16 percent) unmarried mothers were involved in a cohabiting relationship. Some couples explain cohabitation and the postponement of legal marriage by their inability to afford the *lobola*.

In most rural areas and in some urban areas, couples may out of tradition and obligation live with the extended family of the man most often or the woman occasionally even if they have sufficient financial resources to live independently. Once married or cohabiting, the couple adds on to their parents' home. This provides a level of social and financial security to the entire family in an environment in which sharing of resources is expected. The presence or absence of parents is one of the most significant features of family life for children. Among African families, the proportion of mothers living with biological fathers of the children is in a minority. First, 48.2 percent of the BTT children were born to mothers who were never married to their fathers. By the time the children were six years old, only 40.2 percent of them resided in homes together with both biological parents. In about 6.2 percent of cases parents were divorced or separated, and in another 4.2 percent of the cases the fathers had died. The high rate of unmarried motherhood and the proportion living away from biological fathers could conceivably have profound implications for the support and raising of children.

Mothers and Partners
Because a mother is not legally married and living with the child's biological father does not mean that she lives without a heterosexual partner. In fact, 46.5 percent of the mothers who describe themselves as not living with a spouse report having a partner. In the BTT birth cohort, the likelihood of the mother living in a cohabiting relationship depends on the reason the mother is single. Never-married mothers are more likely (16 percent) to have a cohabiting partner than formerly married women who are divorced (3 percent likelihood) or widowed (2 percent likelihood). Across the entire BTT cohort, 40 percent of mothers are legally married and currently living with their spouses, 9 percent are in cohabiting relationships, and 51 percent are living without partners. This last group includes those who are widowed, divorced, or separated.

Men's Roles: Increased Invisibility of Men in Families
The migration to urban areas has brought an important benefit to women. It has contributed to women's autonomy and independent access to employment, money, and other resources such as land. Thus

it has increased the possibility that women can sustain households on their own. The role of men within the family, particularly in the raising and socialization of children, continues to be symbolically important but in reality may be diminishing. Even for employed men, the span of involvement within the household with their children and partners is shrinking. Under apartheid, a migrant labor system was imposed upon blacks seeking employment in industries such as mining. The men could come to the cities and to mining areas to work but they could not bring their families. For months at a time, men lived in single-sex dormitory-style hostels with only a bed or mat for themselves. The intent of the migratory labor policy was to keep black families from migrating permanently to white-controlled areas near mines. Mamphela Ramphele highlights the tragic conditions of families who attempted to defy this policy by accompanying their husbands and fathers in a book, *A Bed Called Home* (1993). With the policy, the long absences of fathers from the home effectively limited their ability to influence the household consistently. Many became shadowy figures who provided for the family without much direct involvement. The situation of men living with other men away from their families led to the predictable problems of substance abuse, prostitution, and the creation of second families with women living closer to the mines. All of these served to undermine paternal involvement in the raising of their children. Alternatively men who are underemployed or unemployed experience stress in the provider role and may withdraw from families and children. Many drink excessively and may be involved in the abuse of other substances. As a consequence, it was difficult for many men to maintain any significant and meaningful role in the care and socialization of their children.

Single Mothers

Caution must be taken in forming conclusions about household composition when mothers designate themselves as single and without partners. The absence of a heterosexual partner does not mean that mother is the sole adult in a household. Many women in this circumstance live with their parents, siblings, or other adult relatives in extended family configurations. Even so, the number of unattached mothers is relatively high and is caused only to a limited extent by marital dissolution or loss of a spouse through death. Admittedly many young men were casualties of violence associated with the struggle against apartheid, random violence, and of AIDS. Altogether these are not sufficient to account for the magnitude of single mothers. Explanations used to account for high rates of unmarried African-American mothers in the United States may serve as a guide to understanding this phenomenon in South Africa. For example, men's high unemployment rates and inability to contribute financially to the support of children may reduce the appeal of marriage both for them and their potential partners. When doubts exist about the capacity to meet the financial obligations of marriage, hesitation to enter into a legal marriage is understandable. Nevertheless, having children is an important rite of passage for women in several African cultures in South Africa. Until she passes that milestone, she is not accorded full status as a grown woman. With the dim prospects for male employment and the improved access of women to the labor markets in cities, some women apparently decide to have children and forgo marriage rather than assume the many risks to their well-being from the control and possibly excessive demands of a husband and his extended family. As a consequence of many different factors, fathers live with their biological children in only two out of five BTT households. Irrespective of the cause, the high proportion of single-parent female-headed households is a source of concern for policy makers and social planners. The specter of father absence raises many questions about the efficacy of the family unit and socializing, monitoring, and preparing young children for adult life. In some parts of the world, for example, in the United States, father-absent female-headed households have been viewed as a spawning ground for academic, behavioral, and emotional maladjustment of children, particularly young boys. On the other hand, any assertion that single-parent female-headed households are innately ineffective with respect to raising children is clearly not justified by the evidence. Nevertheless, that single-parent female-headed households are much more likely than other family units, particularly multiadult households, to be poor poses a worrisome social policy issue.

Leaning on a Cypress Tree: Increased Reliance on Grandparents

One of the most curious and ironic outcomes of the impact of modernity on the black family is the expanded and increasingly important role of grandmothers. After all, the notion of extended family matriarchies is associated with the past rather than the future. The elderly have traditionally played an important role in African families. As the heads of households, they were looked to as a source of wisdom, authority, and social control, and as arbiters of conflicts. As members at a stage of life in which their personal needs were minimal, they had time that could be devoted to the care of children when the children's parents' obligations left them little time. They were also a source of accumulated wealth that could be passed on as a legacy to their children and grandchildren. Consequently grandparents, particularly grandmothers, were an important source of financial and social resources to the young developing family. However, life followed a natural and expected progression in which the younger generation gradually assumed greater responsibility to the point where they took over and reciprocated by caring for aging parents and relatives. Thus as grandparents aged, they became increasingly dependent on their youngest or oldest to care for them.

Several forces of modern life and public policy have undercut that process and prolonged the time period over which younger generations remain dependent on the elderly. These include the economic policies of apartheid, which constrained employment opportunities for blacks, policy-related restrictions on the supply of housing in urban areas, and the AIDS epidemic. These forces have protracted the period of dependence and delayed indefinitely the passing of the baton of responsibility from the elderly to the next generation. High rates of poverty and unemployment have made it difficult for the younger generation to gain financial footing, forcing them to rely on the meager pensions of the elderly for the financial support of entire households. With the elderly's increasing fragility and approaching death, household economic status becomes precarious. This dependence on the elderly has been fittingly compared to leaning on a rootless cypress tree that could fall over at any moment. Nevertheless, grandmothers provide much-needed social and financial aid. In about one in every three African households, the grandmother lives in the home with the children and the mother. This is an important feature because it adds not only physical and financial resources and assistance in monitoring children, but also the wisdom of the elderly, the kind of experience that enriches the lives of the children, the mother, and the grandparents. The opportunity for cross-generational exchange is quite important and critical.

Grandmothers as Caregivers and Surrogate Parents

The contribution of grandmothers to the welfare of their unmarried daughters and grandchildren has been well-documented. For example, the effects of teen pregnancy and motherhood are much less devastating when young women with children live with their mothers. Grandmothers provide assistance that permits young mothers to remain in school and to participate in social activities that promote their continuing development. Grandmothers provide resources needed to maintain the independence of young mothers and the healthy development of their children. In many cases, grandparents take over the role of full-time caretakers from their daughters. When adult children are not able to care for their own children because of serious illness, abuse of substances, or even irresponsibility, grandmothers are usually the first ones to step in. In urban South Africa, where housing is so limited, single women with children often live in the homes of their mothers.

Data from the BTT study show that hunger is a reality for one of every five urban African children. Furthermore, additional evidence suggests provocatively that in the townships, grandmothers buffer children against hunger to a greater extent than the male partners of their mothers. Perhaps this occurs because the elderly receive small but reliable pensions, which for many households have been the only regular sources of cash income. With pension income, grandmothers often help to meet the basic needs of grand- and great-grandchildren who reside with them.

The benefits that accrue to all from living in households with grandparents is a blessing that comes at a cost. When adult children and their own children live in the home of their parents, ambiguity of roles and lines of authority and responsibility can create misunderstandings, hurt feelings, and mire relationships, particularly between grandmothers and their daughters. Questions arise about whether a mother or father can parent in the home of a grandparent in the face of subtle but inevitable pressures to conform to the wishes, expectations, and rules of the grandparents. How difficult it must be for young single mothers to insist on being the final arbiter and authority when inevitable conflicts arise with parents about how one's child should be raised. The protracted state of dependence makes it difficult to question or challenge grandparents, and many parents end up surrendering or being undercut by grandparents in efforts to direct the socialization of their offspring. Many grandmothers hold their tongue, and against their better judgment yield to the decisions of their adult children about rules and discipline. However the ability to bite one's tongue when one thinks that a grandchild is being raised incorrectly may be more than some grandparents can manage. Grandmothers are especially likely to step in and take over when the mother is an adolescent and still in school. In many cases, the grandmother completely usurps the role of parent and raises the grandchild as though it were her own biological offspring. Grandparent usurpation of the parental role or even conflict over the socialization practices are much less likely to occur when the mother is older and when she works and contributes to the financial resources of the household. In the end, necessity requires that many walk this tightrope and negotiate the differences over how to raise children. Often the degree of support that is provided and the gratitude regarding the access to resources that would not otherwise be available to the young mother and her children make it possible to smooth over the rough edges that result from the conflict over authority and hierarchy in the family unit.

In many cases, this arrangement is not completely satisfactory for the grandparent either. Grandmothers are often required to share resources that are barely sufficient for their own needs. Grandparents are essential sources of economic support and child care for their parents. Meager pensions must often be stretched to satisfy fundamental needs of grandchildren and sometimes adult children for food and shelter. In the worst cases, grandparents' own children abandon their responsibilities as parents, leaving to the elderly tasks that they are not well-equipped to handle given their physical frailty and limited resources. Grandparents are sometimes thrust into the role of principal parent and caregiver by default. No one else is available because of death, incapacity, or abandonment by biological parents. Necessity requires and makes heroes of many of these grandparents. Take, for instance, the case of two children with AIDS abandoned by their own father.

When thrust in the role of default caregiver for young grandchildren, grandparents recognize the bind they are in as a consequence of their age. They are caught between the desire to be responsible and loving caretakers and the realistic appraisal of their physical and social limitations. They fully appreciate and understand the vulnerability imposed by their age and physical condition, the breach between the needs of the children and what they can provide; between the joys of being a parent and the fear of failing to meet its obligations. They want to be responsible but recognize how handicapped they are in relation to the immense tasks of preparing the child for the challenges of life as an adult in a world that is out of their reach and beyond their imagination. One grandmother commented, "I like being a parent, taking care of him very much. I want to do so much for this child, but I feel too old." For this grandmother, one overriding concern gnaws away at her, disturbing her peace of mind. "I often worry about what will happen—if I die, there's nobody" (she spoke of her health: an ulcer, high blood pressure). The overriding fear among many grandparents is that they will die before the job of parenting the child is done. "That's why I want someone to take him on, to care for and train him—not just anybody. . . ." Acceptable alternatives are elusive. The difficulties for grandmothers are not limited to physical and financial demands but can also be psychological and cultural. Normally the transition of the child from home to school poses a significant challenge to the child's adjustment. Things do not always go easily. However in families where grandparents are the principal caregivers, particularly grandparents who grew up in isolated rural settings, this transition can be difficult for them as well. Consider the case of Zolile.

The entry of Zolile into school has been smooth and good. He loves school. According to the teacher, he is a very good student. However, the issue of language use emerges as an important one. Until recently, when Zolile and his cousin who is living with them started school, Zulu was exclusively spoken at home. Zulu and English are spoken at school. Initially children are instructed in one of the African languages, but over time English becomes the preferred medium of instruction. In time, academic success requires that the children acquire facility in the use of the English language. In Zolile and his cousin's case, the "mistress" (teacher) told their grandmother she must speak English at home. Now she does, but it's "very hard." As a child growing up in rural areas, she never heard English spoken. She was not exposed to it until she "was very old." Now that her grandson is learning English at school she is forced to hear and learn it too. For the grandmother raising Zolile and his cousin, the education and care of her grandchildren has forced her to make difficult changes late in her life. These challenges are taken up with zest and commitment even if they cannot be done with great skill.

Household Composition and Size

South African families are relatively small in size by comparison to the rest of Africa, yet large in comparison to the Western Hemisphere. Although African household size in the BTT cohort ranges from two to twenty-five, the most common household size is six persons. Over three-quarters of the households have eight or fewer persons living within them, with about 20 percent of African families reporting four or fewer persons, 32 percent reporting five to six persons per household, 22 percent reporting seven or eight per household, and 17 percent reporting nine or more persons. An important indicator of the status of urban African households is the ratio of dependent children to adults. The South African population is comparatively young. Approximately 47 percent of South Africans are under age nineteen, and 36 percent are under the age of fifteen (South African Dept. of Nat. Health and Pop. Dev. 1994). Although this is less than the 45 percent average for the entire African continent, this results in a relatively high ratio of children to adults than experienced in, say, Europe, which has a 20 percent average. Moreover, 17 percent, or almost one in five, South Africans is under the age of five. This translates into a much greater dependency ratio and strain on health, educational, and other human services. This is an important indicator because it establishes the extent to which there may be unmet needs in the family. Each individual in a family has material needs that must be provided for by the family. It is often assumed that adults are the main sources of resources to meet a family's needs. Children have high needs but relatively limited capacity to meet them. In households with many children and few adults, the strain of providing for children will be greater than it is for households with a lower dependency ratio. The ratio among African families is approximately .52, suggesting that there are approximately two children for every adult in each household. Even these numbers represent the most rosy scenario. In light of the high unemployment rate, many of these adults may be unable to assist the household in meeting the needs of its members. A more likely scenario is that one person carries the burden of supporting a large household without assistance from others. Not uncommonly, this role falls to an elder retired on a pension of R600 per month. The significance of this dependency ratio of children to adults is that it suggests that fewer adults are available to support more children. However, only 41 percent of the children in the BTT sample have siblings. This suggests the possibility that they live in multiple mother-child households so that, while they do not have siblings, they have the equivalent of them in terms of cousins and other relatives who are of similar age. Until children are old enough to attend school, many live with grandparents or extended family who provide full-time child care so parents can work. Once they reached school age, almost all the children in the BTT cohort lived with their mothers.

One of the ways that the high dependency ratio is managed at the household level is living in extended family units that have multiple adults and their offspring rather than in nuclear family units. Extended family structures defined this way are much more common than nuclear family households in South Africa. Approximately 68 percent of African families from the six-year-old sample live in nuclear family households, while and 32 percent live in extended family households.

Quality of Family Relationships

Satisfying Family Life
Family life satisfaction indicators reveal a great deal about the overall quality of family functioning. On this indicator, African families in urban townships of South Africa scored high. Over half all households indicated that they were satisfied with family life the way it was. Only 12 percent felt that the family had a lot of problems. In contrast, the overwhelming majority (88 percent) were extremely proud of their families. Table 8.2 presents data on family relationships with respect to satisfaction, cohesion, conflict resolution, and privacy versus isolation.

Similar data are presented separately for differing household configurations. With regard to satisfaction with family life, widowed and divorced parents were less frequently satisfied than intact couples. Having a partner and living in a nuclear or extended family made no difference in satisfaction. However, households with grandmothers were satisfied slightly more often than households where there were no grandparents. Thus the overall the quality of family life is quite high. Over 80 percent of families report a very high level of satisfaction with the way the family is functioning. Relatively few believe that their family has many problems. This may suggest a strong identification with family.

Table 8.2: Percentages of Parents Reporting High-Quality Family Relations by Household Configuration and Composition

	High satisfaction with family life	Family very cohesive	Amicable resolution of family conflict	Family very private/ isolated
All households	57.7%	39.0%	79.7%	29.3%
Never married	55.4	38.3	77.4	28.8
Widowed or divorced	38.7	32.3	79.3	22.6
Currently married	58.8	39.7	83.8	30.8
Mother with partner	55.9	41.9	84.5	30.4
Mother without partner	55.7	36.0	75.5	28.1
Nuclear family	55.9	38.8	82.5	30.3
Extended family	55.8	39.4	78.9	28.8
Grandmother in home	58.4	35.7	84.0	24.4
No grandmother	54.6	40.6	78.2	31.6

Cohesion and Emotional Closeness

An important function of families is to provide social support and closeness and intimacy. It is the family that is seen as a refuge, although it is often a place where we are at both our best and worst selves. It is within the context of family life that we make assumptions about the ready access to close and intimate connections with others. Along this line, the quality of supportive family relationships within African families again appears to be high. Only one-third suggest that they ever have difficulty expressing themselves in their family, most agree that their family is fun and congenial to be with, and a large majority feels that the family is almost always easy to get along with and like one another. While irritations and difficulties in getting along occur and are to be expected, they seem not to be a significant problem for many of the families. Most of the families would suggest that it is not true that their families irritate or upset them and they do not wish that their family would get along better. Most importantly, three of every four African mothers report that the family is there when she needs them. In all, almost 40 percent of families in the BTT cohort described themselves as extremely cohesive. The principal exception to this pattern are families in which the mother is widowed or divorced. Mothers with partners are slightly more likely than mothers without partners and, for that matter, all other groups, to describe the family as extremely cohesive. Moreover mothers and families in which no grandmother resides more often rate the family as extremely cohesive than those in which grandmothers live.

Attachment between parent and child also surfaces in connection to family relationships. Attachment has become an important way of conceptualizing the relation of the early caregiving environment to emotional and behavioral functioning. Developmental researchers have often pointed out that, given the exposure of black children to multiple caregivers, the routes by which they attain the benefits of secure attachment may differ. In infancy, comparisons are made about the view of children and attachment, the acceptance of extended parent-child separations, and the reliance on multiple caregivers for infants. In South Africa, it is not uncommon for children to live with and be cared for by grandparents from birth until it is time for them to go to school. They are separated from parents, who must spend long hours in commuting and working. These extended separations of children from biological parents from birth to age six raise questions about how attachment develops and the impact of early sustained separation for social relations and adjustment of children once they return to live with biological parents when they are old enough to attend primary school. The remarkable differences in cultural and ethnic orientations make it possible to engage in a dialogue about how difference in perspectives and values about children and socialization, parental roles, and family relations create unique circumstances that shape child development and adjustment.

Conflict Resolution and Problem-Solving

Public violence perpetrated by unrelated persons within the community is not the only source of threat to the physical welfare of South Africans. Violence within the private domain of the family is equally prevalent and inimical to the well-being particularly of women and children.

Although the family is the place for the greatest support, love, sharing, and identification, it is also a locale where people experience extreme threats to their physical well-being and violence when families do not function well. Conflicts might not be easily resolved, and external strains become expressed in terms of internal conflict and fighting. Even though the use of violence in political and criminal activities is often denounced, many acts of violence go unchallenged because they occur within the private domain of the family. In many quarters, violence remains an acceptable means of social influence and resolving conflict within the intimate setting of the family (Glanz and Spiegel 1996). Violence in families takes many forms, including the use of physical, sexual, or psychological force, exploitation, emotional humiliation, economic deprivation, and the use of harsh measures to discipline and socialize children (Swarts 1997). Although levels of violence in South African families are not epidemic, it does occur. Within the entire BTT sample, over a five-year period 13 percent reported spousal abuse. Within this sample, the hitting or hurting of other family members was reported in 30.4 percent, fighting in about 20 percent, and throwing things in 8.8 percent. Moreover, family members are gradually speaking out about the wave of sexual abuse of children as well. In the Kaiser Health Inequality Survey data, sexual abuse was reported at a rate of 3 per 1,000 households among African families residing in urban areas of Gauteng. Interestingly, spousal abuse was the only form of violence, as reported by the BTT sample on table 8.1, that increased between 1990 and 1995. There was only a modest overlap in the households that affirmed that spousal abuse occurred at least once in each of the two reporting periods. Approximately 30 percent of all families reported that the hitting and hurting of other family members occurred in their home. Fighting as such is infrequent. Only 5 percent reported that fighting occurred regularly in the family; 20 percent of mothers reported that fights occurred occasionally. The most reasonable conclusion from these data is that peaceful resolution of conflict is commonly practiced in South African families. However family violence does occur. Amicable resolution of conflict is reported commonly, with higher rates occurring among women who lived either with the legal spouse or a cohabiting partner. The lowest rates of amicable conflict resolution occurred in homes in which mothers lacked a partner or were widowed or divorced.

Reports of family violence have increased slightly over the period from 1989 to 1995. In addition, the suspicions often voiced by child welfare advocates about the widespread use of physical punishment of children have been borne out by these reports of violence and abuse within the family. Given the taboos about such sexual misconduct and the value attached to family privacy, these data are undoubtedly tempered by underreporting. The actual rates are possibly much higher. Urban life, poverty, and the demands of work may increase the strain on adults and lessen their ability to provide monitoring and guidance for their children. These conditions are contributing to an increase in child abuse and neglectful endangerment, which themselves are forms of violence that deserve attention because they are so inimical to the welfare of children. This situation originates in several sources that are long-standing and pervasive. They are at once internally supported and externally imposed. They are cultural and historical. Messages about violence as an acceptable means of resolving conflict and as a legitimate means of social influence, unfortunately, are reflected in the intimate setting of the family (see Glanz and Spiegel 1996).

Privacy and Isolation: Relationships with the Outside World

Another critical feature of family life is the way in which families manage relationships with persons outside of the family. Few families are completely self-sufficient. They need to be able to look to the outside for assistance. As important as a family is, as consistent as it can be in providing support, most individuals must rely on people outside of their families to supply some of its needs. Almost half of mothers indicated that they depend on people outside of their family. A common form of interdependence is the reliance on community members for financial credit to tide one over when financial resources are short. Credit cooperatives, called "stokvels" operate among street vendors and in communities to provide cash flow because formal banking institutions are often unwilling to lend to poor people. (Some women comment wryly that banks only loan money to people who don't need it.) Nevertheless, privacy seems to be highly valued in many families. For example, about 57 percent of the families reported that they do not disclose much about family matters to outsiders and about 29 percent suggested that the family provided such good support that no one else outside of the family was needed. About one in five mothers indicated that the family has a hard time accepting help from the outside. The issues of privacy and isolation appear to be least well-resolved in families in which there is no grandmother. In contrast, mothers who were separated or divorced reported higher levels of dependence on and lower levels of isolation from persons outside of the family. (See table 8.2.)

In summary, the familial environments in which Mandela's children are being raised are quite diverse and fully reflect the influence of modernization and social stress. The increased role of grandparents and the diminished role of men in the lives of children is potentially troubling because of what it may mean for the children's development of children. In spite of the economic and social strains on family life and the distortions they bring about in household composition and family structure, family life for Mandela's children appears to be quite robust and satisfying. Thus there is every reason to conclude that, on the whole, South African families constitute propitious settings for the socialization of children and are a source of hope and promise for the children of the nation. Data related to the validity of this conclusion will be presented and discussed in the next chapter.

Chapter 9

Family Influences on Socioemotional Development

Family Tasks Associated with Raising Children

Although the family has many different functions in society, the contribution it makes to the care and socialization of children is easily its most important mission. In South Africa, as in many societies, the family has few rivals with respect to the depth and breadth of its impact on children's lives. More often than not young children spend most of their young lives in and around their homes, often under the watchful eye of the family. Consequently the family is the most significant determinant of the quality of care and the adequacy of material and psychological resources available to a child. Under optimal conditions, the family is the ultimate refuge, the safe haven, a shelter against a harsh, indifferent world. Clearly the family is expected to provide adequate monitoring supervision and to protect children from dangers. It must assure that infants and toddlers do not fall prey to accidents or harm that might threaten their lives. Older children must be educated so that their talents and capacities are developed to the fullest.

The family must meet children's basic physical, social, and emotional needs. This includes at the most basic level provision for food, shelter, clothing, and health care. Specifically this means: obtaining financial support to maintain the child; securing adequate food; protecting the child from harm; and the socialization of values and transmission of cultural resources. Families differ in the levels at which they are able to accomplish these tasks for their children and in the means that they must use to accrue the required resources. All the while, conditions of poverty, joblessness, community violence, and racism makes the tasks much more difficult to carry out successfully. In spite of the overwhelming odds that many families face, society judges harshly those which fail in their most fundamental duty of providing shelter, guidance, basic necessities, and nurturing for their children.

This is evident in the views many hold of the families of homeless children. A large proportion of the street children in South Africa, for example, are thought to be fleeing abusive and deprived conditions at home to take their chances sleeping and panhandling in the streets of South Africa's urban areas.

This chapter reviews the evidence gathered by BTT regarding the success of families in carrying out the essential tasks related to providing financial support, safety, food, and cultural/spiritual values. In addition, it examines whether success on these tasks vary by household composition and structure. The previous chapter presented an organizational systems model as a metaphor for understanding family functioning. This model was invoked as a way of proposing relationships among components of family life and between them and child outcomes such as behavioral problems, emotional adjustment, and social competence. Data from the six-year supplement to BTT were utilized to test these relationships. Items from the Family Relations Scale (Barbarin 1992) and demographic information from the larger BTT study provided information about family task performance and family composition.

Obtaining Financial Support to Maintain Children

Overall, black families experienced a relatively high rate of success in securing financial support for children. Table 9 presents the portion of families which effectively carried out child socialization tasks. Although it is not possible to evaluate the adequacy of support to meet the needs of children, we can attest that an overwhelming majority of mothers, approximately 85.5 percent, receive support from partners and/or biological fathers to help defray the cost of feeding, clothing, and sheltering their children. Even with high unemployment and low rates of residing with children, three out of five fathers were significantly involved in the financial and material support of their children, whether or not they were legally married to the child's mother. Nonmarried partners contributed at a similar rate to the financial support of children who were not their biological children. The highest rates of support occurred in families in which the mother was currently married and those in which the family structure was nuclear. In these cases, slightly over 92 percent of mothers reported receiving support. The lowest rates occurred, understandably, among mothers who were never legally married to the fathers of the children, those who were currently living without partners, and those living in extended family structures.

Table 9.1: Percentages of Parents Reporting Effective Family Task Performance by Household Configuration and Composition

	Obtain child support	Provide adequate food	Reside in safe area	Family values/ spirituality
All households	85.5%	78.5%	68.5%	72.7%
Never married	80.6	73.4	66.2	71.9
Widowed or divorced	85.0	75.0	65.7	77.4
Currently married	93.2	87.9	72.9	73.3
Mothers with partner	89.9	82.7	71.7	73.1
Mothers without partner	80.4	74.0	65.2	72.4
Nuclear family	92.3	85.4	69.8	73.7
Extended family	82.1	75.8	67.8	73.7
Grandmother in home	86.8	82.4	73.2	69.8
No grandmother	84.6	77.1	66.2	74.2

Even though a preponderance of African children lived in families in which their mothers were not married to their fathers or in which fathers did not live with the children, this does not tell us much about the likelihood of her receiving financial support or predict the father's social involvement with his children. Across the entire sample, 61.9 percent of mothers reported that the biological fathers are actively involved in the financial support of their children. Moreover, for mothers who were cohabiting with nonspouse partners, about the same proportion of cohabiting partners contributed to the financial support and care of the child. Thus when biological fathers are in default, the mothers' partners typically step up and assume their responsibilities. In 62.2 percent of the cases where mothers live with cohabiting partners, financial assistance is provided by those non-parental partners for the support of the child.

In the South African context, too much may be made of the critical importance of the father or male presence for the economic well-being of children in a family. An interesting paradox occurred with respect to the relationship between childhood hunger and the presence in the household of the mother's partner and her own mother. Child hunger was more likely to occur when there was a father figure in the home. Hunger was more often experienced by children living with biological mothers and their partners, but no grandmother, than those residing with their single, unattached mothers and grandmothers. The protection often afforded to children by the presence in the home of the mother's spouse or partner does not obtain in the case of children growing up in South African townships. Children are more likely to experience hunger when a male partner is present than if he is absent. The high rates of unemployment among adult males in the townships render the usual financial advantage of males in the labor force moot and irrelevant. In time, they can even become a drain on the family's meager resources. Bomela has explained this apparent paradox by suggesting that when women control the financial resources, they are more likely to be expended on behalf of the needs of children than when men have control (Bomela 2000).

Securing Adequate Food

The ability of African families to meet the basic needs of their children has been severely constrained. As noted earlier, one in five African children experience significant hunger regularly and meet the criteria for moderate malnutrition. This high rate of hunger and malnutrition is hardly surprising in light of the data presented in chapter 3 on the allocation of household financial resources. Recall that the total monthly financial resources for black families is R1,812 for a household, or approximately R342 per person living in the household. For whites, the total monthly expenditure is R4,742 or R1,845 per person. Although the typical black household allocates more than half of its income to expenditures for food, it has only about R181 ($30) each month per member of the household. Colored households are only slightly better off with respect to the resources they are able to allocate to feed themselves. This compares to food expenditures of only 22 percent of total income for whites and 32.9 percent for Indians. Even with the small proportion of total income devoted to food expenditures, whites spend almost twice as much on a single person within the household than blacks will spend on their entire household. Some scholars make the argument that black families have much less discretionary income to make available for purchasing health care and food. Overall, 78.5 percent of all households are able to provide minimally adequate food for the children. The groups with the lowest ability to secure food for children include never-married mothers without partners and families in which there is no grandmother in the home.

Children have many other needs in addition to food. It is instructive to review data on poverty contained in chapter 3 to explore how families allocate financial resources to address other needs and obligations. Blacks, for example, spend much less for shelter (9.9 percent) than do any of the other population groups. This is true not because the cost of housing is lower for blacks, but because high-quality and adequate housing has been inaccessible until recently. For example, people who live in informal settlement areas in shacks have lower housing-related expenses. Another important need is health care. Blacks spend 25 percent of what whites spend for health care and most take advantage of free or low-cost primary healthcare services through clinics or rely primarily on home remedies. Child care is one domain where blacks also allocate a relatively small proportion of their income. In this area, they spend 0.9 percent, whereas whites spend 5.8 percent and Indians 6.2 percent of their income. Most notable is that many black families have culturally defined obligations to provide assistance to extended family members. In this case, blacks spend about 3.3 percent of their income on remittances or the sharing of financial resources with persons outside of their households. Whites and Indians spend less than blacks both in absolute amounts and as a portion of their total income (0.5 percent) on remittances.

Protecting Children from Harm

Most central among different concerns is the need to provide for the physical safety of children. The very essence of childhood is its dependence, its inability to meet its own needs, particularly provisions for its own physical safety. Children often lack the physical strength and ability as well as the foresight and knowledge to identify potential dangers and to take the steps that are needed to protect themselves. Therefore one of the most critical duties of families is to provide for their safety. We will comment below on the severe strain with respect to providing protection and security for children, either because of threats from the outside world—political violence and interethnic conflict around economic matters—or from threats that emerge, unfortunately, from within the family. Data from BTT and other studies suggest that the ability of the family to provide a safe, orderly environment for children and the well-being of mothers and primary caregivers are critical sources of resilience for children in distressing environments. Note the following case:

> An entry in the archives of the South African Press Association describes a 16-month-old baby burnt to death in a squatter shack. The child was in the hut with his two brothers aged 3 and 6. The fire allegedly started when a blanket near an open fire caught alight and the two older children managed to escape but could not save their younger brother. In addition to the egregious loss of life, there will likely be other damage resulting from this infant's death. We can only imagine the sadness and guilt experienced by the surviving children, who may carry for a lifetime the psychological sense of responsibility for the death of a sibling because they were unable to rescue him.

Value Socialization and the Transmission of Cultural Resources

The transmission of values and culture to children is a way of passing on a legacy to children. In one sense, it is a way of providing meaning for children about the dilemmas of life and death. It is a means of connecting them to the social network and to provide a set of perspectives by which they are able to organize and order their relationships to one another. The socialization of cultural values is a way of transmitting a sense of responsibilities, obligations, and rights that are central to knowing one's place in the world. Most often this is thought of in terms of ethnicity or cultural groups and language. These are not the only ways in which cultural values are transmitted.

Family Socialization of Values—Teaching Social Motives and Self-Regulation
From birth, Nora was taught to eat all kinds of food so that she would learn to value and appreciate what she had and was given. Her family would not tolerate her being a picky eater. She was taught to eat porridge (oatmeal) without sugar and sometimes without milk, even though the family could afford to put sugar in her porridge most of the time. The family understood that many of their friends and extended family were very poor and could rarely afford milk and sugar. When visiting them, they would offer food out of a sense of hospitality and obligation to attend to the needs of their visitors. Nora's

family did not want her to hurt the feelings of their host by her asking for sugar or other things. For that reason, they omitted sugar at home so that she was prepared to accept food without sugar when she was a guest. This approach to socialization through self-denial was done for multiple reasons but mostly out of concern for the feelings of others. The value this taught to Nora is to learn to modify one's own wants so that one can be happy with fewer material things. It was an effective way to prepare her to address conditions in which material goods were limited. For the child, the goal was to teach her in a way that she could grow to feel comfortable in a variety of circumstances, to be at home with a range of people. As the mother reported in the interview, "I don't want Nora to be satisfied only with high society food."

Culture and Spirituality

An important task of the family is to maintain and pass on cultural traditions, such as knowledge of and respect for ancestors, to support individual spirituality, and to perform important cultural rituals, particularly those that mark the movement from one developmental phase to another or afford protection against illness and harm from the supernatural world. Spirituality is an important aspect of the cultural heritage of African families. Across time and the continents, religious beliefs have been a principal organizing theme, a means of fashioning a community of faith and action and strengthening identification with and loyalty to family. This continues to be true for African families, who have inculcated children with a reverence for deceased ancestors. More than 73 percent of mothers indicate that religion is very important in the household. Religious beliefs and practices are a central aspect of the lives of a majority of urban African families. Over 62 percent indicate that prayers are a routine feature of their lives. Songs of praise are offered for the good things that happen to families, and penance as the price of their failings. The active practice of those spiritual values and religious behaviors speaks to the ability of a family to pass on its legacy of spirituality to its children. Through observations, imitation, and active participation, children acquire a set of values and cultural resources that serve as a legacy that they can draw upon as they progress toward adulthood. This cultural legacy provides an ideological framework or wisdom that guides them through the universal dilemmas of life and death. The data from the BTT suggest that spirituality is valued slightly more in households led by widowed and divorced mothers and homes in which no grandmothers reside than it is in other households.

For one grandmother, religion and involvement in the church is very important. The entire family attends Zulu Holy Benediction

Church of Zion on Sundays. Grandmother "is in the habit of attending services four times a week: Thursday, Friday, Saturday, and Sunday." It is a central part of her life, and this is something that she is passing on as a legacy to her grandson. At this point in her grandson Zolile's life (age six), it has made a favorable impression and he likes to go with her. Spirituality has become an important part of his identity and behavior. He is developing his own inclination toward spirituality. He prays before taking food. He prays when someone is sick. He frequently enjoys singing religious songs. Zolile has internalized his grandmother's value for religion and has taken on her aspiration for him. By himself, he seems to have arrived at the wish of becoming a man of God, Mfundi—a man who takes on the special role of praying for church. She concurs and approves of this calling. But she is open to other possibilities at the same time: "I would also like him to be a doctor." Then she turned to Zolile and asked him playfully, "Want to be a tsotsi, a medical doctor?" (smiling broadly), and he said clearly, laughing, "No, no, I want to be Mfundi!"

Cultural resources are likely to promote resilience in the face of hardship. Protective factors within the environment or social context include family functioning characterized by warmth, cohesion, enlightened discipline, culture and ethnic identification, supportive extrafamilial relationships, and effectively promoting competence in social and cognitive domains (Reid et al. 1989). Social support in the family acts as a buffering agent to reduce emotional strain on parents and also helps to decrease the presence of punitive, coercive, and inconsistent parenting behaviors (McLoyd 1990; Ogbu 1981). Thus these social networks have an indirect effect on the child's socioemotional development. The most common factor mediating developmental outcomes include: sociocultural resources such as ethnic identity, religiosity, extended kin networks, and individual coping styles. The relations of these factors to one another and to developmental outcomes are not clear. It is likely that the interactions among these personal and environmental factors facilitate or enhance children's ability to accommodate to adverse circumstances and remain on course toward normal social and emotional development.

Family Life as a Mediator of Child Outcomes

In the previous chapter, other potential problems were raised regarding the composition of households, particularly the role of fathers and grandmothers, which may be a threat to the effectiveness of families in carrying out their important roles regarding the socialization and care of children. As noted earlier, the strains of apartheid, urbanization, and the resulting modernization of family life were theorized to be most keenly reflected in urban household membership and structure. Specifically, these social factors would give rise to high proportions of single mothers and their children either living alone or in households of the grandparents. These family configurations would lead in turn to grandparents, particularly grandmothers, assuming considerable responsibility for children. This leads to questions about whether the effectiveness of family functioning and the favorableness of child outcomes are related to these aspects of household composition and structure. (For example, see Naidoo and Pillay 1995; Skuy, Koeberg, and Fridjhon 1997) The dimensions of family life included in the organizational systems model introduced in chapter 8 conceivably impact development by moderating the effects of environmental strains on children. Accordingly differences in how family structure, roles, and relationships are related to differences in how families approach and in how well they carry out the principal tasks of nurturing and socializing children. Within the context of this theory of family life, it is assumed that the effectiveness of family task performance is influenced by the family's structure and composition, which in themselves impact child development. Family effectiveness in performing these tasks impacts child health and development. Within this framework, the social risks discussed in previous chapters—racism, poverty, and violence—are viewed as environmental stressors that can impact children's emotional, behavioral, and academic adjustment. However these effects can be buffered or moderated when the family functions well. Thus in spite of the significant threat posed to children, family life represents a source of hope for protecting children and permitting them to develop normally.

Effects of Household Composition/Membership on Development

The data in table 9.2 present information on the relationship of marital status to child problems. The differences due to marital status are small and significant for only four indicators: often crying, having specific fears, starting fights, and bullying others. Children living with mothers who have never been married more frequently present with maladaptive behaviors and emotions in these domains. In essence, children growing up with unmarried mothers more often had specific fears and cried, fought, and bullied more than children growing up with mothers who were married. In other words, children of unmarried mothers are more fearful and they cry and fight more. This pattern gave rise to speculation about a possible relationship between fearfulness, crying, and bullying. Could the bullying and fighting that occur at higher rates among children of unmarried mothers result from or be related to their fears and crying? Alternatively the crying may be suggestive of temperamental issues such as irritability, frustration, and deficits in self-regulation rather than fear. Could crying represent another form of being undercontrolled? This question was examined for children of unmarried mothers. Significant associations were found for crying with bullying and fighting. Of those who cry often, 50 percent fight a lot and 70 percent bully others. From the other side, 20 percent of children who fight a lot, and 22 percent of those who are described as bullying, also cry a lot without good reason. In line with the speculation, fearfulness was also associated significantly with bullying and fighting. Bullying occurs in less than 30 percent of children overall, but 40 percent of children with specific fears engaged in fighting and bullying. While this does not conclusively establish a causal relationship between fear and fighting, it does point us toward a more complex explanation of bullying in terms of fear and proposes an interesting set of processes that may underlie children's fighting and aggression. Such explanations might be easily missed or overlooked in favor of simpler formulations involving social risks such as poverty and violence.

A similar pattern of problems obtains for children of mothers who did not have partners in the home irrespective of whether or not they

Table 9.2: Prevalence of Child Problems at Age 6
by Mother's Marital Status

	Marital status		
Developmental problems	Never married	Married	$\chi^2(df=4)$
Fearful	35.1%	23.8%	7.97[a]
Cries without good reason	13.5	7.0	5.80[a]
Starts fights	40.2	29.4	6.70[a]
Bullies, mean	42.4	33.2	4.78[a]

[a]$p \leq .05$.

were married. These are presented in table 9.3. Children of parents without partners in the home had significantly higher levels of aggression, crying, and clumsiness than children of mothers with partners in the home. Differences are also observed between children living in extended family households and those living in nuclear families. Children in extended families had higher prevalence of problems such as aggression, bullying, crying, clumsiness, thumb-sucking, and fears than children in nuclear families. (See table 9.4.) The effects of a grandmother in the household on emotional and behavioral symptoms were minimal. There are slightly higher rates of aggression, eating difficulties, and thumb-sucking, but lower rates of fears and language difficulty among children living in homes with grandmothers than children living without grandmothers in the home. Only the differences in aggression and language were statistically significant. (See table 9.5.)

Table 9.3: Prevalence of Child Problems at Age 6 by Presence of Mother's Partner in the Household

| Developmental problems | Domestic partner | | $\chi^2(df = 4)$ |
	No partner in home	Partner in home	
Starts fights	20.5%	15.8%	8.8[a]
Cries without good reason	14.4	8.8	7.5[a]
Clumsy	9.4	4.5	7.4[a]

[a] $p \leq .05.$

Table 9.4: Prevalence of Child Problems at Age 6 in Extended and Nuclear Family Structures

	Extended family structure $(N = 372)$	Nuclear family structure $(N = 175)$	χ^2 $(df = 3)$
Temper tantrums	19.1%	18.6%	9.05[a]

[a] $p \leq .05.$

**Table 9.5: Prevalence of Child Problems
at Age 6 by the Presence of Grandmother in the Household**

	No grandmother in home	Grandmother present in home	χ^2
Starts fights	34.0%	40.0%	8.4[a]
Difficult to understand	22.1	13.4	6.95[a]

[a]$p \leq .05.$

Relationship Quality and Child Development

The analysis of the impact of family functioning on child development was extended to quality of family relationships and task performance. The dimensions of child development that were used in this analysis were as follows:

Anxiety-Depression	Unusual level of fear, worry, and tearfulness, excessive sadness, irritability, and loneliness
Opposition	Disobedience; defiance, stubborn refusal to comply with rules and accept adult authority
Affability	Social attractiveness, which includes qualities such as being affectionate and lovable, and having a sense of humor
Resilience	Personal adaptability, self-esteem, relaxed easy temperament, frustration tolerance, and acceptance of correction and things not going his or her way

These scales were based on reports of parents of BTT children when they were six years old. The results presented in table 9.6 show that the model of family functioning proposed in chapter 8 is partially supported by the data. Again, single motherhood is related to a higher

Table 9.6: Pearson Product Moment Correlations between Dimensions of Family Life and Child Developmental Outcomes

	Child Psychological Outcomes			
	Emotional	Behavioral	Social	Adaptation
Dimensions of family life	Anxious-Depressed	Oppositional	Affable	Resilient
Household configuration				
Single mother	.057	**.133^c**	.044	−.046
Grandmother in home	−.063	−.005	.042	**.097^b**
Dependence ratio	−.099^b	.090^a	−.072^a	−.047
Household size	.061	.070^a	−.039	−.067^a
Family relationship quality				
Satisfaction with family	**−.077^a**	**−.153^c**	**.145^c**	**.152^c**
Family cohesion	.036	−.064	**.133^c**	**.080^a**
Family conflict	.065	**.145^c**	**−.090^b**	**−.147^c**
Privacy/isolation	.035	−.004	**.098^b**	.046
Family task performance				
Adequate food	**−.180^c**	−.056	.065	**.136^c**
Spirituality	.016	−.017	.044	.023
Safety	.043	**.111^b**	**−.120^c**	**−.152^c**

$^a p \leq .05$ $^b p \leq .01$ $^c p \leq .001$

incidence of behavioral problems, and, on the positive side, a grandmother in the home to higher levels of flexibility in the child. In addition, the dependence ratio or the proportion of children to adults in the household is related to emotional and behavioral and social outcomes. The more children there are the lower anxiety-depression, affability, and social competence, and the more behavioral problems. Larger household sizes are also associated with a greater opposition and lower resilience in children. The family's effectiveness in securing an adequate food supply for children is significantly related to child outcomes. To the extent that children experience hunger, they are higher on anxiety-depression and lower on social competence and adaptability. Cultural values are unrelated to children's early developmental outcomes. Family conflict and fighting are related to oppositional behavior and lower levels of social competence adaptability.

Satisfaction with family life stands out as particularly important to outcomes of early development. For example, satisfaction with family life is inversely related to anxiety-depression. Children from families that are high in satisfaction, with supportive relationships, have lower levels of anxiety and depression. They also have lower levels of oppositional behavior. Conversely satisfactory and supportive family relationships are also associated with higher levels of affability and resilience. Thus greater satisfaction with family life is associated with more socially adept and psychologically adaptive children. Cohesion in families is important but not as important as family satisfaction. Cohesive families have children who are more affable and resilient than families that are not. Amicable resolution of conflict is similarly predictive of children's psychological outcomes. Lower levels of conflict in families are associated with lower rates of oppositional behavior and higher rates of affability and resilience in children. Privacy/isolation is also important to social outcomes in children: The better families manage this issue of privacy/isolation, the more socially competent and affable the children are.

Task Performance

Table 9.6 shows that the effectiveness with which the family is able to perform the task of providing adequate resources to feed children is significantly related to the degree of anxiety-depression reported for the child. Children are more likely to be depressed and anxious if their parents were unsuccessful in providing the adequate resources to prevent hunger in them. Hungry children were more depressed and anxious. Providing a peaceful, nonviolent environment within the family was highly related to whether or not the child had an oppositional disorder. Families that were not successful in resolving conflicts amicably and that used fighting and aggression as a means of dealing with issues tended to have children who were more oppositional and defiant. Conduct problems such as aggression and youthful offending have strong relationships both to qualities of the child, including temperament and cognitive ability, and to aspects of family life, such as parent-child attachment and socialization practices (Yoshikawa 1994). Clearly the ways in which families address the early indication of problems, the values they transmit, the degree of support and direction they provide, and the love they exhibit all make a difference ultimately in whether or not children will have difficulties and persist in them once they arise.

We began this chapter with a keen interest in discovering how family life affects children's development. We were particularly interested in identifying the features that distinguish families that are able to safeguard the development of children. What is it about some families that allow them to minimize the effects of social ills while others are overcome by them? What features of families enable them to affirm their children and help them develop physically and psychologically in spite of the suboptimal conditions surrounding them? We have advanced an argument that the transforming forces of racism, urbanization, and modernization have adversely affected the family life of black South Africans. Moreover if these social forces affect child development, they do so indirectly through their impact on family composition relationships and task performance. Furthermore we have argued extensively that social transformations in the form of urbanization and the modernization of family life have significant impact on the composition structure and tasks of families. There is increasing acceptance of women raising children on their own outside of marriage and movement toward nuclear family households and the pairing of unmarried mothers with grandmothers as a household configuration for raising children. The latter give grandmothers expanded but not altogether welcome responsibility for raising grand- and great-grandchildren. Several unanticipated findings emerged from the data on urban South African families. Although the majority of mothers were not legally married, about equal numbers lived with and without heterosexual partners. In addition, although one-third of the households had grandmothers, they tended much more often to be in households with unmarried daughters without partners than with married daughters.

Almost no one disputes the assertion that families are important to child development. In fact, they are thought to be so important that persons drafting the United Nations Conventions on the Rights of the Child argue that the significance of family life to child development is so great that it should be considered a right under the conventions. But what is it that children need most from families to grow up healthy? Is it the socialization families provide regarding human values and the meaning of life? Could it be the structure and resources through which families provide for safety and the meeting of children's basic physical needs? Is it the sense of connection and supportive relationships that provide for attachment and a sense of belonging? Are there optimal ways of organizing and functioning to make some families better at promoting development than others? Are all effective families alike in some way, or are there different ways for a family to be effective? We think that there are many ways to be effective and to carry out the responsibilities of raising children. Do these aspects of family life affect the early development of children's capacity to regulate behavior and emotions and to become socially competent and adept? To address these questions, we assessed the relationship of the dimensions of family functioning to developmental outcomes. According to the model we proposed, child emotional, behavioral, and social adjustment should be related to household configurations, quality of family relationships, and effectiveness of task performance.

Four separate analyses were conducted. Each employed one of the four developmental outcomes as the dependent variable and the dimensions of family life as the predictor or independent variables. These analys is permit inferences about the relative contribution of model parameters (viz., household composition, task performance, and relationship quality) to account for child behavioral, emotional, social, and adaptational outcomes. With respect to children's *social competence,* the family's ability to effectively resolve conflicts is also related to affability in children. Children tended to be more affable when the family did not fight as a means of resolving conflicts. Thus prosocial resolution of conflict was important to the development of social competence in the form of affability in children. Other factors that significantly predicted social competence in children were dependence ratio, family cohesion, and conflict and boundary maintenance. Children are more likely to be affable and have higher levels of social competence in homes with a low dependence ratio—that is, fewer children per adult; in families in which relationships were characterized as cohesive and family conflict was low and which tended to maintain privacy and to have less permeable boundaries between themselves and the outside world. On the developmental outcome of *adaptation* or resilience, the family tasks of providing resources and prosocial conflict resolution were significant predictors. Families successful in securing adequate resources so that children were not hungry tended to have children who were more resilient. In addition, families that utilized prosocial means of resolving conflict (avoiding fighting) had children who were also more resilient. Other factors related to resilience included grandmother presence, and family satisfaction, cohesion, and conflict resolution. Specifically adaptive, resilient children tend to come from families with the presence of a grandmother, that were also highly cohesive and satisfied, and which resolved conflicts amicably. The results of the analyses can be summarized as follows:

1. On emotional outcomes, dependence ratio and child hunger were most significant;
2. On behavioral disorders, single-parent female-headed households were most significant;
3. For social competence, the degree of family cohesion was most strongly related; and
4. For adaptation/resilience, a grandmother in the home and amicable family conflict resolution were most significant.

These results should be interpreted cautiously. Though each regression model tested was significant, the evidence does not support assertions that family life as represented in these analyses is the most robust predictor of early child development. The percentages of total variance explained were small and in each case under 5 percent.

Although families do protect children from the adverse consequences of racism, it too has subjected them to pressures that have strained their capacity to cope and adapt. Unfortunately the twin challenges of urbanization and modernization have exacted a heavy toll on individual well-being and have contributed to significant adjustments to traditional family structures, household memberships, and family role assignments. The impact of modernization on families has become evident in the timing of and method used in the formation of new family units, eroding or transforming traditions of familial reciprocity and communal sharing, and altering the composition and structures of households. The tradition of living in extended family households, an artificially restricted housing policy, and poverty and joblessness among young adults has led to a more varied combinations of related and unrelated individuals living together, along with their children. Migratory labor policies and high male unemployment have figured in an erosion of male commitment to children and to partners and to the propensity of biological fathers to live away from their children. As a consequence, men are becoming increasingly invisible and uninvolved in the children's lives. Often it is grandparents, particularly grandmothers, who must step into the breach and fill the vacuum created by uninvolved or ineffectual fathers and partners. Thus the responsibility of elderly women for their grand- and great-grandchildren has increased. In some cases, adaptation to imperatives of modern urban living has sharpened families' ability to cope with the stress of poverty and to provide nurturing and protection to their children. In other cases the consequences have been less felicitous, as evidenced in rising reports of alcoholism, domestic violence, sexual abuse, parents abandoning their children, and children taking to the streets to run away from the pain of family life.

It must be emphasized that no single family structure or configuration emerged as superior to every other across every dimension as a context for promoting favorable child development. Each has its strengths and weaknesses, its advantages and disadvantages. These data suggest that there are many ways of configuring households that help families adapt to the pressures of modern living and social change. Each alternative affords the possibility of creating an optimal environment for child development. For example, growing up in single-parent female-headed households does not seem to have negative consequences for emotional, social, or adaptational outcomes. However with respect to behavioral outcomes, children from single-mother households did tend to be more oppositional and defiant. Moreover having a larger number of children in the family relative to adults tended to be associated both with higher levels of depression and affability in children. Data from these and other studies also suggest that the ability of the family to provide food security and a safe, orderly environment for children are critical determinants of healthy adaptation and resilience for children growing up in distressing environments.

Conclusion

Social transformation is undeniably accompanied by a high level of stressful demands on families. At the same time, it presents children and their families with challenges that ultimately strengthen them as they adapt to life under an evolving set of circumstances. The psychological demands and strains that accompany political, social, and economic change create the motivation for adaptation. How well the family responds to these challenges has significant implications for children. In the next chapters, we explore how poverty and violence influence and shape behavioral and emotional development among South African children.

Chapter 10
Poverty and Child Development

What Does It Mean to Be Poor in South Africa?

Poverty affects people in different ways. Some it softens, granting them patience, grace, and wisdom, deepening their humanity and sensitivity toward others. Others it hardens, making them callous, cynical, indifferent to others, self-interested, and rapacious.

The situation of Issak and Ibrahim recounted in chapter 1 provides just one window to the experiences of the poor. Poverty does not have to deprive one of life, as in their case, to have a devastating impact on development. Material hardship in South Africa has many different facets, each with its own challenges. To be poor and South African usually means to be unemployed with no dependable means of support, to live with a single mother or Grandmother, and to survive primarily on the grandmother's pension. To be poor is to experience hunger frequently, to live on a diet of tea and bread without milk or sugar and to be grateful to have cabbage soup at night. It means living in a one-room shack without electricity, heat, a refrigerator, or a television, and relying on candles for light at night. It means having to rely on taxis for transportation when you can afford it, and to go places by foot when there is no money.

To blacks, poverty means insufficient money for school fees and books, and having to staying out of school for several weeks until funds can be found to purchase shoes and school uniforms. Probably it means not having savings for life insurance, and if a parent dies, the family left is even further tested. It means worrying about how to bury relatives who die.

It means having to borrow money just to get by, and pay exorbitant interest rates. Poverty means children being left at home by parents who must leave for work before they wake up, with the children getting themselves up on their own and out to school without breakfast.

Poverty means coming home after a long day at work or school to find that your home has been burned and you've lost all of your possessions. It means having to squeeze in for a night's sleep at the crowded home of relatives. And it means being hopeful in spite of one's wants, and thinking that prospects may not be good for you, but may be better for your children.

Poverty has many faces in South Africa. One of them is Dumisane, who goes to school with hunger pangs. Another is Tina who must stay home from school until her mother can afford to buy her school uniforms. And Michael, who shares a one-room shack with his mother and four siblings, unbearably cold in the winter and swelteringly hot in the summer, with no space to play or study. The face of poverty is Mandisa, whose breakfast of white bread and tea may be the only food for the day if her father is not fortunate enough to be picked by one of the contractors who drives to the edge of the township looking for cheap day laborers. It is Ishmael, for whom dreams of toys, books, electricity, and an indoor toilet are out of reach. It is Tsepo, whose parents worry about where they will find money for his grandmother's funeral.

Importance of Living Standards for Children

Poverty and Children's Functioning

The manifestations of poverty may be idiosyncratic, and its definition elusive but its effects palpable. Evidence from research on living standards[1] and child development conducted in the United States is clear and unmistakable. Poverty is associated with human suffering from disease and lower life expectancy to stigma and psychological distress. Poverty and inadequate living standards have particularly devastating effects on the development of children. Research on the consequences for children of inadequate living standards concludes unambiguously that disease, stunted growth, impaired cognitive functioning, and early death occur at higher rates among very poor children. This research fuels concerns that standard of living is associated not only with chronic malnutrition and illness, but also that it impacts more broadly cognitive development, psychosocial functioning, academic achievement, and employment than originally thought (Pollitt 1994). Living standards are also implicated in a host of problems faced by children, including: prematurity, exposure to environmental pollution, slowed development of language skills, and delayed acquisition of behavioral and emotion regulation. They may also be linked to social ills such as community violence, substance abuse, and disintegration of family life (Barbarin and Soler 1993). In all, living standards have important implications for the health and development of children.

In most cases, the hardships associated with poverty are so patently aversive and obvious that claims about the benefits to children's lives of *improving living standards* are widely accepted without question. Nevertheless, social scientists are beginning to accumulate evidence that lays an empirical foundation for claims of adverse consequences of low Socioeconomic Status (SES) for children and their families. They have found that for children, economic hardship and resource inadequacy are among the most consistent predictors of poor outcomes in children. Serious adverse consequences occur across most domains of development—cognitive, academic, behavioral, emotional, and social—to children who grow up in poor living conditions. Poor children are at greater risk of developing mental health problems than children who come from financially advantaged backgrounds (Langner et al. 1970). For example, Duncan, Brooks-Gunn, and Klebanov (1994) have shown that conduct and emotional problems occur more frequently among poor than nonpoor children. Similarly, in a review of research literature on poverty and emotional disorders, Hammen and Rudolph (1996) conclude that a reasonable case can be made linking poverty to elevated levels of depression and anxiety.

Even though poor children do not meet criteria for diagnosable emotional disorders more frequently than nonpoor children, they report symptoms classified within the syndromes of depression and anxiety more frequently than children from economically advantaged backgrounds (Gore et al. 1993; Valez et al. 1989). Poverty has an especially pronounced effect in the domain of externalizing disorders (Capaldi and Patterson 1994). Data show that an even stronger case can been made linking poverty to children's conduct problems and academic failure than has been made for emotional problems (Capaldi and Patterson 1994; Felner et al. 1995; McLoyd 1998). Poverty has been linked to conduct problems, aggression, delinquency, and adjustment problems of children because it increases family stress and conflict.

Economically disadvantaged children often exhibit difficulty on dimensions of psychological disorders such as anxiety, depression, somatic problems, shyness, attention deficits, aggression, oppositional behavior, and thought disorders. Since almost all of this work was conducted using income poverty as the criterion, it is not possible to discern whether the psychological problems result from the material hardship itself—stress, and the limited resources to cope with or exert control over unpredictable aspects of life—or from the stigma and lack of status often attached to being poor in an affluent society. There is reason to believe that material hardship is implicated in the suboptimal emotional, behavioral, and academic outcomes of poor children. Take the case of Paballo as an illustration.

Paballo is a seven-year-old boy, residing with his mother and ten-year-old sister, Nolunkcwe, in a newly established squatter camp in Johannesburg. Their home consists of a one-room shack without electricity or running water. At night they use candles. Wood and paraffin are used for cooking. The wood-frame home has plastic and heavy cardboard for walls and a galvanized steel roof. The dirt floors have to be swept and dampened with water to keep the dust down. When the rains come or the sewers overflow, the house's floors flood. They get water from a tap and use a toilet that is shared with all forty families in the squatter area.

Paballo's mother works as a domestic in an affluent home in Parktown. She is not paid much, but is sometimes able to bring home food that is left over from the family. Paballo missed the first month of school because his mother did not have money for the school uniforms, pens, and paper. He never caught up with the rest of the fifty pupils in his class. His performance is thought to be impaired, because he often comes to school looking tired and unwashed, and seems irritable, cranky, argumentative, and displays a short temper with his fellow students. When the teacher noticed his behavior, she reprimanded him and indicated that she would not tolerate it in the class. However, she also noted that the behavior was atypical. He was usually shy, though well-mannered and agreeable. She inquired about why he was getting to be so grumpy and naughty. Why did he seem so tired? At first he looked down and did not answer. She waited patiently for an answer. With some hesitation, he admitted that he had not slept well for the past week. The floor of their home had been flooded with water, which happened periodically whenever it rained heavily. To avoid getting wet, he had to sleep sitting up in a wooden chair rather than down on the mat. He kept falling off the chair. He could not get comfortable, and whenever he fell asleep he would lose his balance and fall off the chair and wake up. Although he is motivated and follows directions, he seems very shy and retiring with the other students.

A growing body of research fuels concerns that economic deprivation and its sequelae, such as malnutrition and hunger, have enduring detrimental effects to children's physical and cognitive development (Pollitt 1994). Moreover low living standards and economic hardship are linked to adverse outcomes such as high rates of behavioral problems, low school achievement, and a host of social ills such as community violence, substance abuse, and disintegration of family life

(Barbarin and Soler 1993; McLeod and Shanahan 1993; Valez et al. 1989). Housing quality in South Africa is related to psychological functioning. Children living in shack communities displayed stress-related symptoms at significantly higher rates than children living in relatively formal housing communities (Robertson and Berger 1994). One of the difficulties, of course, is that these different dimensions of poverty may be correlated and thus their effects similar to one another. In any event, a lethal combination of economic hardship and limited access to supportive services combine to disadvantage poor children and place obstacles in the way of their continued academic and emotional development. There is convincing evidence that suggests that they double children's risk of emotional and academic problems. The sequelae of these conditions can be observed across the life span: increased morbidity and mortality, mood disturbances, academic underachievement, aggression, premature sexuality and childbearing, substance abuse, delinquency, underemployment, high rates of divorce, and instability of family life.

Poverty and Social Competence

In contrast to the prodigious efforts to understand the effects of poverty on psychological disorders, very little research has explored its relationship to social competence. Consequently claims about the nature of such relationships rest on uncertain grounds. In the absence of empirical data and a convincing theoretical rationale, at least three alternative relationships between adversity and competence can be argued: no significant effect, a direct positive effect, and an inverse effect. Arguments that low socioeconomic status has no relationship to social competence and academic adjustment rest on the assumption that adverse conditions are as likely as propitious conditions to give rise to social competence.

Assertions of an inverse relationship between adversity and competence assume that children's social and cognitive development are stunted as a result of the stress and adaptational demands associated with household poverty. In propitious environments characterized by material adequacy, the balance of resources and needs engenders a basic trust in and reliance on others. As a result, such environments free children from preoccupation with requirements of physical survival to invest their creative energies and emotional capital in the development of empathetic and cooperative social relations. In contrast, poor children face high adaptational demands with limited resources, receive less cognitive stimulation, exhibit premature self-care and self-reliance, and ultimately become unresponsive to direction from adults (Kellam et al. 1975). Moreover in an effort to protect their children from danger, parents living in poor and dangerous communities may adopt practices that are physically restrictive and dependence-inducing (Jarrett 1995). With this pattern of social adaptation, children overreact to provocation from others, perceive threat where none exists, and approach social and academic situations with suspicion, fear, shyness, or social withdrawal (Dodge and Price 1994).

Claims of a positive relationship rest on the assumption that hardship challenges children in ways that promote social competence and academic motivation (Chesler and Barbarin 1987). In this view, an orientation toward mastery is just as likely to arise from hardship and community danger as demoralization. The strain of an adverse environment elicits resourcefulness that might not be required or developed in its absence. Accordingly growing up in adversity presents children with opportunities for mastery and self-sufficiency not available to children in more advantaged circumstances. They may be confronted early on with adult challenges, and forced to be more planful and adaptive in the face of deprivation. As a result, children growing up in such difficult circumstances may mature more quickly than their more advantaged counterparts. Similarly economic disadvantage may motivate interest in and effort at academic tasks as the means of upward mobility and as the principal means of escaping from the hardships of material poverty. Evidence from studies of children in families challenged by life-threatening illness provides strong support for this argument (Barbarin 1990). Children challenged by such adversity evidenced high levels of maturity; an enhanced capacity for empathy; planfulness and perspective-taking; and a more focused and purposeful engagement in academic pursuits (Barbarin et al. 1995). Of all the domains, evidence of impact on cognitive and academic functioning is most striking, particularly when poverty occurs early in life (Brooks-Gunn and Duncan 1997).

Chronic versus Acute Hardship

The duration and timing of the poverty experience may be an important determinant of its effects. For example, the chronic multigenerational poverty that occurs among large numbers of blacks in South Africa is especially detrimental to academic, behavioral, and emotional functioning (McLeod and Shanahan 1993, 1996). Early and persistent poverty adversely influences the course of depressive and conduct problems. Chronic poverty is associated with depressive symptoms, and contemporaneous poverty alone is related to externalizing symptoms (McLeod and Shanahan 1993). Recent evidence suggests that the impact of economic hardship on children may be time-limited and influenced by its duration and timing in the life span. Children living in poverty at the time they were assessed (contemporaneous poverty) were more likely to exhibit disordered conduct than children who were no longer poor or who had never lived in poverty (McLeod and Shanahan 1993). In some cases, chronic poverty is associated with fewer problems than short-term acute poverty (Korneman et al. 1995). Other evidence suggests that the earlier poverty occurs in a child's life and the longer it persists, the more pronounced and enduring the academic and behavioral difficulties (Brooks-Gunn and Duncan 1997). For example, Werner and Smith (1989) found that children who are chronically poor from birth have significantly higher rates of psychological, social, and academic impairment through adolescence and into early adulthood than their more advantaged counterparts. Though the observed effect sizes of poverty and its sequelae are sometimes small, risks associated with poverty are hardly trivial. When poverty is chronic, it augurs a lifelong pattern of maladjustment involving such outcomes as poor school performance, early termination of education, juvenile crime, substance abuse, teen pregnancy, and chronic unemployment (Dryfoos 1980).

Generalizability of Poverty Research to Africa

Much of the evidence reviewed here on the relationship of income poverty, material disadvantage, and child development has been gathered on the poor living in countries with high standards of living. Should we expect that the effects of poverty observed there can be applied globally? How safe is it to assume that data, for example, from the United States, accurately characterize the conditions faced by the poor in Latin America or Africa? On one hand, food and nutrition are recognized universal needs, and deprivation no matter where it is experienced should lead to identical consequences. Consequently health researchers and policy makers seem confident in accepting the assumption of generalizability in regard to the physical and health consequences of poverty. The case for the cross-national generalizability of the psychosocial consequences of poverty is much less clear. Historical, cultural, economic, and social differences in the experience of poverty in developing and industrialized nations give poverty different meanings. The varied contexts of poverty may create a very different social and psychological status for the poor. For example, the psychological consequences of material hardship may differ considerably when poverty is a common and widely shared experience, when it is treated with empathy as opposed to moral censure, when it is not stigmatized or racialized, or when it is attributed to external and mutable rather than internal causes. Because of these differences, reluctance to take the leap of faith in applying findings on the developmental consequences of poverty in the United States to Asia or Africa is justified and wise.

Assessment of Poverty in South Africa

What are the principal threats poverty poses to the physical and psychological well-being of children? The outcomes of Ibrahim and Issak make clear the high stakes involved in the struggle against material need and deprivation. Who are the poor? They are those who lack sufficient assets to meet their basic needs. Most of our knowledge about the effects of poverty come from examinations of a single dimension of living standards, low or inadequate income. Though important, low income and the material deprivation that accompanies it are probably not sufficient *in se* to account for the pervasive and disruptive consequences low living standards have on the lives of the poor. Moreover, as we argued in chapter 3, the use of monetary income alone as an indicator of material well-being and hardship affords a restricted window onto the life quality of the poor.

But what is meant by assets? Income is most often used as the principal asset considered in determining who is poor. In these terms, the poor are those whose income falls below what is required to meet basic needs such as food and shelter. This approach has its advantages with respect to the evaluation of public policy and to poverty reduction programs; it has major disadvantages for developmental research. Among households that fall below the poverty line, there are significant differences in social and material circumstances that profoundly affect well-being. An identical level of income may be deployed in a variety of ways across households with widely varying consequences for children. Consequently the depth of poverty as a concept and the wide diversity among people who are designated as poor is missed if its assessment stops at the dichotomous distinction implied in a poverty line or threshold and no information is gathered about additional hardships associated with low income.

Moreover the ramifications of poverty extend beyond a dearth of household material resources. The poor defined on the basis of income are not all poor in the same way. The diverse experiences of poverty may account in part for the differences observed in the development of poor children. The focus on a single dimension such income poverty, particularly in a dichotomous form, overlooks differences in the social and material conditions of poor people that may prove crucial to an explanation of why some poor children evidence a healthy developmental trajectory and others do not. An implication of this line of reasoning is that aspects of poverty may differ in their importance to a specific child outcome or their influence may vary with the age and developmental stage of the child. Particular configurations of material and social disadvantage may lead to some adverse outcomes but not others.

Other traditions for defining poverty seem better suited for capturing the aspects of poverty that track differences in lifestyles and circumstances that may impact child developmental outcomes. These traditions focus on consumption and wealth, with wealth including both human and financial assets. Consumption goes to the heart of the matter in characterizing the material conditions of a family. It concerns the material resources a family has access to and not how they acquired them. Related to material consumption is the notion of financial capital or material assets. In this tradition, poverty is conceptualized primarily as material hardship and measured in terms of household access to material possessions and financial resources. But material resources are not the only or necessarily the most important resources that potentially affect child development. Human resources or assets are equally critical. Included among human assets are education and employment status. These two indicators are commonly used in measures of SES.

An example of this tradition is the Hollingshead social class rating, which combines parents' education and a rating of their occupational status (Hollingshead 1975). In this tradition, poverty is indexed by low income, and deficits in material goods, housing, and food. Thus differences in a household's access to both human and material capital will be examined and comparisons made about the strength of their relations to favorable and unfavorable emotional and behavioral development of children. By itself, income poverty provides fewer details of actual life quality, household living standard, and material hardship than is available from a variety of financial or material indicators combined with measures of human capital. Because of our interest in determining whether some aspects of poverty might have a greater impact than others on children's development, the measures of SES in this study include measures of consumption and wealth, through financial and human capital.

It is still unclear, for example, whether the adverse consequences of poverty on children's psychological development are associated more with insufficient material resources and the lack of financial assets (for example, income, wealth), than with limitations of human or social capital that precede or accompany poverty. This question and its answers amount to more than the testing of academic theories or indulging in pedantic nitpicking. These questions have considerable relevance to social intervention and policy. For example, emotional, behavioral, social, and academic outcomes that are of concern to families, schools, communities, and policy makers may be differentially related to each of these domains. Answers to questions about what aspects of living standards are related to specific outcomes will make it possible to focus attention and target interventions on the dimensions of living standard most closely linked to the outcomes about which they have concern. Resolution of this issue would provide direction to poverty alleviation programs that must choose where to focus efforts to change the lives of poor children. For example, very different strategies would be enacted if it were clear that increasing income and material living standards of families would have a greater impact on children's health and development than concentrating resources on the development of human capital in job training or adult education programs to raise the educational and occupational levels of parents. Consequently a more complete understanding of the relations of economic conditions to children's developmental context may result from extending this analysis to other dimensions of poverty such as housing quality, material possessions, and asset accumulation. Moreover analyzing these dimensions of poverty separately may lead to more precise charting of the pathways through which poverty compromises child development.

In this chapter, assessments of developmental outcomes for children include information on biological self-regulation related to feeding problems and bladder control, emotional regulation (fears and anxiety-depression), behavioral regulation (aggression and problem behavior), and developmental disorders related to speech and motor skills. The descriptions of these dimensions have been provided in chapters 6 and 7.

BTT Indicators of Poverty and Hardship

No matter what terms are used to characterize hardship in the unfortunate Ibrahim's life, or what dimensions of poverty are used as indicators—lack of income, consistent joblessness, low educational attainment, poor housing, low material consumption, chronic hunger, or absence of wealth—the conclusion is the same and effects are just as devastating. In this chapter, we revisit and resolve in a small way the controversies and issues surrounding the conception of poverty and hardship. We found that indicators of consumption and wealth were helpful in describing the living standard and characterizing the degree of hardship experienced by children and families. These dimensions include consumer goods, hunger, housing, education, job status, and financial assets. We examine how the poor look on these dimensions and how the dimensions manifest themselves in the lives of families in ways that might impact child development. In this chapter, we end with a focus on two dimensions: consumption and capital, consisting of human resources and wealth or accumulated assets.

Poverty and Psychosocial Development in South Africa

The data to be presented on psychosocial development and poverty are at the heart of this chapter. With them, we will address questions raised about the relative importance of human and financial capital in the assessment of poverty. Effects of deficits in financial and human capital on development are examined independently. Specifically social and material deprivation are separated into their constituent forms such as consumer goods, financial assets, housing quality, employment, and educational status in order to assess their independent contributions to the prediction of children's social, emotional, behavioral, and academic adjustment. To address questions about the relationships of dimensions of poverty to development, indicators of psychosocial development obtained when children were between ages two and six were analyzed using multiple regression with the five principal poverty indicators, as predictors. The developmental outcomes were all related to poverty indicators, but not at every age. At age two, only developmental disorders of feeding and speech were significantly related to poverty. At ages four and five, bladder, feeding, speech, and behavioral problems were significantly related to poverty indicators. At age five, bladder, speech, emotional, and behavioral problems were predicted. At age six, poverty predicted problems with feeding, motor and speech, behavioral problems, emotional disorders, and social competence. Table 10.1 presents the standardized betas for the poverty indicators that were significantly related to developmental problems at each age.

Feeding
Feeding problems were associated with material well-being among children at each point from ages two to six. The relationships between poverty and maternal reports of feeding problems were the opposite of what might have been expected based the literature. Surprisingly mothers in households with higher levels of material goods and accumulated assets reported more difficulties with feeding. At ages two and four, mothers in homes that consumed more reported more problems than those in materially disadvantaged homes. In addition, household wealth was associated with problems of feeding at age four. Thus instead of protecting children against feeding problems, material advantage seems to have promoted them. Alternatively it is possible that material comforts simply lowered the threshold for maternal concern and that children in materially advantaged households did not objectively have more eating difficulties. This interpretation suggests that mothers had high expectations and were more sensitive to or anx-

Table 10.1: Dimensions of Living Standards Most Strongly Related to Psychosocial Development between Ages 2 and 6

	Age 2	Age 4	Age 5	Age 6
Feeding problems	Consumption*	Financial assets*		Consumption*
Speech problems	Consumption; Occupation	Consumption; Maternal education	Housing; Maternal education	Financial assets; Maternal education
Bed-wetting		Consumption; Maternal education*	Consumption; Housing; Financial assets	
Motor control/ clumsiness				Financial assets; Consumption; Maternal education; Occupation
Fear			Financial assets	Financial assets
Problem behaviors		Financial assets; Occupation	Financial assets; Occupation	Consumption

*The direction of the relationship is such that higher living standards are predictive of greater problems.

ious about eating than mothers of poor children who may have other things that concerned them more than feeding.

Speech Problems

Language development problems were predicted by indicators of poverty at each age at which children were assessed. The number of consumer goods and the occupational prestige of the head of household also predicted language problems. In contrast to the result for feeding, the direction of these relationships comported well with existing views of the adverse effects of poverty. In general, the higher the level of material well-being in a household, the lower the level of language difficulties in the child. Children from homes with fewer human resources were also more likely to demonstrate early language deficiencies. At age four, consumer goods continued to predict development, as did maternal education. At age five, the type of home and maternal education predicted language difficulties. At age six, household wealth and maternal education were predictive of language deficiencies. Thus at each point of development, lack of access to both financial and human capital are implicated in the likelihood of language deficiencies early in life. It is widely accepted that early language development depends greatly on the level of stimulation and enrichment available to the child in the critical early stages of life. Mothers with higher levels of education have been shown to interact more and provide more verbal stimulation to their children than mothers with less education. Moreover access to material resources also contributes to an enriched, interesting, and complex environment that apparently promotes language skill development.

Bladder Control

A relationship between poverty and bladder control did not arise until age four. This late emergence of the relationship is noteworthy. Even though many children are toilet trained by age three, bed-wetting is not uncommon as late as age four. By then, children are thought to be capable of bladder control during the day and at night. Somewhere between ages three and five, the ability to regulate bladder functioning at night shifts from being normative to being a symptom of biological, behavioral, emotional dysregulation. Like the case of feeding disorders, children of more highly educated mothers were less likely to have attained bladder control than children of mothers with less education. Perhaps educated mothers are more permissive and laissez-faire in making demands that their child control wetting since the social consequences may not be as severe or detrimental. Unlike maternal education, material advantage is inversely related to bladder control. Children from households with high levels of consumer goods were less likely to attain bladder control by ages four and five than children from materially disadvantaged backgrounds. Similarly at age five the quality of housing and degree of accumulated assets were also inversely related to bladder control, such that those children and homes with lower levels of material resources were more likely to have difficulties. Perhaps highly educated mothers may be more tolerant of their children's delay in attaining bladder control. Tolerance of bed-wetting may be more protracted among more educated mothers who may be more flexible and lenient in imposing the demand for bladder control. Their reluctance to demand that the child exercise control may lead to children in these households going longer before attaining self-control in this domain. Thus children of more educated mothers may not be expected or required to practice a high level of control and the choice to exercise self-regulation in this domain may be left up to the child. At age five, this is no longer the case, as material disadvantage and poverty are associated with enuresis.

Motor Skills Development/Clumsiness

Clumsiness or problems with motor skills were not related to poverty until age six. Motor skill deficits were predicted by indicators of both financial and human capital. Motor problems were related to low levels of consumer goods, maternal education, and occupational prestige. Low levels of capital are associated with high levels of difficulty. Specifically the lower the level of assets the family has accumulated, the fewer consumer goods it has available, the less maternal education, and lower occupational prestige, the greater the likelihood of clumsiness and motor control problems.

Fears

A relationship between material hardship and fears did not arise until age five. At this age, the level of fear reported by mothers in their children is significantly related to asset accumulation. The fewer the financial resources the family had accumulated and had at its disposal, the more likely it was that the child would exhibit fear. Take, for example, the account of a very distressed mother with low income and no assets residing in an informal housing area. She described with grave concern the disrupted anxious pattern of sleep she observed in her five-year-old son:

> He shakes; his whole body shakes when he is sleeping. Sometimes, not all the time. In his sleep he moves all over the place. Since March of last year he has been shaking in his sleep. It wakes me up. We sleep together. When I wake him up, he will

say he wants water or something to eat; that he is not frightened anymore.

Data from BTT show convincingly that material disadvantage is associated with high levels of emotional difficulties, which also take the form of a chronically sad and depressed mood. Thus children in families with fewer material assets are more likely to have symptoms of depression. One interviewer was so struck by the affective presentation of six-year-old Pumla that she made the following notation in the margins of the interview protocol after a visit with the child and her family:

> Pumla looks very sad, very quiet. She is a beautiful slight girl; her hair was braided painstakingly in light corn rows. She is very neatly dressed and she is on the thin side. Pumla does not smile. Her biological mother is her primary caretaker and she has never spent time away from their home where she resides with her little brother and 16-year-old-sister. She is often quiet and motionless. She looks, she takes in but she does not respond. She gets cross when she tumbles and hurts herself. Reports from her mother and older sister suggest that she is very compliant. Her communication skills are very good but she is quiet most of the time. She avoids eye contact. My efforts to reach out to her were not responded to, when I intrusively looked at her and greeted her with "Hallo" she looked down and away. This is one of the *saddest and least responsive* children I have worked with.

In many ways Pumla is very much like other South African children, particularly when they go to formal settings such as clinics and hospitals. However the interviewer picked up on an aspect of her reticence that was qualitatively different in its affective or emotional tone than the self-controlled demeanor often observed in poor children. These qualitative impressions were supported by our empirical data. Alternatively wealth can serve as a protective factor against the risk of depressed mood, fears, and excessive anxiety.

Symptoms reported above such as bed-wetting, feeding problems, clumsiness, and fears occur so commonly among young children that some observers may question whether they should be of concern. Admittedly for many young children such symptoms are normative, transient, and developmentally insignificant over the long term. Many of these symptoms fail to be sufficiently intensive enough or last long enough to be disruptive or to cause long-term damage to children.

Although often harmless, they can impair normal functioning. They may precede more serious difficulty and may serve as the early warning signs of later emotional and neurological impairments that considerably impede development. It is often difficult to discern whether they constitute a passing phase of normal development or augur a protracted course of suboptimal functioning. Such distinction about whether a symptom is normal or deviant ultimately must rely on fine judgments based on the intensity, frequency, duration, patterning, situational appropriateness, impact, and context in which the symptom is displayed.

Problem Behaviors

It is much easier to make a case for concern about disordered behavior when a child is aggressive, destructive, dishonest, disdains adult authority, deliberately violates rules, and shows blatant disregard for the rights of others. In regard to such conduct problems, wealth and possession of material goods were significant predictors beginning as early as age four. At the same time, occupational prestige, a human resource, was also predictive of behavior problems at both age four and five. The lower the occupational prestige, the more behavior problems. Consequently children who live in households with low levels of material goods, with mothers who are less well educated, and in which the primary wage earner is employed in a low-status job, tended to have more behavioral and emotional difficulties. Such is the case for Lerato, who is growing up in one of the poorest areas of Soweto.

Lerato is described by his mother as very observant and talkative. He is also very naughty; he fights and screams. He does not know his father, but is very close to his mother and a sister who also helps to take care of him. His mother worked and he attended creche (preschool) since he was one year old. Now his mother is unemployed. As a toddler he suffered so badly from bronchitis that he was admitted to Chris Hani-Baragwanath Hospital, where he remained for six months to receive treatment. The air was polluted around his home and the doctors felt he would not get better without being hospitalized and receiving an extended course of treatment. This early sustained separation from his mother and family may have created separation anxiety and disrupted the maturing of the attachment relationship to his mother. He usually gets cross when his mother leaves, but only for a few minutes, then he goes to play. His bronchitis stopped when he was two years old.

Now he likes to run and fight. He particularly enjoys soccer. When he plays he likes to make noise. He fights and screams when you try to chastise or punish him for fighting. He doesn't sit down and he can be difficult. Lerato is too active; at age five, he climbed onto the roof of the house. He doesn't want to listen. His mother must get cross and strict before he will stop doing things. She says, "If you smile and are not cross he does not listen. He has a major problem running out into the road. If he likes a car that is driving down our street, he takes off and runs behind it. He runs fast also behind big delivery trucks. It can be dangerous. He does not listen when I tell him to stop. His sister has good control over him, he listens to her."

The interviewer captured several observations of Lerato in her field notes. "When asked questions in the interview he pointed a lot to his mother, rubbed his eyes, talked a lot to his mother. During the interview, he showed a lot of interest in the drawings on the wall; moved around the room a lot. He needed a lot of attention from his mother. Lerato was curious about what I was doing; however, his curiosity lacked the endearing quality that sometimes accompanies a child's expressions of interest and curiosity. Perhaps this was so because he came off as intrusive in a way that is unusual for many African children. He did not observe personal boundaries or observe social rules about keeping a respectful distance between himself and a stranger. He pressed up against me, almost aggressively, looking to see what I was writing.

"He likes school; and he is doing well there. He is obstinate he will not practice writing at home. His biggest problem is that he fights too much. Sometimes he can sit down and be quiet; watches what is going on carefully. If there is something he doesn't like, he won't go to play again. The teacher says he has problems concentrating. He gets tired easily; he can't write for a long time; however he is able to listen to Mom tell a story. When he was in a creche, he was able to count and read the recitation; he can tell me a prayer he learned from school. However he cries a lot if you don't give him something he wants, or if he gets a spanking."

Additional data were available on the scales for psychological disorders and for social competence. These scales were completed by parents and individual interviews on a subset of the sample for approximately 625 children when the children were age six. To address the question of the relationship between dimensions of poverty and child developmental outcomes, we computed several simultaneous regressions in which we regressed dimensions of poverty (material or financial capital and human capital) on the developmental problems and social competence including anxiety-depression, aggression, opposition, affability, resilience, and school readiness. (See table 10.2)

Table 10.2: Standardized Betas
for the Eight Regression Analyses Using Living Standards Indicators (Consumption and Assets) as Predictors and Each Indicator of Psychological Disorders and Social Competence Taken at Age 6 as the Dependent Variable

	Human capital		Material resources		
	Maternal education	Occupational prestige	Financial assets	Material consumption	Housing quality
Psychological disorders					
Anxious-depressed			-.15	.13	
Aggression		-.17			
Opposition				-11	.10
Attention disorder		-.17			
Social competence					
Affable	.34	.10			.57
Resilient	.37				
School ready	.36	.14		.09	.52
Physical growth Weight/height	.01				

Psychological Disorders at Age Six

Each outcome was significantly related to a specific set of poverty indicators. Anxiety-depression at age six was most strongly associated with material and financial well-being but in an unusual way. High levels of anxiety and depression are associated with low levels of accumulated assets or wealth but high levels of consumer goods. Low accumulated wealth in the form of savings and insurance may increase parents' sense of economic vulnerability, which might be passed on to children in the form of anxiety. At the same time, a high level of material possessions may engender families with concerns that their material possessions may make them a conspicuous target for criminal activity. Whereas emotional difficulty was related to material advantage or financial capital, behavioral difficulties were more strongly associated with the absence of human capital. For aggression, attention problems, and oppositional behavior, occupational prestige was a significant predictor. Children living in households in which the primary wage earner held a low-status position or no employment at all were more likely to be aggressive and have difficulty concentrating than children in households where the principal wage earner was employed in a high-wage, high-status position. At the same time, children living with an unemployed primary wage earner or one in a low-prestige occupation and in poor-quality housing were more likely to present with oppositional behavior. This is exactly the situation in which Ishmael was growing up.

According to his mother, "Ishmael is naughty; don't know where it comes from. He likes to be a boss, he shouts, they must listen to him, even when they are older, but he does not fight. He is also very stubborn; he shouts back at me when I tell him I'm going to beat him. He says defiantly that he is going to beat me. He is the only child; he breaks my heart when he defies me. He behaves the same with father; he is not afraid of him and he is used to threats. They do not work. Every day he does something. For example, he was kicking some children, fighting for a ball, the teacher says he is not adjusting well to school. At preschool when it is time for writing, he says he is tired and that he doesn't want to write." One day, Ishmael's father went through his mother's purse looking for change; Ishmael said that he would do it for the father. The father said no because he knew what he was looking for. Ishmael pulled the purse. He went through it while the father was not looking. He spilled sweets. He took them and hid them in his pants. The father came after him. Ishmael lied and denied that he had anything. At first, Ishmael's mother defended her child, saying he did not do anything. Ishmael repeated that he did not have anything. His father pulled the sweets out of his pants where he had tucked them.

His mother then told him that he was bad and that he should get a spanking for taking the candy from her purse. The father spanked him. Ishmael angrily ran out into the yard and pulled his father's clean clothes off the line and threw them in the dirt. Ishmael then told his mother not to wash his father's clothes.

Social Competence

Although maternal education did not make an independent contribution to the prediction of emotional and behavioral problems, it was related to each domain of social competence and to physical growth. Children of women with lower levels of education were lower in social competence and deviated from the norm for weight-to-height ratios more than children whose mothers were well-educated. Levels of affability were lower for children from families with low occupational prestige and living in lower-quality housing. As an example, Prudence's mother complained that her daughter is extremely shy and unassertive, she pulls back, shrinks from conflict. She is very tender in that all someone has to do is to look at her sternly or raise their voice and Prudence will break down and cry. Her mother feels that she developed this way because the home is very quiet. No one raises their voice, so the daughter is not used to sternness, conflict, or raised voices. She fears disapproval. Her mother worries that Prudence will fall apart in school if she gets a mean, strict teacher, but realizes that she can't be there to protect her from feelings of being injured by an insensitive, uncaring, or emotionally abusive adult. She thinks her daughter is more sensitive than she should be for her age and for her own good.

The mother leaves Prudence regularly to work in Pretoria, where she works three weeks (six days a week) and is off one week; during the one week she stays in Johannesburg and works in the credit inquiry section of a business. Although she does not say so explicitly, the mother and Prudence have a similar problem—lack of self-confidence, reticence. At work, she is given an opportunity for advancement that involves public customer service, but she is frightened that someone who only speaks Afrikaans might come up to the window and she won't know what to do or say since she doesn't speak that language. Later when other people are given a chance to do this who don't speak Afrikaans, they succeed and she regrets not trying.

Children from households with low levels of consumer goods also were less resilient than children growing up in households that had higher levels of consumption. The children judged to be academically ready tended to come from households with greater access to human capital in the form of maternal education and occupational prestige as well as with high-quality housing.

Distinguishing the Effects of Financial and Human Capital

These analyses were undertaken in part to discover differential effects of deficits in financial and human capital on children's development. Both financial and human capital have proven to be important predictors of psychosocial development between ages two and six. Surprisingly human capital seems to be just as important (and possibly more important) as material advantage in accounting for outcomes measured. Moreover there were even differences within the category of financial capital in that the quality of housing was the least predictive of all the poverty dimensions tested.

Access to human capital seems to foster early maturation and self-regulation. For example, occupational prestige is related to development of speech and motor skills and the self-regulation of behavior. Maternal education appears to be a protective factor in promoting speech and motor development; however it may be a risk factor in other areas. It is associated with delayed bladder control and feeding problems. Another possible generalization pertains to the differential role of human and financial capital, in that human capital is more consistently related to social competence and financial capital or material hardship than to behavioral and emotional problems. An implication of this principle is that improvements in children's social competence are more likely to come from increasing the human capital available to the household. Conversely improvements in material well-being by reducing income poverty are more likely to contribute to the reduction of emotional symptoms and behavioral problems.

At What Ages Do Economic Status and Living Standards Make a Difference?

The results from these data analyses reveal an important difference in the pattern of relationships between poverty and development that occurs prior to and after age five. Financial resources (particularly wealth) seem more important before age five than after. Conversely the role of housing quality seems much less important before age five than it does after. These differences in the relative importance of financial assets and housing before and after age five may relate to the relative role that the neighborhood schools and community at large play in the adjustment of children. Prior to age five, the child may spend most time within the confines of the home and with family.

As a child approaches age six, particularly after enrollment in school, the social environment outside of the household plays a much more influential role than it did when the child was younger. The quality of the neighborhood and schools depend to a great extent on the quality of housing. Better housing in established neighborhoods with private homes is likely to indicate much more resource-filled and positive schools and neighborhoods than in squatter communities or hostels where housing quality is poorer. Finally by age six, human capital seems to be more highly related to the development of social competence, and financial material capital is more highly associated with psychological disorders.

How Poverty Achieves Its Effects on Child Development

Significant gaps exist in our ability to explain why poverty is so detrimental to children—more importantly, to account for why some children are adversely affected while others seem to have immunity from its effects. Although childhood poverty is clearly linked to undesirable developmental outcomes, the processes through which these effects on emotional and social development are achieved or forestalled are not well understood. The effects of poverty on children's adjustment may be traced to early trauma, low birth weight, malnutrition, and iron deficiency (Werner and Smith 1992). In addition, poverty is associated with food insecurity and malnutrition (specifically protein, energy, and iron insufficiency), which can contribute to developmental anomalies, low birth weight, poor physical growth, compromised neurological development, and, ironically, obesity in late childhood and adolescence. These lead in turn to long-term deficits in physical health, motor coordination, problem-solving, attention, and academic achievement, as well as to shy, passive, and withdrawn behavior. Consider the description provided of Princess by her mother during the BTT interview: "She is very slow; if you tell her something one minute, she can't tell you the next minute! She forgets everything at school. If the teacher gives a message she forgets to tell Mother. She can't tell colors. She has learning problems. She can't do anything. She is immature, behaves like a three-year-old, when asked to do something she will not, she will look shy, she cries a lot at school and home, has problems with motor coordination. She is unable to hop on one foot; can hold a pencil, but has fine motor learning difficulties; has speech problem, has difficulty saying things that other children her age can say."

The stress diathesis model provides a compelling approach to depicting the ways poverty contributes to behavioral and emotional dysfunction. Clearly low income is central insofar as it contributes to the economic insufficiency that leaves parents and families in situations in which they lack the resources to meet basic needs and unexpected demands. But the disruptive or impaired functioning of poor children is not entirely attributable to financial insufficiency. Financial insufficiency is accompanied by other disadvantages and stresses that influence family life and the quality of the neighborhood environment (Brooks-Gunn and Duncan 1997). Consequently this model asserts that life among the poor is replete with stressors that have their basis not only in material deprivation but also social disadvantage.

The quality of parents' psychological functioning and the nature of community life are strong determinants of the psychological well-being of the child (Rutter 1990). Some observers suggest that the effects of poverty on child adjustment may be indirect in that they occur as a result of poverty's direct impact on family and community life. For example, family structure, parental distress, limited cognitive stimulation, and residence in dangerous neighborhoods are often implicated in adjustment problems found in early childhood. These factors are also highly correlated with poverty. In examining the effects of poverty-related risk, Brooks-Gunn and Duncan (1997) have demonstrated the importance of other risks associated with poverty, such as single parenthood, the mother's age, and the mother's level of education.

Children from single-adult households exhibited anxiety-depression, oppositional behavior, immaturity, and difficulties with peers more often than children living in two-adult and multigenerational households (Barbarin and Soler 1993). For example, McLoyd (1990) argues that poverty and economic loss diminish a parent's capacity for supportive, consistent, and involved parenting, and at the same time leave parents more vulnerable to the debilitating effects of negative life events. The poverty-related events give rise to parental distress and depression that drains parental energy and reduces their involvement in the monitoring, nurturing, and guiding of children in ways that promote their ability to cope with distress and develop self-regulation and social competence. In this way, economic hardship is indirectly linked to children's socioemotional functioning via its impact on the parent.

To the extent that parents are themselves distracted by financial need, their availability to stimulate and reinforce their child's learning may be undermined and in this way adversely affect the child's academic performance (Slaughter and Epps 1987). Thus it is quite possible that living in an impoverished environment may impact negatively parents' ability to provide the socioemotional resources needed for the child's emotional and cognitive development. Parents may despair about their ability to change the family's situation, strain the resources of extended family, or may lack the needed respite and experience poor health themselves.

Single-adult female-headed households fall disproportionately within the ranks of the poor. The high rates of maternal depression observed among this group may in part account for some of the effects of poverty on children. Poverty may reduce the emotional availability of the parent to establish a close and guiding relationship and to comfort a child faced with emotional difficulties. In this way, poverty reduces the capacity of parents to engage in relationship-sustaining behaviors and thus compromises their ability to guide, protect, and support their children (Lempers et al. 1989).

How Poverty Contributes to Conduct Problems

Similar explanations may apply to the role of poverty in the etiology of behavioral problems—namely, poverty-induced impairments in parental behavior and in parent-child behavior may account for the high rates of conduct problems in poor children. Sampson and Laub (1994:523) speculate that poverty influences conduct problems by "reducing the capacity of families to achieve effective informal social controls." They assert that family interactions related to parental control, discipline, and supervision such as the use of integrative shaming, punishment in the context of love, and respect and acceptance within an attached relationship, predicted whether or not a child would exhibit oppositional behavior, conduct disorder, and a persistent pattern of antisocial behavior.

Erratic, coercive, threatening, and harsh discipline; low levels of supervision; and ineffective or weak parent-child attachment seem to be implicated in the strong positive relationship that poverty often has with delinquent and problem behavior in children and youth. In a literature review on the effects of parental socialization, Steinmetz (1979) reviews evidence of the close link between parents' control strategies, such as contingent reinforcement and reasoning, to childhood aggression. Although research often reveals a strong statistical effect for poverty on these behavioral and emotional outcomes, this effect is most likely achieved indirectly through its impact on parental functioning and parents' socialization practices for their children.

This is probably the case for Noludwe, who is being raised by a single mother marginally self-employed as a street hawker of homemade traditional African crafts. Her long hours and meager living make it difficult to sustain what she knows is a more effective approach to raising her daughter. She finds the persistent pattern of oppositional and behavioral problems difficult to manage. In the words of her mother, "Noludwe is so stubborn. When you tell her don't touch, she touches anyway." Her behavior at the interview in the clinic corroborated her mother's words. Noludwe was an extremely difficult child, who appeared to have a lack of self-control symptomatic of hyperactivity. In response to her misbehavior, her mother shouted at her. The mother thinks Noludwe may be spoiled. "I have used a big voice [shouted] from the beginning, she may be used to it now. She got into a lot of trouble as a little child. Once she put a toy in the nose and it got stuck." At age five, Noludwe was very active. She climbed on top of the refrigerator and jumped off. Noludwe also experiences difficulty in formal academic settings. She is not cooperative with the teachers at creche and has a difficult time sharing with the other children. She seems a bit clever but wants to have her own way and often appears sad. Her mother summed up her frustration and disappointment in saying, "She is a lot of work, I had a lot of trouble, I don't think I will have another child." The toll of financial hardship and the fatigue of living and raising a difficult child is perceptible in words. It seems as though she has little energy left for the arduous task of socializing her child and redirecting her from a developmental trajectory that seems destined to lead her to a difficult adolescence and adulthood.

Poverty Effects Occurring via Community Life

Although the linkages of poverty to impaired parental functioning have gained wide acceptance as an explanation for adverse child development, some researchers have cast the explanatory net even wider. In addition to its influence on parental functioning, poverty may also influence child development through a broader impact on the family as a unit or system, on the neighborhood, and on the schools the child attends. Poverty increases conduct problems by contributing to instability of household composition and effective task performance. It also creates a social climate in neighborhoods in which violence and crime are rampant and antisocial norms become a standard. Community and neighborhood norms may give form to a child's proclivity to engage in antisocial acts and provide opportunity to enact those proclivities.

Some parents recognize that as a consequence of living in certain areas their children will be exposed to behavior, language, and attitudes that they would rather they not adopt. Such is the case with Fikile's mother, who is frustrated in her attempts to socialize her child in ways that are not respected and adhered to by most of the families living nearby. She wants her child to grow up with moral religious values and to observe proper traditions, for example, women going to funerals in hats and men in jackets to show respect. She wants to teach him how to be a real man and to behave properly. However, the negative influences of other children who are not taught properly makes her job more difficult. She gets particularly frustrated when she recounts how a neighbor's child is a bad influence on Fikile and teaches him to use curse words. "He is a bad child from bad family . . . they use vulgar language, fight too much, and misbehave too much." However, she reserves her criticism for his parents and family. "You can see that, he is badly brought up. But, don't blame the child, it is the parents' fault. Fikile brings vulgar language into our home that he hears from the neighbors . . . he does not even understand the words he is saying."

These are not unusual experiences for young children living in poor communities surrounded by substandard housing, attending underresourced chaotic schools where crime, violence, and problems of physical safety are ubiquitous (Halpern 1990). However the overall composition of the community seems to make a difference. The degree to which poverty is concentrated in a community determines its impact. Although children who reside in urban neighborhoods are at greater risk of developing behavioral and academic problems, diversity of income levels in a neighborhood appears to mediate the impact of poverty on emotional and cognitive development.

Higher IQ scores and lower levels of externalizing symptoms were observed among poor children when concentrations of poverty in a neighborhood were lower (Brooks-Gunn et al. 1997). Speculation about aspects of the neighborhood ecology that amplify the risk of academic and socioemotional maladjustment include adult and peer socialization and limited outlets for stimulating, cognitively enhancing, and recreational activities. In many urban schools, poor children may face an instability of teaching staff; low teacher morale; ineffective instructional programs; discipline problems; weak, distrustful relations between schools and families; and limited caretaker involvement in the children's lives at school. In addition, empirical evidence has shown that crime victimization is associated with emotional disturbance in children, but chronic exposures to violence such as witnessing violent acts in the community is not (Fitzpatrick 1993).

To summarize, poverty influences the functioning of parents, family, and community, and these in turn impact the social, psychological, and academic development of children. The multiple sequelae of poverty impact the family's and the parents' exposure to unanticipated life stressors and daily hassles. The high level of stress in daily living directly impacts parental well-being, and through its effects on the parents, impairs the psychosocial development of young children.

This portrayal of the lives of poor children and their families is not intended to resurrect discredited notions such as a "culture of poverty." A culture of poverty posits personal characteristics as fundamental to the etiology of poverty and its role in the lives of children and their families. It minimizes the impact of racism in accounting for how poverty effects come about and how they are maintained. And worse, instead of recognizing their creativity, resourcefulness, and energy many display in dealing with their circumstances, it pushes us toward the slippery slope of blaming victims for their oppression. Rather this model emphasizes that children growing up in impoverished communities live under conditions of extreme familial and community stress that limit families' capacities to cope and support their children's development.

Notes

1. Living standards refer simultaneously to several related concepts: resource adequacy, food and economic security, material deprivation or economic disadvantage and income poverty. The term "living standards" is used here to connote the relative economic and social status of families or households that implies the level of material hardship endured or degree of well-enjoyed.

Chapter 11

The Impact of Violence on Children

Violence in Children's Lives

Safe environments that provide stability and protection from physical harm are essential to the optimal development of children. Yet in South Africa and elsewhere around the world, political strife, ethnic conflict, and criminal violence have proliferated in ways which seem indifferent to the hardships they impose on children and their families. As a result, countless children grow up without the stable and protected environs that best promote healthy development. Many still do well in spite of the conditions in which they are raised. Nevertheless it is clear that exposure to violence on such a scale is unquestionably detrimental to their health and well-being.

Young children seem particularly vulnerable to its effects (Magwaza, Killian, and Peterson 1993). All too often innocent children are caught in the crossfire of adult conflicts, with deadly consequences. The most direct and immediate way that violence impacts children is by depriving them of life. Untold numbers of infants, toddlers, and young children have become unintended victims of random acts of violence that serve political or criminal purposes. In the past, the most frequent causes of death among children could be attributed to the combined effect of infections (mainly measles, acute respiratory infection, malaria, and diarrhea) and undernutrition. Over the last twenty years this picture has changed drastically in urban areas, and in Soweto, trauma is now the major cause of death for children under the age of five years. Take, for example, the tragic case of the Sithole family, whose lives were brutally ended in an incident that is increasingly common and which galvanizes the collective concerns of the nation.

Everyone who knew them thought of them as an ideal and loving family. Themba, his wife, Ayanda, and their five-month-old daughter and three-year-old son were on their way to visit family when their car was hijacked. From the available evidence, the family was driving along Potchefstroom Highway out of Soweto, and when they stopped for a traffic signal, bandits forced their way into the car at gunpoint. The car sped off, and along the way the infant was thrown from a window and probably died soon after impact from multiple wounds. Several miles away, the bodies of Themba and Ayanda were found facedown in a ditch, shot through the head. Their son, who probably witnessed the events, was the only survivor. He was found wandering the fields close to where his parents were shot. The family's car has not been located.

These brutal murders are typical of the violence that is causing so much alarm among citizens of urban areas in South Africa. The long-term impact on the surviving son is inestimable. It is highly likely that this early and tragic loss of family that will become a defining moment that will leave an indelible mark on his personality and haunt him for the rest of his life. Especially adverse consequences happen to children when violence results in serious injury to or the death of parents. Parental death (particularly of the mother) constitutes one of the most devastating losses a young child can sustain. It is one that has both emotional and instrumental implications.

For children, such loss may mean progressing through life without that nurturing individual who is deeply and overwhelmingly committed to one's care and socialization. Parental loss also has consequences for the standard of living, as surviving family members struggle to replace resources once provided by the now-deceased parent. For extended family structures already stretched to their financial limits, death or incapacitating injury to a child's parents almost always results in an unrecoverable decline in a child's standard of living. Moreover the senseless and brutal nature of such incidents and their random, unexpected occurrence leaves a lasting impression on the community as it reinforces a general state of anxiety and confirms the belief that citizens must constantly be on alert for potential danger.

Children may also be impacted by violence as they witness the killing or injury of others. In South Africa, many children have witnessed the physical harassment, injury, and killing of their family members and friends. The effects of violence extend beyond physical loss, and include severe disruption of family life and community relations, and can lead to such psychological problems as traumatic stress disorders (Smith and Holford 1993). In Eastern Europe, East Asia, East Africa, and Central America, violence may transform children into refugees and sometimes combatants. Once children are refugees, all semblance of normality built around routines at home and at school is swept away by a process of displacement, exodus, and resettlement, often under conditions that pose great physical peril.

Refugee or not, violence disrupts every aspect of children's lives at home, and in school, recreational, and community settings. Phillip, a student from Soweto, describes the ways that violence impacts the children in his community:

> Our students are not going to school because teaching and learning is difficult. There are Hippos [a pickup truck with a covered rear cab used by police to hold and transport persons arrested on the streets] everywhere around Soweto. These men which are called Boers [Afrikaans-speaking whites] run, shoot, beat, and kill our students. They even rape them. Our students are burning cars and stoning buses. If you go to school having books, they burn your books. The soldiers are very cruel and when we see Hippos coming we run away because we are afraid that they would arrest, shoot, beat, or kill us. I don't like what is happening in Soweto.

The impact of war and violence takes many different forms: starvation, injury, torture, imprisonment, life disruption, psychological trauma, and death. Chronic exposure to and participation in violence may also cause developmental delays and anomalies that do not resolve on their own even after the violence has ceased. But children are not only victims, they can also become perpetrators of violence. For example, children may participate as child soldiers by force or voluntarily because to do so secures food, clothing, and shelter for them. Similar motives for survival and safety propel children toward membership in gangs and criminal syndicates. Driven by necessity and coercion, many come in time to ultimately accept crime and even killing as a way of life, without thought and without remorse. They learn to anesthetize any stirrings of empathy for their victims and excise any nascent sensibilities about the value of human life. Moreover their combat experiences as child soldiers or members of street gangs scar them emotionally. They suffer psychological trauma and encounter social alienation, resentment, and suspicion from family and community as a consequence of their involvement in the victimization, injury, and killing of others.

Violence: Types and Modes of Exposure

Detecting the systematic developmental effects of violence on children is complicated by the great diversity of children's experiences with violence and the many different forms that violence can take. Even within the same city or suburb, exposure to violence is not the same for all children. Nor are its effects equally disruptive and enduring because of the wide variations in access to familial and social resources that offer children protection to children against violence's potential effects.

Our examination of violence in South Africa, has centered on four principal types that characterizes most BTT children's experience with violence: political, direct victimization, ambient community, and family violence. These types may differ from one another along two dimensions that we label *locus of violence*, that is, the setting in which the violence occurs (family or community); and *mode of exposure*, the manner in which the violence is experienced (direct or vicarious). We believe that these dimensions may ultimately prove important in illuminating why some experiences of violence may influence one aspect of development and not another, or explain the timing and duration of the impacts of violence in children's lives.

Locus of Violence

Family Violence

As noted earlier, family and neighborhood settings are the most likely ways in which children encounter violence (Boney-McCoy and Finkelhor 1996). Of the two, the family is undoubtedly the most common venue through which young children encounter violence. For example, Loening (1981) reports that 49 percent of the children referred to a trauma clinic in South Africa arrived there as a consequence of family violence. This contrasts with the 31 percent whose trauma resulted from political violence, and 20 percent from criminal violence. The number of cases of family violence against children reported to the Child Protection Unit of the South African police has risen steadily since 1988.

While family violence is the most likely form in which young children encounter violence, that occurring within the intimate relations of family life is also likely to affect their development most fundamentally. This is because the family is traditionally seen as the place where children develop working models for what intimate relationships are supposed to be about. Moreover for most children, the family represents the place of refuge, the last resort in seeking protection from harm. Where else can the child turn when his or her last hope for safety becomes the major source of peril?

In the case of Mandela's children, reports of family violence most often centered physical abuse of the mother. In chapter 8, we noted the moderately high levels of intrafamilial violence reported in our BTT sample. To summarize those data, over a five-year period, about 13 percent of children were living in families in which spouse abuse had occurred. About 5.4 percent reported that the abuse occurred in the first year of the child's life. By the fifth year of the child's life, 7.6 percent reported abuse. Other less severe forms of intrafamilial violence and conflict that involved hitting and physically hurting family members were also reported in 30 percent of families by the time the child turned six years of age.

Interestingly the likelihood of such violence in family life seems strongly influenced by contextual factors. Certain community contexts tend to be associated with higher levels of family violence. We have seen that family violence is more likely to occur in communities that are dangerous and which experienced high levels of political violence. For example, family violence is much more common in communities. which might be characterized as poor and disorganized, and in which violence in the broader community itself is relatively high. Ironically the more commonplace violence becomes, the more it becomes legitimized as a method for managing conflict (Coulton et al. 1995; Farrell and Bruce 1997). This parallelism in the rates of poverty and violence in the family and community might be explained by the high levels of strain and hardship that accompany low living standards (Aber 1993). It is impossible to say with certainty that poverty causes violence, but it is clear that the two are interdependent, have high rates of concordance, and may be mutually reinforcing (Cicchetti and Lynch 1993; Durant et al. 1994).

Social Distance and Violence

Nevertheless important differences exist between violence that occurs within the family and violence that is experienced in community life. For example, the social relations among perpetrator, victim, and witness are frequently more distant in community incidents than they are in family violence. This social distance possibly mediates the effects on the lives of those touched by violence. The closer the social relationship, the greater the impact of a violent incident (Boney-McCoy and Finkelhor 1995). Osofsky, and colleagues (1993) found that adolescents showed psychological distress only when community violence involved someone they knew. Similarly, Pynoos and collaborators (1987) reported that the most severe reactions to a sniping incident in a kindergarten were among the children who were emotionally close to those killed.

Physical distance also contributes to differences in outcomes. Independent of the closeness of their social relationships to victims, children who were physically closest to those killed were more severely traumatized than those who were farther away. In addition, violence that occurs within the family appears to be more detrimental to development of children's emotional functioning and social competence than violence that occurs in the community beyond the family (Campbell and Lewandowski 1997; Osofsky et al. 1993). At this time, we can only surmise the ominous long long-term implications for society as these traumatized children mature.

Mode of Exposure to Violence: Direct Victimization and Ambient Danger

Experiences of violence occur in several modes; exposure to violence may be direct, vicarious, and/or ambient. Direct experiences of violence occur when an individual or someone close to the individual is victimized or in immediate danger, or when the individual is an eyewitness to incidents of violence such as assaults or abuse. Vicarious experiences of violence occur not by direct exposure but through intermediaries—word of mouth, media reports, and other narrative accounts of incidents. We have advanced a view shared by many that vicarious but chronic threats to safety (such as exist in crime-ridden communities) pose threats to development that are as parallel to and perhaps as serious as war and civil strife. A diary entry by a Soweto youth demonstrates clearly the emotionally evocative and disturbing power of vicarious images of violence:

> Going back home—saw four policemen hitting two boys who were smoking dagga [a marijuana-like drug] in the street. They took them to the police station. . . . When I went to sleep, I saw them again in a dream arresting me. (Mtshali 1988:10)

Through identification and empathy, vicarious exposure can have powerful and emotionally disruptive effects (Farrell and Bruce 1997; Taylor et al. 1994). Violence can also impact individuals through a general ambience of danger or residue of fear created by high levels of conflict and violence in a community. As such, exposure to ambient violence is not tied to specific incidents or encounters, but to a generalized conviction of a high probability of harm. Nevertheless ambient violence profoundly shapes the culture and reputation of a community and influences child development through its impact on social processes and interpersonal relations within the community (Aneshensel and Sucoff 1996). It is manifested by social withdrawal, restrictions on children's explorations outside the family home, retreat from public domains, fear and suspicion of strangers in the neighborhood, and a readiness to interpret stimuli such as noises as indicators of violent or potentially violent episodes. Even though the sources of ambient community danger are difficult to pinpoint, their consequences are far from trivial.

Community danger exposes individuals to anticipatory loss and trauma. These experiences trigger unpleasant emotional arousal, which can become chronic and interfere with daily functioning at home, at work, and at school. Such a climate of danger not only robs individuals of a sense of well-being and life satisfaction, but may also interfere fundamentally with biological, psychological, and social functioning. Worst of all, violence is thought to create an environment inhospitable to the healthy development of children and has particularly negative impacts on emotional and behavioral adjustment. It contributes to impairments that are not easily reversed and may result in damage to psychological function that persists into adulthood.

The children of Soweto are targets of special concern because some seem surrounded by the specter of violence. Although most seem blissfully unaware of it, legitimate questions can be raised about its impact. Danger and violence in the lives of children come in many forms: Accidents, cruelty to animals, theft, and family arguments are some examples. Just how common it is in the lives of some children is made clear from one week of entries in the diary of a Soweto youth. On each day, the child was exposed to some form of death and danger:

- Sun., Sept. 12   I read about the children who were killed by a hit and run driver on Dube Street Within minutes after the killings several motorists chased the man and arrested him.
- Mon., Sept. 13   Going to school I saw a crowd of people running—they were wearing green polo-necked sweaters and black trousers. They were the Baygon Greens (street gang from Meadowlands) they were going to fight the people who live at Dube Hostel. They were carrying axes and knives. We were all frightened and ran away.
- Tues., Sept. 14   Going to school—saw a man fighting with his father. They broke all windows of the house and those were big windows. The police came and he was arrested.
- Wed., Sept. 15   On my way home I saw the taxi drivers and a bus driver fight for passengers.

- Thu., Sept. 16   While we were at the Ikwezi Railway Station, we saw people looking at a man who was dead. He was killed overnight by thieves.
- Fri., Sept. 17   Going to school—on my way I saw a cat lying in the road it was dead—all the fur was taken off.
- Sat., Sept. 18   . . . went to town to buy some shoes. On my way I saw a bad accident. The children were playing in the trenches [dug for the electrification of Soweto]. One of them didn't realize that his friend was in it. So he pushed a big stone in it and the other was badly injured and unconscious. Till now I don't know whether he is still alive.

Although the youth reporting these events was not directly involved in any of them, the constant barrage of violence, injury, and death occurred within her psychological space and likely take their toll on her emotionally and physically. As we have noted earlier, violence is common but it would be a mistake to conclude that it is ubiquitous. As pointed out in chapters 4 and 5, great variations exist among communities in rates of violent incidents and in the perception of communities as dangerous. Many mothers regard their communities are as very safe for themselves and their children. They have witnessed no violence and they experience little anxiety about danger. These favorable views are corroborated by independent ratings used in the BTT study. In fact, only about 40 percent of the BTT children either live in communities rated as dangerous or have parents who have been victims of or witnesses to violence.

Now we turn to observations made within the BTT about the relationships of violence to the development of Mandela's children from birth to age six. These will be used to address questions about the extent to which types of violence such as victimization, family violence, political violence, and community danger are associated with children's development. We also wanted to know whether different forms of violence exposure had differential impacts on how well children managed the critical developmental tasks related to feeding, bladder control, language development, and behavioral, emotional, and social functioning. We began this exploration with an assumption that the depth and nature of any effects would depend on the locus of the violence and the mode by which children were exposed to it.

Previous research would lead us to conclude that direct victimization would have the biggest effects because of the salience of violence. If the salience of violence was critical, then family violence too would have a consistently strong relationship to developmental problems.

Given the dearth of information on the early effects of violence exposure, we were not certain what to expect with regard to how early in life effects of violence would emerge and what domains would be affected at what points in development. Our approach is also founded on the assertion that the degree to which violence impacts the child can be attenuated by the level of distress suffered by and the coping resources available to the child's mother or primary caregiver. With respect to coping resources, we explore the abilities of mothers and primary caretakers to protect children against the adverse consequences of violence by helping them manage the life disruptions and psychological distress that often accompany violence. To assess the veracity of these suppositions, we examine the differential effects of family and community as distinct loci of violence, and alternative modes of exposure as represented by direct victimization and vicarious or ambient danger.

Our discussion will focus on whether, how, and when different forms of violence disrupt or alter the development of children in areas that are key to early development: feeding, language, bladder control, motor development, fears, and behavior.[1] When we began we expected that violence would have a negative impact on development between birth and age six. In addition, we expected that violence would be associated with children's negative affect, including expressions of anxiety and depression. Violence might also have consequences for cognitive functioning but we were less certain about how these might manifest themselves. We reasoned that negative heightened arousal associated with violence may contribute to difficulties in concentrating and maintaining focus that are symptomatic of attention deficits, and these may be expressed in low levels of academic motivation. At the same time, arousal may have a disinhibitory effect on children's behavior, making it less controlled and more resistant to norms and direction from authority figures. Therefore children living in conditions of violence may become noncompliant and exhibit problem behaviors such as aggression, behaviors that are often associated with deficiencies in the development of self-regulation.

Violence and Psychological Functioning

Although violence is not ubiquitous in the lives of Mandela's children, concern has been raised about the possible long long-term effects it might have on their development. Evidence from studies around the world consistently demonstrates principal effects of violence in two domains of children's functioning: developmental regressions and post-traumatic stress. Effects in the first domain occur for a class of symptoms that can be thought of as detours from a normal and expected developmental trajectory, along with chronic, unexplainable somatic complaints such as aches and pains. Effects in the second domain consist of psychological symptoms that commonly occur together as an aftermath of some discrete, significant, and often unpredictable trauma. Events that have been known to produce such psychological reactions include natural disaster, fires, rape, and other stressful life events. The pattern of symptoms associated with these traumatic events have become so well recognized and understood that, if severe enough, they constitute what mental health professionals deem a mental disorder called post-traumatic stress disorder (PTSD).

Developmental Regressions: Detours from Normal Development

The term *developmental regression* conveys a moving backward to a more primitive level of functioning or a slipping back to an earlier stage of development. It suggests functioning at a lower and less-mature level than might be expected for a given chronological age or because the behaviors represent a reversal of previously attained developmental milestones. Developmental regression is the inability to perform tasks or master demands that were once handled with facility and mastery.

Robertson (1994) observed such symptoms among children living in informal settlements in South Africa, which are characterized by extreme danger as well as poverty. These children presented with somatic complaints such as headaches and dizziness, as well as symptoms of regression such as bed-wetting at higher rates than children living in relatively more secure communities.

Episodic loss of bladder and bowel control among children growing up in situations of violence is particularly striking, since many urban South African children acquire such control as early as one year of age. The presentation of symptoms refers more to occasional or episodic loss of control as opposed to full-blown cases of enuresis and encopresis in which children totally lack the ability to hold their urine in their sleep or who regularly soil themselves during the day. Accordingly the effects of violence are more likely to be evidenced as children occasionally soiling themselves or episodically wetting the bed at night. Problems in this domain may also be expressed in terms of high levels of unexplainable somatic complaints such as aches, pains, and dizziness, which have been observed in unusually high levels among children exposed to community violence (Campbell and Schwarz 1996).

The indicators of developmental regression available in the BTT study include feeding problems, bed-wetting, and speech difficulties. Analyses of the effects of violence on such developmental regressions among Mandela's children reveal several interesting findings. First, no signs of developmental regressions manifested themselves at age two. This is not surprising, since psychosocial and motor development are still in their early stages at this point in life and it would be difficult to discriminate what is normally uneven performance at this stage and what represents a problematic reversal. The effect of violence on competence and performance would have to be dramatic to be noticed, and such large effects are unusual. Most tend to be subtle and too small to notice until much later when parents are able to contrast a child's current competence with what she was able to do in the past or to compare the child to others his age.

By age four, speech and feeding problems emerged as developmental difficulties associated with violence. Also at age four, children growing up in communities with high level of political violence evidenced more difficulty with feeding than children in communities less disturbed by politically motivated killings, injuries, and arrests. Similarly, children in households with high levels of family conflict and violence were reported to have more difficulty in the area of speech development. One can only speculate about the processes that account for the relationship between family violence and speech difficulties. Perhaps in violent families, the level of stress may be so high that children are not provided with sufficient stimulation to develop their verbal abilities fully. Where violence prevails as a method for resolving conflicts, the stimulation of children in speech discourse may be limited. In this way, poor linguistic development is the most obvious and the earliest sign of what may be a more pervasive problem. Alternatively, children may be reluctant to test their emerging speech skills in a home where speech may be toxic and where it is better to be quiet and not draw attention to oneself.

By age five, violence was related to all three indicators of developmental regression, including bed-wetting, feeding, and speech problems. Children in households with high levels of family violence and conflict were more likely to have speech and feeding difficulties at this time. Similarly children in households in which a family member was a victim of violence had more speech difficulty. Bed-wetting was more common in communities which were subject to political violence.

By age six, only feeding and speech problems were predicted by violence. Again family violence predicts feeding difficulties, and victimization of a member of the household predicts speech problems. This latter finding suggests that stress related to violence my underlie its relationship to speech difficulties. (See table 11.1 for a list of developmental outcomes related to violence.)

Psychological Effects of Violence on Children: Post-Traumatic Stress Disorder

Rutter and Garmezy (1985) have suggested that that post-traumatic stress disorder (PTSD) is a useful analog for summarizing the psychological effects of violence on children. This disorder consists of a set of psychological symptoms that arise after exposure to trauma. Most often, these traumatic events are salient, discrete, and significant. In the case, of violence this means experiencing symptoms such evidence as fears, sadness, difficulties in concentration, and in some cases that makes it so interesting aggression. One of the interesting features of PTSD is that the psychological effects present with the same intensity as though one were presently experiencing the trauma. By recounting and ruminating about the event, the child suffers the effects as though

Table 11.1: Dimensions of Violence Related to Development—Ages 2 to 6

	Age 2	Age 4	Age 5	Age 6
Developmental regression				
Feeding problems		Political	Family	Family
Bed-wetting			Political	
Speech problems		Family	Victimization family	Victimization
Post-traumatic stress				
Attention/ concentration	—	—	—	Community victimization
Aggression		Community victimization family		Community
Fears/sadness	Political			Community

it were still happening. In this way, children may react emotionally and behaviorally with the same intensity as when it originally occurred. Distress included includes symptoms of depression and anxiety, as well as, lack of attention; daydreaming; loss of desire to do fun things; not caring about anything; worry about being safe; intrusive thoughts; having a hard time getting up in the morning; fitful, disturbed sleep; having bad dreams; difficulty avoiding fear; feeling lonely, nervous, scared, upset, easily bothered, and afraid one might not live.

Another interesting feature of PTSD is that most individuals try not to relive the traumatic event, but images and recollections of it break into their conscious thoughts in spite of efforts to divert attention away from the event and not to ruminate about it. One result is that traumatized children such as those exposed to violence either by witness or victimization report high levels of distress, and these are often corroborated by parent observations of distress symptoms in their children (Osofsky et al. 1993).

Other studies have independently demonstrated that children exposed to violence experienced a range of similar symptoms, including: (1) difficulty concentrating because of lack of sleep and disturbing imagery; (2) avoidance of intrusive thoughts; (3) anxious attachments to mothers, being fearful of leaving them or sleeping alone; an unrealistic, preoccupying worry about harm befalling attachment figures; worry about some event causing separation from attachment figures; (4) becoming more aggressive while playing, imitating behaviors they have seen; (5) acting tough to deal with fear and developing counterphobic reactions; (6) acting uncaring because they have to deal with loss and hurt; and (7) becoming severely constricted in activities for fear of reexperiencing traumatic events (Osofsky et al. 1993).

For the BTT sample, the results were very consistent with the findings reported by others. Violence was related to parental reports of child fears and sadness at age two and at age six. Children growing up in areas with high levels of political violence and that were rated as dangerous were more often described as sad and anxious than were children growing up in safer communities.

For Mandela's children, fear was a common reaction to chronically violent conditions. Children often gave voice to their fears in ways that creatively integrated fantasy, exaggerated concerns, and reality. This process is reflected in the words of children who were preadolescents during the height of the political violence. ". . . We boys, especially . . . we have sleepless nights being afraid of being taken away from our families. . . . If you are a boy, whenever you hear a knock on the door at night you start panicking without knowing why. All that comes into your mind at once is a man wearing a greenish helmet, green camou-flage clothes, a pair of dark brown boots, a pistol in a holster on his waist, and a rifle in his hands with a red face hunting you like a beast." This fear has a pervasively disruptive effect onto children's activities and daily life. Often they adapt to the threat by over-reacting to even normal events such as the sound of a delivery truck or a knock on the door. "We are forced to lock ourselves in the house for the whole day. When playing with friends and you just happen to hear a truck's engine coming in your direction, you don't even waste time wanting to know what it is, even if it's a coal truck. You just run like mad for safety. You no longer have the opportunity to visit your friends the way you like. The minute you go towards the door and happen to think about the 'Casspirs' [a military vehicle used for transporting troops and patrolling] you just lock the door right away." Conditions of violence such as these may also create a psychological environment that pro-motes wariness, chronic fear, and concern about threats to the physi-cal safety of self and one's family.

> These army troops pretend to be our friends. They play football
> with us in order to get us unaware. They are always bribing us
> with sweets in order for us to think they are our friends and
> trust them . . . on the other hand, they are killing us like dogs.
> I am not going to trust my killers and destroyers. (Open School
> 1986)

The high levels of emotional arousal associated with violence con-tribute to negative mood states that take the form of sadness and irri-tability (Fitzpatrick 1993). Mason and Killian (1994) studied black schoolchildren in in KwaZulu/Natal and found that 17.8 percent of children met criteria for emotional problems (8.7 percent for depres-sion and 12.9 percent for PTSD). Sadness, low morale, hopelessness about life, and despondence about one's future prospects follow from the many ways in which chronic and unpredictable violence disrupts normal life (Durant et al. 1995; Freeman et al. 1993). The anxiety and depression often resulted from reliving the trauma, ruminating about it, or having it intrude against one's wishes into conscious thought.

Nozipho shows many signs of traumatic stress. In the BTT inter-view, she seemed very sad. She almost appeared depressed. Nozipho's father died two years ago, killed on his way to work in political violence on the commuter train. Nozipho cries a lot. She talks to herself when alone. She is easily frightened by a scene of fighting on the TV. She is afraid at night of the dark. She screams out loud in her sleep.

However important the emotional reactions to victimization and violence exposure may be, the behavioral consequences are compelling. There is mounting evidence that exposure to violence is not only associated with depression, but also with increased levels of behavioral and social problems in children (Gorman-Smith and Tolan 1998). For example, Nozipho's mother reports that Nozipho her daughter avoids other children and seems to prefer playing alone. Her mother also describes her as naughty. She does not want to listen. "I [mother] say to her 'Don't do this,' but she will do it, anyway. I repeat it, she still does it. If you tell her in a smooth calm voice, she won't listen. But if I say to her 'I will take a stick [to beat her],' then she will listen."

The toll of violence on psychological functioning can also be expressed in attention difficulties. The effects of violence may also spill over to relations with peers in the form of emotional withdrawal and aggressive behavior, both of which may contribute ultimately to rejection by peers. (Cooleyquille et al. 1995; Garbarino et al. 1991). Attention problems did not appear in connection with violence until age six. At that point in development, children in communities with high levels of ambient danger and those growing up in households with members who have been victimized by violence had higher levels of attention and concentration problems than children growing up in safer communities and whose family members were not victimized. Problems of concentration result from intrusive ruminations and preoccupation with the details of the traumatic event. As a consequence, cognitive function is slowed and inefficient. Children become distracted and unable to concentrate because they are unable to clear their minds of the trauma.

Fear and despondence over loss of loved ones or over loss of what was perceived as a normal life are typical reactions to trauma. In children, these may be expressed in terms of fears; reliving or reenactment of distressing incidents; heightened arousal; irritability; anger; fear of being alone; nightmares about separation; and recurrent distress characterized by crying, tantrums, misery, emotional numbness, apathy, or social withdrawal. Psychological reactions such as being chronically scared were much more frequent among children in informal settlements where housing consisted mostly of temporary shack dwellings than among children living in formal housing areas. The informal settlement area was rife with crime and violence.

Chronic exposure to violence thus appears to stimulate a hyperaroused emotional state and contributes to cognitive disorganization. The composite symptom profile resulting from violence is highly consistent with a diagnosis of PTSD.

Effects of Types of Violence

It was expected that proximal, direct, and personal exposure to violence would have stronger relationships to adverse social development than exposure to violence that was distal or vicarious. In fact, proximal violence such as direct victimization was no more adverse in consequences than distal or vicarious forms such as political violence and ambient community danger. Victimization was related to aggression, attention, and speech problems. Another proximal type of violence, family violence, predicted feeding problems, speech problems, and aggression. Indirect or ambient community violence did not contribute to the prediction of any of the indicators of developmental regression, but it did contribute to each symptom of PTSD used in the BTT study. This is an unusual finding in that PTSD is conceptualized as resulting from a discrete event, but community danger is a nondiscrete quality of the climate of the community that is more suggestive of a threat to safety than it is a real and discrete threat .

McKendrick and Senoamadi (1996) provide a plausible explanation for why this chronic ambient violence may have the effects normally associated with discrete traumatic events. They argue that if the experience of violence is chronic, it may lead to a pattern of adaptation that interferes with children's normal functioning at home and at school. The long-term disruptions and adaptations to it may limit opportunities for experiences that are uplifting and constrain the development of competence. Moreover, the strain of the adaptation to chronic ambient violence may lead to distractibility and irritability, which are incorporated into children's adaptive styles. The resulting emotional states may also find expression in dysthymic mood, trait-like anxiety, social reserve and alienation, oppositional behavior, aggression, and low school achievement (Aneshensel and Sucoff 1996).

Although the distinctions among types of violence exposure were not related to the magnitude of effects on children, different types of violence did produce distinct outcomes. For example, family violence is linked to problems of feeding, speech, and aggression. With ambient community violence, an atmosphere of danger is strongly associated with symptoms of PTSD, but not developmental regression. In contrast, political violence was associated with developmental regressions and sadness in children. The form violence takes does make a difference in its impact on children. Today, in light of the demise of political violence, family and community violence represent the most likely threats to children's development. Consequently we should expect that the principal continuing threat to Mandela's children will be the emotional and behavioral sequelae of violence.

Figure 11.1 summarizes what we have learned about the effects of different forms of violence on children by age six. Two points are emphasized in interpreting this figure. First, the form that violence takes determines the nature of its impact on children. Second, mothers' functioning can make a difference by muting some effects of violence. While some forms of violence affected children directly, the impact of ambient community violence was filtered through or mediated by its impact on mothers. Note that family violence and victimization, the two proximal forms of violence, have direct effects on children that are not moderated by mother's coping. Recent data reported by Paschall and Hubbard (1998) also suggest that family stress and conflict are risk factors, and harmony and effective coping may act as protective factors for children and youth exposed to violence. Perhaps the trauma associated with the injury or death of a family member is so arousing that it is distracting for the child. Such attention problems may not be significantly debilitating in early childhood. However if they persist into the school years, they may interfere with learning and academic achievement. Family violence is directly associated with higher levels of aggression in children—the higher the level of family violence, the higher the aggression. In this way, family violence may serve as a source of modeling as children learn to be violent by witnessing violence among family members. The effects of ambient community violence characterized by a nonspecific but palpable sense of danger are mediated by maternal functioning. The extent to which children exhibit PTSD-related symptoms vary with how distressed mothers are themselves.

**Figure 11.1: Types of Violence,
Maternal Coping, and Child Development Outcomes at Age 6**

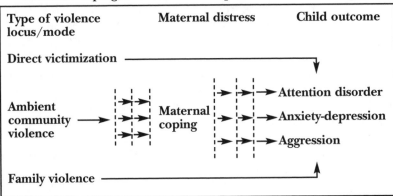

Family Resources Can Diminish the Psychological Impact of Community Violence

These data show that caretakers, principally mothers, play an important buffering role in limiting the effects of ambient community violence on children. The capacity of caretakers to lower the adverse impact of violence was most likely related to parents' effectiveness in coping, and their involvement in helping the child deal with violence. Mothers who were coping well and able to regulate their own negative emotional arousal to danger seem to pass on a capacity for self-regulation to their children (Ackerman et al. 1999). Thus the impact of violence on children may well be related to the quality of relationship to the child, and how parents responded behaviorally, emotionally, and cognitively in the face of violence. Specifically the effect of community violence on attention problems, anxiety-depression, and aggression were muted when mothers themselves coped well with the impact of violence.

Avoiding Victim-Blaming

In highlighting the relationship of maternal well-being to child outcomes, there arises the possibility of attributing responsibility for children's outcomes to maternal distress and coping failure rather than social conditions that are the root cause of both maternal distress and poor child outcomes. This would be a classic example of blaming the victim. Blaming mothers for the aggressive behavior and poor school adjustment of their children in dangerous environments betrays an emphasis on individual causality in human behavior and ignores the influence of the social environment. In reality, maternal distress is also influenced by the types of resources and supports available to them. Mothers do not automatically develop immunity to the adverse effects of violence by virtue of their caretaking role. Mothers who lived in communities rated as dangerous and who described high levels of conflict and physical violence in their own household situations often reported symptoms of depression and anxiety. To be fair, explanations of mothers' capacity to cope with the effects of violence must go beyond them as individuals and encompass the environment in which they are nested. Mothers and caretakers need support themselves in dealing with the trauma of violence. They do not exist in a vacuum, but rely instead on a network of social resources and access to cultural strengths and practices that help to maintain equilibrium. These resources may include extended family structures and family spirituality. Perhaps mothers who were protected emotionally themselves were more able to safeguard their children from the otherwise harmful effects of violence. Seen in this light, mothers' functioning is probably a proxy for family functioning and supports. When these broader supports are not available, it is likely that both caretaker and child will adjust poorly in dangerous and violent environments.

This interpretation is highly consistent with observations that the sense of threat and danger emanating from experiences of violence can be reduced by the variety of strategies families develop and the social resources they have to cope with violence (Berman et al. 1996). Key personal, familial, and social resources enable families to assist children to manage the stress of violence and moderate its adverse effects on adjustment. Among the possible resources are competence in the use of emotion-regulating strategies, spirituality, access to transcendental ideologies that help the child to interpret violence in a constructive way, and instrumental and emotional support, particularly from family members (Wallen and Rubin 1967; Garbarino and Kostelny 1996).

The coping resources of parents and family members are therefore important in predicting the impact of violence on children. Presumably young children have limited internal resources of their own with which to cope and often must rely on external support from caregivers and family to manage stress. This is just one of the ways that parents and other caregivers mitigate the potentially negative influence that experiences of violence may have on children's social development. Because a very young child's experience of the world is filtered by parents and dependent to a large measure on what they allow to permeate the child's psychological space, the child's experience of violence is largely a function of the family's ability to filter and serve as a barrier to disturbances. Moreover families can be important resources to children in maintaining equilibrium in the face of life disruption, personal loss, and physical harm, and can equip them with an ideology by which to interpret and transcend danger (Garbarino and Kostelny 1996). As a consequence, the capacity of primary caregivers to transmit effective coping strategies and to maintain their own emotional equilibrium are particularly important to children in situations of violence. Consequently knowledge about how well the mother and family cope can reveal a great deal about how the child will experience and respond to distress.

These observations permit us to end our consideration of the impact of violence on children on an optimistic note. Not all children respond to violence adversely, and the possibility of adverse or positive developmental outcomes may depend on qualities of resources made available to the family. To the extent that these supports are available to the mother and the child, the impact of ambient community danger on children will be diminished. When mothers and families have the personal, social, and material resources to cope and to avert excessive anxiety and depression, they are better positioned to protect their children against the consequences of violence. From the perspective of social policy, therefore efforts to promote the well-being of mothers through supportive interventions could pay dividends with respect to enhancing the adjustment of their children.

Notes

1. The details of these analyses are available in the list of published articles presented at the end of this book.

Chapter 12

Comparing the Social Development of South African, Ugandan, and African-American Children

A Cross-National Perspective on Development

The social development of South African children has been discussed in chapters 6 and 7, where we noted deficits in the behavior regulation as exemplified in high levels of aggression and opposition by the time children were age six. Recall that 19 percent of South African children were described by their parents as often disobedient and 36 percent were often aggressive. Also, problems were noted with regard to emotional regulation. Thirty percent of Mandela's children were rated as frequently fearful when they were six years old. We have tried to make the case that conditions in South Africa relevant to poverty, racism, community violece, and family life are signifcantly implicated in these adverse developmental outcomes. Arguments linking these conditions to elevated levels of opposition, aggression, and fear could be strengthened by examining the extent to which the same relationships between social risks and development are observed among children growing up in slightly different cultural contexts. Accordingly this chapter compares the quality of psychosocial development among children in South Africa, Uganda, and the United States and examines the extent to which poverty continues to have a relationship to poor outcomes.

In general, outcomes of psychosocial development among Mandela's children seem quite consistent with those reported in studies of children elsewhere in the world. Compared to children in Western societies, data on Mandela's children collected in the BTT study suggest that South Africans as a group do not differ in prevalence of symptoms of emotional distress. However they do evidence somewhat higher levels of attention and behavior problems (Costello et al. 1996; Mash and Barkley 1996). Moreover except for aggression, the developmental trajectories of South African children fit a pattern consistent with healthy development in six-year-old children. Unlike the data on South African children, most studies of developmental psychopathology in Western and highly developed countries reveal developmental patterns in which the prevalence of aggression decreases between ages two and six.

Should this pattern of increasingly aggressive behavior be viewed as a warning signal about trouble ahead for South African children? Alternatively should it be overlooked as a typical and normal adaptation within an African context? Comparative data obtained on a general population of children in Western countries such as the United States, Great Britain, or Canada are not a strong and sufficient basis for drawing conclusions about the adequacy of adjustment of South African children. A more effective strategy is to compare BTT children to children of African descent with roughly similar social histories and demographic profiles. With cross-national data, we can interrogate more convincingly the role of social risks in susceptibility to psychosocial impairment. In chapters 10 and 11, we demonstrated that poverty and violence place South African children at risk for aggression and socioemotional difficulties. In this comparative analysis, we inquire whether children who share social risks show similar developmental effects of those risks. By positioning the status of South African children within a broader cross-national context, we can strengthen our understanding of the quality and normalcy of their behavioral, emotional, or social development and the role of these social risks in South Africa.

Before proceeding to a discussion of the developmental outcomes of South African, Ugandan, and African-American children, we review briefly the procedures for gathering information in each country and summarize information that informs us about the relative risks experienced in each of the three groups. Specifically we discuss information comparing the sociohistorical context, family life, socioeconomic status, and social risks in each of these three settings. Understanding similarities and differences among the groups on these dimensions will facilitate interpretation of differences across national lines in developmental outcomes.

Developmental Contexts in Uganda and the United States

Social Context in Uganda
Making a case for comparability of the developmental contexts of Ugandan and South African children is easy and straightforward.

Although Uganda is far from South Africa in distance, historically and socially they have much in common. They share a legacy of white hegemony and colonial rule as members of the British Commonwealth. Although both countries have substantial numbers of whites and Indians, their populations are overwhelmingly composed of African blacks. Even within the indigenous African population, multiple ethnic groups exist with their own cultures, languages, and identities. Moreover both countries have experienced significant interethnic group conflicts that have exploded into extended periods of bloody civil warfare. Both are now ruled by stable, effective, democratically elected governments that are attempting to enact social policies emphasizing human development and to improve the lives of their children. Both have economies robust and strong enough to make them economic leaders in their regions: Uganda in East Africa and South Africa in the southern part of the continent. Nevertheless a substantial proportion of citizens in each country live in poverty.

Procedures for Gathering Data in Uganda

The Ugandan children whose data are reported in this chapter are residents in the city of Kampala. A representative sample of 520 school-age children in Grade 1 was obtained in 1997 using a multistage, random sampling technique. Kampala is divided into five municipal districts. Two schools were randomly selected from each of the five districts. All children enrolled in Grade 1 in each of the elementary schools were recruited for the study based on lists provided by the schools. At the time the study was conducted, the policy of free universal primary education was just recently instituted by the Ugandan Ministry of Education. As a consequence, children entering school for the first time and enrolled in Grade 1 spanned a wide age range. Only the 165 children who were six years old at the time are included in this comparison with African-Americans and South Africans. Measures identical to those used in BTT were employed in Uganda. These measures included assessing the demographic questions and the psychosocial development questionnaire. Measures were translated into the local language (Luganda) and back-translated for accuracy. The interviews were conducted with parents in their homes or at the schools. In addition, information about experiences with violence and community safety were gathered from parents and expert raters using a method similar to the one described in the BTT study.

The Social Context of African-Americans

The parallels between South Africans and African-Americans exist more at a symbolic level than in the material details of their daily lives.

The similarities are not as obvious as the parallels between South Africans and Ugandans, but they are just as compelling. This is especially true regarding life in urban communities of black America and black townships in South Africa. Even a cursory examination of the social and historical conditions endured by urban South Africans reveals striking parallels to the situation of African-Americans. The similarities between the two groups can be traced to a common history and shared experiences of institutionalized racism and material hardship. The economic disadvantages endured by South Africans and African-Americans relative to whites can be traced to a similar history of racial oppression fueled by educational inequality and sustained by excessively high rates of unemployment.

Both groups have undergone rapid urbanization and suffered from its adverse effects on family ties, economic pressures on family formation and stability, and high poverty rates. Institutionalized racism against both groups has resulted in residential segregation, economic disadvantage, and inequality of opportunity. Both have experienced long-standing patterns of disadvantage in important domains of life: health, education, social welfare, access to decent affordable housing, and safe communities. As a consequence, both populations suffer inordinately from hunger, nutritional deficiencies, inadequate housing, cycles of rural-urban migration, degradation of the physical environment, exposure to pollution and toxins, and unequal access to health care (Offord et al. 1989).

Consequently the social challenges and community problems confronting South Africans resonate strongly within African-American communities. The litany of problems recited for South African blacks are echoed in concerns historically expressed for African-American communities: unemployment, lack of quality education, substandard housing, concerns about crime and violence, teen pregnancy, exposure to pollution and industrial waste, chronic health problems, and a low life expectancy compared to whites.

In addition, African-Americans and South Africans have similar worries about the well-being and development of their youth. Both communities view with alarm the spiraling rates of gang activity, juvenile crime, and premature termination of education. The demographic trends that impact South Africans also are found among African-Americans: high proportions of children born to mothers without partners; violence within the family, particularly spouse abuse; child abuse and neglect; high morbidity and mortality rates from preventable causes; and an epidemic of alcoholism and substance abuse that tears apart the fabric of family life.

Data on the African Americans were collected as part of the 1988 National Health Interview Survey, the Child Health Supplement (NHIS-CHS) under the auspices of the United States Department of Health and Human Services, and the National Center for Health Statistics. The NHIS provided a summary of children's physical and social development and targeted, specifically, symptoms of physical illness, emotional difficulties, and behavioral disorders. The purpose of the NHIS was to gather information about children's physical, developmental, and psychological conditions. Trained project staff visited children's homes to conduct face-to-face interviews with parents or parental surrogates. The information was used to identify service needs of children and their families. Additional information was gathered on household composition: demographic status of the biological mother, father, and primary caretaker; and data related to pregnancy, birth, and child care. The sampling methodology involved a multistage probability sample from 1,924 geographically defined primary sampling units. When more than one child resided in a selected household, a single target child was randomly selected from each household. The resulting sample is therefore a representative sample of the population of the United States, with a large national probability sample of African-American children ages zero to seventeen. The data used in these analyses were for 306 children who were six years old at the time the survey was conducted.

Sociodemographic Profile

Table 12.1 summarizes the sociodemographic status of South African, African-American, and Ugandan children used in these comparisons. Although the South African and African-American children were roughly evenly divided between males and females, the Ugandans consisted of more females than males. The South African and African-American children had mothers who were quite similar with respect to educational attainment. About 17 percent of mothers in these two countries graduated from high school; in Uganda, less than 3 percent of mothers completed high school. The same is true with respect to mothers' participation in the labor force. About two-thirds of mothers in South Africa and the United States were employed or seeking employment, but only 43 percent of Ugandan mothers had or had sought employment outside of the home.

The biggest sociodemographic differences among the three groups are reflected in marital status. Twice as many Ugandan mothers are married and living with spouses as African-American and South African mothers. For the latter two groups, only about one of three mothers was in a marital relationship. This suggests substantial differences in the living circumstances of Ugandan children and those

**Table 12.1: Demographic Profile
of African-Americans, South Africans, and Ugandans**

	African-American (N = 306)	South African (N = 625)	Ugandan (N = 165)
% Male	52.3%	49.6%	42.6%
Mother's education			
< H.S.	83.0c	83.0	97.4
Mother in labor force	63.7	65.9	42.7
Marital status			
Never married	40.4	59.7	24.1
Divorced/separated	23.9	5.2	10.7
Married	35.7	35.1	65.2
Father figure in home	49.7	60.3	71.5
Grandmother in home	19.0	32.8	—
Single adult, female-headed household	39.2	33.4	17.8
Hollingshead 2-factor social class rating			
Class I (highest)	10.5	.3	—
Class II	8.2	13.0	6.1
Class III	18.3	17.8	26.2
Class IV	26.1	31.6	14.0
Class V (lowest)	36.9	37.3	53.7
Percent living in poverty	44.1	57.1	76.4

experienced by the other two groups. This is particularly true with respect to the presence of father figures in the house. Among African-Americans, about 50 percent of the children had a father figure in the home, but 72 percent of Ugandans had father figures living with them. Also African-Americans were much less likely to have grandmothers living in their home than the South African households. The high marital rates and differences in household composition between Ugandans and the other two groups may also explain why fewer Ugandan women were in the labor market.

Table 12.2:
Living Standards of South African and Ugandan Households

	Soweto, South Africa	Kampala, Uganda
Adequacy of food supply Hunger		
Often	6.1%	22.8%
Sometimes	15.0	61.4
Never	78.9	15.8
Consumption		
Phone	56.2	4.9
Refrigerator	88.6	15.9
Car	26.1	3.9
TV	91.0	43.0
VCR	27.4	3.1
Washing machine	20.8	0.2
Microwave	9.8	1.4
Inside flush toilet	25.4	—
Type home		
Private home	88.5	81.9
Shared home	1.4	11.8
Apartment/room	7.0	4.2
Capital/wealth		
Savings	48.5	50.1
Life insurance	28.2	0.6
Pension	16.8	9.8
Own home	42.6	24.0
Community safety		
Dangerous	31.5	1.6
Safe	22.2	74.6

Substantial differences existed among the three groups in poverty levels and socioeconomic status. A substantial proportion (44 percent) of African-American children were living in poverty. However the figures for Ugandans and South Africans were even higher. Among Ugandan children, the poverty rate is excessively high. More than three of four Ugandan children lived in poverty. A similar pattern is reflected in the social class index. Approximately 18 percent of African-Americans were in the top two social classes, and 37 percent were in the lowest social class. Among South Africans, 13 percent were in the top two classes and 57 percent in the lowest class. Among Ugandans, only 6 percent were in the top two classes and 76 percent in the lowest class. Thus with respect to poverty, Ugandans are the poorest, followed by South Africans and then African-Americans.

These poverty figures are reflected in hunger rates experienced in Uganda and South Africa. (See table 12.2.) More than one in five Ugandan children experienced frequent hunger, and the overwhelming majority of Ugandan children experienced hunger at least occasionally. This is much greater than the figures for South Africa, where about 21 percent of children occasionally experienced hunger. Differences in living standards of Ugandan and South African children also occurred in the dimensions of consumption (consumer durables) and wealth (financial assets such as home ownership, savings, and insurance) as they were defined in chapter 3. Overall, South Africans had consumer durable items at much higher rates than is true for Ugandans. For example, about 87 percent of South Africans but only 16 percent of Ugandans had refrigerators. Similarly large discrepancies were also evident for telephones, televisions, washing machines, and other durable consumer items. On measures of accumulated assets, South Africans fare much better than Ugandans, and were much more likely to have the protection of life insurance and pensions and to own their homes than Ugandans.

Summary of Comparison

There are many similarities in the social history and living conditions of the three groups of children who are compared in this chapter. Although the similarities are substantial, significant differences are also noted between African-Americans and South African blacks with respect to family life, history, culture, geography, language, minority status, and experience of colonization. Important differences also exist with respect to family composition and living standards. As expected from national data, South African children in our six-year-old sample are less likely to live with a father and more likely to live with a grandmother than African-American and Ugandan children. Grandmothers resided with mother and child in one of three South African families but in only one of five African-American families. The figure for Uganda is much closer to the U.S. figure than to the South African figure. In addition, the socioeconomic status of African-American children is somewhat better than that of the South African children, which in turn is somewhat better than it is for Ugandan children. Nevertheless substantial numbers of children in all three countries live in poverty. The significantly larger household size for South Africans is due not only to the larger number of dependent children but also to the greater likelihood of multiple generations living in the same home.

Another subtle but important difference is that, unlike African-Americans, South African and Ugandan blacks constitute an overwhelming majority in their countries. Majority status may afford them a psychological advantage. In addition, South Africans and Ugandans organize themselves into strong ethnic, clan, and family groupings that forge a common identity through shared languages, traditions, and ideologies. These ethnic group identifications bring with them culturally defined views, for example, of childhood and gender roles, that are reflected in socialization goals, discipline, and expectations of unquestioning compliance with parental, familial, and male authority (Barbarin and Khomo 1997). Remarkable differences in cultural and ethnic orientations raise issues about how perspectives and values about children and socialization, parental roles, and family relations create unique circumstances that shape child development and adjustment. The combination of similar economic situations and differences in cultural contexts between urban dwellers of South Africa and the United States permits comparisons that reveal a great deal about the ways cultures mediate development of behavioral and emotional problems on the one hand, and may illuminate how they serve as a basis for resilience and coping on the other hand.

Social Risks

Violence as a Risk Factor

We have already made the case that violence is a significant issue in South African society. It appears to be equally problematic in the urban centers where the majority of African-Americans reside. However the situation is very different in Kampala, Uganda. With respect to community safety, Ugandans enjoy a considerable advantage over South Africans and African-Americans. Community danger was a much less common experience in Uganda than in South Africa. In fact, about 75 percent of Ugandans were living in communities rated as a very safe, whereas only 22 percent of South Africans were. Violence experienced by urban residents of the United States parallels that reported for the sample of BTT parents in South Africa (Richters and Martinez 1993b). One national study in the United States estimated that about 13 percent of the population sample has been exposed to minor violence and 6 percent to severe violence. In more violence-prone urban areas in the United States, about 50 percent of the residents reported exposure to at least minor incidents of violence and 32 percent to severe violence (Richters and Martinez 1993a).

In *There Are No Children Here*, Kotlewitz presents a disturbingly realistic account of the experiences of children in the urban projects of Chicago, suggesting that violence perpetrated by youth against youth has reached epidemic proportions. It has been an undeclared war without clearly defined political agendas, battle lines, objectives, or adversaries. Disputes related to drugs, gangs, and community tensions often erupt in reckless acts of violence. These eruptions have frequently led to loss of life and the terrorizing of innocent people. Like many other conflicts, they destroy the semblance of civility and give rise to a loss of predictability and optimism about the future. Random indiscriminate acts of violence have become so ubiquitous that homicide has attained the dubious status of becoming the most common cause of death for young African-American men under the age of twenty-four in major urban metropolitan areas in the United States.

Concern over this situation has led former U.S. Surgeon General Joycelyn Elders to designate homicide as the nation's number one health problem for inner-city youth. It is interesting to speculate about differences and similarities in the etiology of juvenile involvement in violence and crime. For both the United States and South Africa, speculation centers on the failure of families and communities to properly nurture youth, and youth's involvement with antisocial peers, early school termination, joblessness, the lack of opportunity, and hopelessness. In the United States, adolescent violence is also identified with loss in early childhood, a history of unremediated academic difficulties, family breakdown, and antisocial peers. In South Africa, juvenile violence seems to result from a breakdown in the contract between adults and children in which care, nurturance, and sustenance are provided in exchange for compliance and respect for adult authority. Some link the breakdown of family life to a legacy of youth involvement in resisting apartheid authority.

In almost all analyses of psychological and social problems in the United States, gender emerges as an important correlate of psychological development. Boys were more likely than girls to experience problems, particularly among young children. Accordingly gender is a robust determinant of behavior and emotional and academic functioning. Though the frequency of very serious problems is low in young children, boys seem to be at higher risk of psychosocial maladjustment in early childhood. In comparison to all other groups, boys aged five to eleven had the greatest risk of behavioral and emotional disturbances. For example, Barbarin and Soler (1993) found that young boys were more likely than young girls to act impulsively, exhibit anger, break things, be withdrawn, feel worthless, have problems concentrating, be disobedient, and have problems getting along with adults. In particular, we examine the consistency of risks related to gender, family structure, and poverty for development of behavioral emotional problems in children and adolescents from the United States and South Africa.

Cross-National Effects of Risk Factors

The extent to which factors identified as social risks in the United States have similar effects in other national contexts is unclear. For example, in the United States single parenthood is associated with relative economic disadvantage; single-parent, unmarried women tend to have lower income or access to financial resources and poorer quality of housing. Consequently growing up as a black, poor child of an unmarried mother may involve a different experience and have a different significance in South Africa than in the United States. Because of social differences in family composition and structure, this relationship between single parenthood and poverty may not be as strong for South Africans as it is for African-Americans. By living with parents and siblings, single mothers tend to provide for their children a quality of housing and security of food support that is comparable to that enjoyed by children of women with partners if not better.

In addition, the effects of economic status and family structure on psychological and educational outcomes appear to be much stronger for boys than for girls. In general, boys seem to suffer more adverse effects than girls. With respect to racial group identity, being among the majority may convey a psychological advantage in the form of self-efficacy and hope to black South Africans not enjoyed by African-Americans. Perhaps majority status confers protection against the effects of racially based social and economic inequality on emotional and behavioral problems. In light of the majority status and cultural differences, will the consequences of economic status, family structure, and gender for behavioral, emotional, and academic functioning be the same for South African blacks as it is for African-American children? The cross-national comparisons undertaken here offer the advantage of controlling for socioeconomic status and racial subordination, thus making possible a clearer test of the relationship of psychological adjustment to other social risks and cultural resources.

Index of Psychosocial Development

The Behavior Problem Index is the principal measure used to assess psychosocial development in this comparative analysis of six-year-old South African, Ugandan, and African-American children. It was adapted from 1988 CHS to the NHIS, a national survey of children's health and development sponsored by the National Center for Health Statistics. South African, Ugandan, and African-American parents rated their children's behavioral and emotional development using this common measure. The measure is made up of twenty-eight items organized into five scales that have reasonable support for their validity and reliability. The summary scales include:

Anxiety-depression	Fearfulness, sadness, mood changes, feeling unloved, and feeling worthless
Immaturity	Excessive dependence and reliance on others, particularly adults
Oppositional behavior	Strong temper, disobedience at home, arguing, and being high-strung
Hyperactivity	Restlessness, inattention, inability to inhibit or control movement
Social problems	Social withdrawal and problems in social situations; shyness

Comparative Data on Psychosocial Functioning

Figure 12.1 presents a graphical representation of the mean scores on the five scales broken down by gender within each country. National differences can be seen on all five summary scales. Overall South African children attain scores that fall between African-Americans and Ugandans. On twelve of the seventeen individual symptoms for which differences were significant, African-American children had higher prevalence rates than the South Africans (i.e., anxiety, nervousness, sadness, disobedience at home and school, temper tantrums, concentration problems, being confused, complaining about love, dependence, clinging to an adult, and crying without reason); African-American children were more often rated having difficulty with these problems. However South Africans had higher prevalence rates for individual symptoms related to social and behavioral adjustment such as breaking the rules, destroying others' possessions, bullying, not being liked by others, and demanding attention. With the exception of social problems, the African-American children scored significantly higher on the summary scales than the South African and Ugandan children. This pattern is particularly evident on the summary scale for anxiety. On this scale, gender differences are minor. In contrast, examine the scores for opposition. Again we observe a pattern where South Africans fall between African-Americans and Ugandans, and again Ugandan children are much lower on the hyperactivity scale. The only area of functioning in which the Ugandan children outscore South African children is social problems. All scores on social problems were low, but Ugandan children had more problems than the other two groups.

With regard to hyperactivity, South African children exhibit high levels of difficulty with concentration and restlessness. In this domain, they are described as having levels of restlessness and inattention that are comparable to African-American children. Gender differences on hyperactivity are also quite strong, at least among South African and African-American children. As might be expected, boys more often than girls evidenced individual symptoms of disruptive behavior such as disobeying, breaking rules, acting impulsively, destroying others' possessions, and bullying or acting with cruelty. Interestingly gender differences did not occur among Ugandan children. The differences between South African boys and girls on hyperactivity were negligible, but African-American boys were much more likely than African-American girls to evidence hyperactivity. There is a similar pattern with respect to bullying behavior. African-American boys scored significantly higher than girls. For the South African children, boys and girls were not different, but as a group, South African scores were higher than African-American scores.

A different pattern occurs with respect to feelings of worthlessness. African-American girls and South African boys are more frequently rated as often feeling worthless. Exactly the opposite patterns occur on demanding attention, where the South African girls and African-American boys rate higher than their gender counterparts. On the full scales, gender differences were found for oppositional behavior and hyperactivity. As expected, boys scored significantly higher on opposition and hyperactivity than girls. However gender differences for African-Americans are much greater than they are for South African boys and girls.

Effects of Poverty on Family Life

Overall differences between the poor and the nonpoor were found on the scales for immaturity, hyperactivity, and social problems. In each case, poor children score significantly higher on problem scales than children from more advantaged backgrounds. The difference in anxiety between the poor and nonpoor for African-Americans is greater than that between nonpoor and poor South Africans (see figure 12.2). There is a similar pattern for opposition and hyperactivity. (See figures 12.3 and 12.4) It is also important to note that family composition and structure were not significantly related to children's functioning at

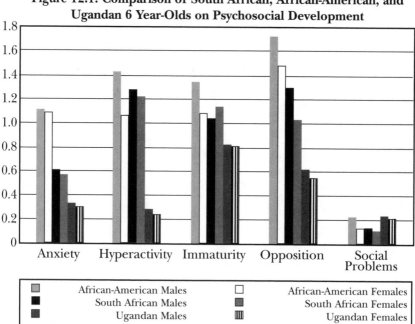

Figure 12.1: Comparison of South African, African-American, and Ugandan 6 Year-Olds on Psychosocial Development

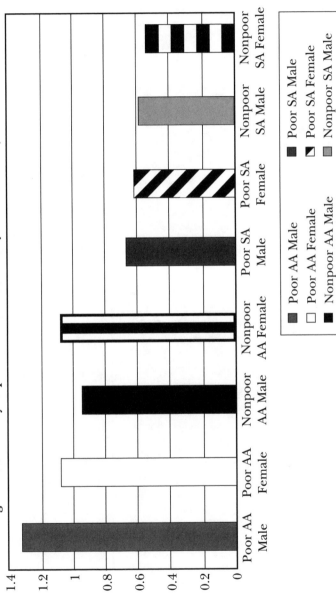

Figure 12.2: Anxiety-Depression—Mean Scores by Nation, Poverty, and Gender

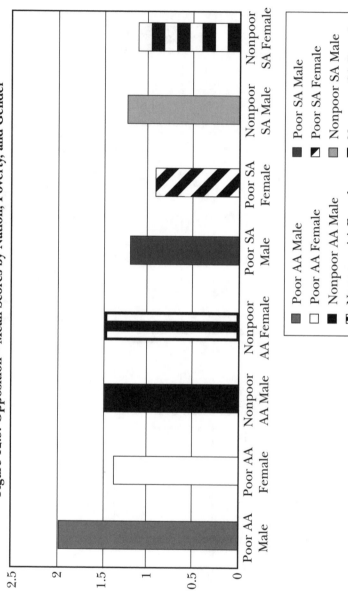

Figure 12.3: Opposition—Mean Scores by Nation, Poverty, and Gender

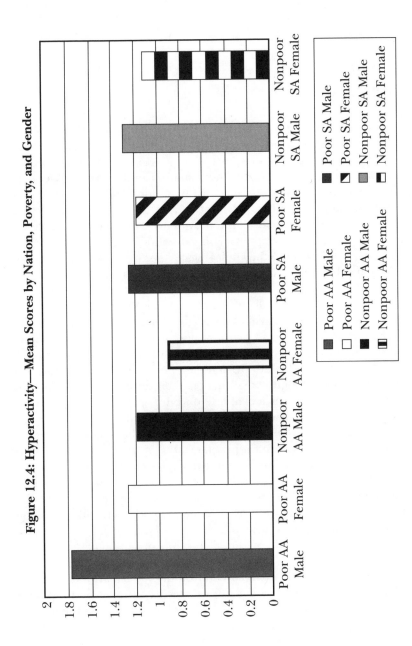

Figure 12.4: Hyperactivity—Mean Scores by Nation, Poverty, and Gender

age six. Once controls are made for poverty level, children in single-parent structures were not different from other children with respect to development. This finding contradicts the widespread belief that growing up in a single-parent, female-headed household is a risk factor.

Implications

In this research, we analyze differences between South African blacks and African-American children in psychological adjustment and evaluate the cross-cultural robustness of several social risk factors. Taken together, the results of the log linear analysis and the MANOVA analyses suggest interesting differences for behavioral and emotional problems among young African-American and South African children. Overall African-American children evidenced greater prevalence for most, though not all, symptoms and scored higher than South African children with respect to the clinical scales. For example, the symptom-level data show that African-American children scored much higher on emotional symptoms such as anxiety, nervousness, sadness, complaining about love, and dependence on adults than the South African children. In addition, African-American children scored significantly higher than South Africans on the scales for anxiety-depression, immaturity, opposition, and hyperactivity. These data lead to the conclusion that African-Americans are, in general, more troubled and more susceptible to psychological dysfunction than South Africans. African-American boys, in particular, evidenced a pattern of heightened vulnerability for behavioral and emotional difficulties.

Of all groups in the study, African-American boys have the greatest difficulty with concentration problems. It is not immediately evident why African-American boys should have more difficulty in this area than African-American girls. Plausible explanations include gender-differentiated socialization, biological vulnerability early in life that makes young males more susceptible to malnutrition, and early exposure to toxins and metals that severely compromise neurological development necessary for the acquisition of self-regulation (Pollitt and Gorman 1994).

Although African-American children display behavioral and emotional difficulties to a significantly greater extent than South African children, South Africans evidence greater vulnerability within a subset of symptoms related to antisocial and disruptive behavior. Specifically South Africans were rated much higher on symptoms such as bullying, breaking rules, destroying others' property, not being liked by others, and demanding attention. These data suggest a differential pattern of dysfunction—namely, African-American children tend to have greater vulnerability with respect to internalizing symptoms, suggestive of overregulation among African-Americans, and South African children have greater vulnerability to socially disruptive behavior, suggestive of suboptimal regulation (Hammen and Rudolf 1996).

The differences may be related to high levels of disruption in family and community life associated with political turmoil in South Africa and the wave of violent criminal activity that has risen in its place (Barbarin et al. 1998). In addition, the excesses of physical punishment at home and at school, ethnic conflict, and a steadily increasing wave of criminal violence may create in children the unmistakable impression that violence and coercion are socially acceptable and sanctioned strategies for resolving interpersonal difficulties (McKendrick and Senoamadi 1996; Swarts 1997). Moreover during the protracted period of the liberation struggle against apartheid, defiance of authority became an accepted norm, particularly among youth. This sentiment may still be commonplace in the post-apartheid transformation period. Some of those who defied apartheid and adult authority as youths are now parents of children in the BTT study. It remains to be seen whether their challenges will make them more sympathetic to or less tolerant of the adult-questioning culture they spawned.

Poverty, family structure, and gender have broad empirical support as risk factors for behavioral and emotional difficulties (Barbarin and Soler 1993). The evidence from this study is relatively consistent with the existing research on these issues. The gender differences expected on the basis of this earlier work were found for behavior and conduct problems. Predictably boys were more often rated as having conduct problems than girls. However our data do not provide support for differences between girls and boys on emotional symptoms. Poverty was also confirmed as a risk factor. Poor children scored significantly higher on immaturity, hyperactivity, and social problems than non-poor children. However family structure, as indexed by single parenthood, was unrelated to children's behavioral and emotional adjustment when poverty status was controlled. This finding is important because so many of the studies that report a relationship between single-adult households and poor development were unable to control adequately for the confounding effects of poverty. If economic status rather than single parenthood is the active ingredient, then policy efforts focused exclusively on reinforcing childbearing within the context of legal marriage are misguided at best.

Although poverty and gender are confirmed as risk factors for

African-American children, this is not the case for South African children. Poverty in particular simply does not have the same adverse effect on South African and Ugandan children as it does for African-Americans. Why are children living on the African continent protected relative to African-Americans? Some may invoke relative poverty as an explanation. In the United States, poverty may carry with it stigma and shame not associated with poverty in Uganda and South Africa. Given such a large proportion of the population who are poor, personal-blame explanations of poverty that make individuals responsible for their poverty may not be as common as they are in the United States, and children and adults may not feel as downtrodden, alienated, and hopeless about their poverty. The degree of income inequality in South Africa may lead people to resort to this explanation as they move further away in time from the era of institutionalized racism that we call apartheid. Other possible explanations include the psychological protections afforded by majority status and the stress-buffering resources of support from extended family networks.

Even though South African children grow up under conditions that are as adverse as, if not *more* adverse than, those for African-Americans, the social and cultural context may afford them some protections not available to African-American children. A different consciousness of self, founded in the perception of self as part of a majority group, may be an important resource for South African children and their families. This notion could be tested by comparisons of African-Americans and Africans to the mixed-race groups in South Africa classified under the apartheid system as Colored. If the supposition about the effect of majority status is accurate, African children would show better outcomes than both Colored and African-American. "Colored" designates a mixed-race group formed from a combination of whites, Africans, or Malay Indians. Through language, culture, and politics, many Coloreds tend to identify more with Afrikaans-speaking whites than with black Africans. In the shifting landscape of South Africa's racial politics, Colored children, situated uncomfortably between whites and Africans, occupy an uncertain position in the black-majority-ruled democracy. Absent the psychological protections afforded blacks by their majority status, the position of Coloreds is analogous to that occupied by blacks in the United States. For this reason, it could be argued that comparisons of Coloreds to African-Americans would reveal less striking differences in psychological adjustment.

Another explanation is that a more adequate foundation of social and material support is available to South African parents who are living in multigenerational households (which tend to be more of a standard than in the United States). By limiting the supply of housing, the forces of apartheid may inadvertently have contributed to a level of family interdependence that makes some form of adult nurturance and guidance more consistently available to children than is the case among African-Americans. Moreover ideological resources may be available to South African families from the resistance struggle to seek liberation from apartheid. Participation in the liberation movement may have unleashed a set of schemas that permit families to transcend the demoralizing effects of adversity by reinterpreting it as an externally imposed condition. Retention of traditional family practices in a modified form (ritualization; family, clan, or ethnic group identification) also affords protection to the developing child. In the absence of confirming empirical data, these ideas amount to little more than plausible speculations. Additional research is needed to test these speculations, and to identify and measure additional cultural resources and the ways in which they impact child development.

The comparisons of South Africans, Ugandans, and African-Americans presented here and the speculations accompanying them might serve as a guide for more focused investigations of the social and cultural contexts of psychological adjustment and development (e.g., Robertson and Kottler 1993). Advancement of knowledge about these issues may result from several lines of research. At the heart of suggestions for future research are efforts to understand how differing conceptions of childhood, socialization goals, parental roles, and family relations combine to create culturally distinctive social environments for children. Future research might examine differences in how adults understand the inner lives and emotional experiences of children. It could document how parents set standards for children's emotional regulation, behavioral compliance, and social competencies. It could explore whether different outcomes result from the tendency of adults to encourage some responses to developmental challenges children face and to sanction others. It would be important to know how much attributes thought to be valued in the United States are related to positive outcomes in the developing world. These attributes include parents' investment in their children's lives and the promotion of psychological autonomy and functional independence. This study also demonstrates that there are identifiable similarities between urban dwellers in Uganda, the United States, and South Africa with respect to socioeconomic situations, and putative differences with respect to cultural mores and worldviews. The differences reported here justify additional research on the ways cultures mediate the development of behavior and emotional problems on the one hand, and how on the other hand they serve as a basis for resilience and coping. South

African children have high rates of opposition, hyperactivity, and moderately high levels of anxiety-depression as compared to Ugandan children. However their problems are not as severe as those observed among African-American children, particularly African-American males. Partial explanation may lie in the role of familial and cultural resources. The potentially health-promoting factors such ethnic identity, family support, and spirituality may provide relative safeguards for Ugandan and South African children from the deleterious effects of adverse social conditions such as poverty.

Differences in these domains are suggested by notable differences in the South African parents' ratings of their children's behaviors, emotions, and social functioning. South African parents are less likely than African-Americans to ascribe aversive cognitive or emotional states to their children. Typically these experiences of anxiety or sadness are not readily observable, and inferences are guided by a conception of childhood that includes differentiated affect.

The views of African-American parents about the emotional experiences of their children are not clear. Therefore the connection between differential views of childhood and ratings of emotional function is speculative and must be empirically tested. Differences between African-Americans and South Africans are most pronounced on symptoms that involve observable and potentially disruptive or disturbing behavior. South African parents make markedly higher ratings than African-American parents on these items. These differences do not occur with symptoms that are cognitive, emotional, or social in nature and that are not easily observable.

South Africans, however, are no more ready to characterize their children as disobedient than are African-American parents. Differences in the behavioral ratings of South Africans and African-Americans may reflect a stricter standard held by South African parents for compliance on the part of their children. Some support for this higher expectation is available in the comparatively high frequencies of South African parents reporting that their children break rules, are impulsive, and destroy things. This interpretation is consistent with the commonly held beliefs that African parents value compliance and demand immediate and complete obedience (Liddell et al. 1994). While the former may be true, it appears that children, for the most part, meet this expectation.

Chapter 13

Between Hope and Peril: Adaptive Families, Resilient Children

The information we have gathered on Mandela's children weaves a complex story of how normal development can occur in the face of acute hardships. The costs of racism, poverty, and violence to children and their families are considerable. Yet in spite of the largely bleak account that has been given to this point, a case can be made for hope and optimism for the future of this new generation of South Africans.

First, in response to how well Mandela's children fared over the course of their first six years of life, we can say that they are doing quite well in several respects. Physically, they are growing at an expected rate as a group. Low birth weights, malnutrition, and stunting affect about one in five. Nevertheless the growth curves representing weight and height for South African children over time are almost identical to the results obtained for children in other parts of the world. Progress is being made with respect to treating preventable illness. Children are being immunized and well-protected against premature death due to infectious disease. But healthy development denotes more than just sound physical growth and freedom from illness. Equally important is psychosocial development, wherein children acquire language, social attachments, interpersonal competence, and the capacity to regulate behavior, emotions, and attention. These psychosocial dimensions of development are critical because they permit children to mature into adults who can live meaningful lives, set and achieve personal goals, develop and live by commitments, demonstrate empathic investment in others, and work in a prosocial manner that can contribute to the building of a peaceful and productive society.

With the exception of stunting due to malnutrition, most of Mandela's children are off to a promising start and seem very likely to reach those lofty developmental objectives. Most began life on an auspicious course of behavioral and emotional development and continued on that path through to age six. However there is considerable variation among children and within children over time. It is clear that children progress on different timelines or proceed along different pathways toward competence in later life. Some children seem to meander or take temporary detours before reaching an optimal level of self-regulation or fully attaining social competence. Of the children who exhibited problems early in life, more got better with time than persisted in negative behavioral or emotional functioning.

For example, at age two about half of the children in the BTT cohort are described by parents as exhibiting behavior that is difficult to manage, but by age four these problems decline. At this age, the proportion of children with behavioral problems is less than 25 percent. Perhaps the high rates of behavioral problems observed during the notorious "terrible twos" are brought under control as a consequence of intensive parental and family intervention, biological maturation, and the social benefits that accrue to children as they develop the capacity for behavioral self-regulation. On one hand, few children were described as temperamental, irritable, fussy, anxious, or emotionally distressed at age two, but over time the number increased to 50 percent and but then decreased by age six. The increased level of emotional difficulty mostly took the form of fearfulness, which is not at all surprising or alarming. To develop fears of dogs, the dark, strangers, or snakes between the ages of three and five is fairly typical. Such a pattern of increased fearfulness has long been recognized as a developmentally normal trend in children of this age across many different cultures (Jersild and Holmes 1935). These more or less universal fears in early childhood resolve without intervention for all but a small minority of children. So it was with Mandela's children. On most dimensions of behavioral and emotional functioning, Mandela's children evidence a commonly occurring pattern of behavioral and emotional adaptations. By age six, only a small proportion of children had problems of any type. When serious concerns did occur, they most often took the form of behavioral dysregulation or deficits in social competence. Disobedience was a culturally significant problem which was reported often. Among the group of children that had difficulties at age six, most had problems related to aggression and opposition. Next in frequency were children with a combination of behavioral and emotional difficulties. With respect to psychomotor development and the acquisition of biological self-regulation, the development of South African children again appears to be in line with that of other children around the world. Moreover on most dimensions of psychosocial functioning, South African children are doing as well as if not better than African-American children. Though superior to African-Americans in regard to regulation of attention and emotions, South Africans developed less well than urban Ugandan children growing up under similarly adverse social and economic conditions. Overall on both absolute and relative bases, South African children appear to be developing normally, but there is reason for some concern over selective domains such as aggression, conduct, and peer relations within subgroups of South African children.

The percentage of South African children who score in the clinical or distressed range in psychological assessments of both aggression and withdrawn behavior is higher than what has been observed in mental health prevalence studies around the world. Even though South African children compare favorably to African-American children on most dimensions of emotional functioning, this is not true for symptoms related to behavioral self-regulation. Mandela's children rate significantly higher than African-Americans with respect to symptoms such as breaking rules, destroying others' property, bullying, and not being liked by others. Furthermore on each measure of aggression used in the study, South African children were rated by parents and teachers much higher than children from the United States and Uganda. Taken together, these results justify concerns about the direction of development for a subgroup of Mandela's children. Interestingly materially propitious circumstances are no guarantee of favorable social development for the children in the BTT study.

This is clearly the case for Lindelihle Shabalala. The Shabalalas are a financially secure family who live in a relatively prosperous section of Pimville in Soweto. Sam and Essie Shabalala had been married for three years and desperately wanted a child. When they conceived Lindelihle they were ecstatic, and both of their families helped to prepare the house for the baby. Lindelihle was born in a private hospital by cesarean section because he could not be turned from a breach position, and he spent six days in the hospital with his mother before they went home. Sam's and Essie's parents were waiting to welcome them and both mother and child were cosseted in the love and care of the family. Very soon everyone became aware that Lindelihle was a strange child—unaffectionate, distant, and odd. But the family was determined to love him on his own terms and to let him be himself. He fought being fed and dressed, cried when he was put down to sleep, and later he had wild temper tantrums.

Explanations about their son's strong character wore thin as Sam and Essie began to feel sad and rejected by their firstborn boy. Essie became pregnant again and gave birth to a girl. Three-year-old Lindelihle was enraged, and Sam and Essie were afraid to leave Lindelihle alone with Girlie. Sam's job became more demanding and he frequently had to be away from home; it was a relief, really, not to have to deal with Lindelihle's temper and the children's squabbles when he came home from the office. Essie loved Girlie but became more and more reluctant to invite people to the house because Lindelihle was bound to bite one of the children or have a tantrum. Essie sent Lindelihle to a preschool but was asked to take him out because he was aggressive and hurt the other children. Essie began to beat her son, hating herself for doing something that relieved her stress but did nothing to improve Lindelihle's behavior. Sam, always away with the other salesmen, began to drink heavily, and he and Essie grew more and more apart.

Lindelihle started school but was soon in trouble with his teachers. Essie dreaded seeing the notes in her son's diary, complaining about him hitting and stealing from the other children, and she was not surprised when he was held back to repeat Grade 1. Lindelihle began to hang out with some of the older children in the street, and would frequently come home after dark. Essie was alone with her fears about her son and retreated into her loving relationship with Girlie. She was dismayed when she found Lindelihle and his friends smoking behind the house, having bought the cigarettes with money he had taken from her purse. Results on the psychological questionnaires administered for behavior at home and school confirmed these concerns. Lindelihle's scores for aggression and opposition were significantly higher than typical for Mandela's children and were very high in comparison to the norms developed for children in the United States.

Even though Lindelihle may be atypical of Mandela's children, his case raises perplexing questions about how to explain his aberrations from the expected developmental trajectory. Clearly the sources of Lindelihle's difficulty are not straightforward. Some theorists suggest that temperamental and neurodevelopmental anomalies provide the best explanation for a small minority of the children who display the significant and early problem behaviors such as Lindelihle did. However there are many more children like Lindelihle whose behavior may be firmly rooted in the social conditions in which they are raised. Throughout this book, we have suggested that community danger, violence, poverty, and racism are heavily implicated in such risks. Unfortunately these problems will not disappear on their own. To the contrary, the evidence accumulating in developmental science makes a convincing case for the enduring costs that conditions such as poverty and community danger impose on children and the peril we face as a society as a consequence of our indifference to their plight.

Poverty as a Risk Factor

Unlike Lindelihle, who comes from a financially secure home, many children who exhibit behavioral and emotional difficulties come from homes where economic hardship, interpersonal strife, and adversity have been inseparable companions. We are convinced that the psychosocial outcomes of these young children are closely linked to the adverse social conditions experienced by their families. In general, the more risks children experience, the poorer their outcomes. Poverty is unquestionably an important contributor to suboptimal development. The widespread social and financial inequities in South African society and the material disadvantage they produce for Africans and Coloreds at the low end of the economic spectrum are reflected in significant educational and employment disparities.

These population group discrepancies are also reflected in differences in physical development. Although the growth charts for South Africa's children as a group resemble the growth curves on children around the world, important population group differences in growth arise from inequities in living standards. Overall the rates of stunting presumably related to moderate but chronic malnutrition among South African children is between 20 and 25 percent. These figures are higher among Africans and Coloreds. Group differences in access to human capital (education and employment) are mirrored in the patterns of physical growth from birth to age five. African and Colored children were well below average in weight-for-height and remained so through age six. Although these two groups were close to the norm at birth, between the ages of one and four they showed a marked increase in the number of children who were malnourished and who experienced hunger.

Physical growth is not the only aspect of child development adversely affected by poverty and material disadvantage. Low living standards construed broadly in terms of deficits in either material or human capital adversely affect emotional, behavioral, and social development. Material disadvantage gauged by relatively low material consumption is associated with speech problems between ages two and four, bed-wetting from ages four to six, and clumsiness, anxiety, and behavior problems at age six. A lack of financial assets is related to bed-wetting at age five, emotional and behavioral problems from ages five to six, and clumsiness and speech problems at age six. On the whole, the effects of inadequate material or financial resources on development are not strongly evident in the first few years of life but seem to emerge later in the lives of these children. They tend to become pronounced and evident close to the time when the children are to begin school at age six. This offers a compelling reason for a national policy regarding early childhood intervention, if only for the most needy of South Africa's children.

Our emphasis on human capital was justified by our finding. Human capital appears to be just as important as material and financial assets, in regard to its impact on child development. When low human capital is indexed by low employment status of the household's principal wage earner, it is related to speech problems at age four, conduct problems from ages four through six, and problems related to motor development, attention, and school readiness at age six. In many countries, job status is highly associated with education. When mothers' education is the index of human capital, low educational levels place children at risk for behavior and speech problems from ages four through six, and for impaired motor development and physical growth as well as diminished affability, resilience, and school readiness at age six. These findings reinforce the importance of mothers' level of education to child development in critical domains related to language, motor skills, and social competence.

Mothers' education does not seem to impact the acquisition of behavioral self-regulation. Children acquire or fail to acquire behavioral self-regulation whether the mother has high or low educational attainment. Except in this domain, we have confirmed what most people have suspected all along about how important mothers and their well-being are to the quality of children's development. Related to this point, we discuss later the crucial role that mothers play in blunting the potentially negative effects of violence on children's behavioral and emotional adjustment. These conditions of low educational levels, material disadvantage, and inequality are perplexing and deeply troubling for all of South Africa. They seem intractable in spite of the nation's best intentions and efforts to redress them. In spite of that, their importance to children and families make it impossible to give up the struggle to neutralize them as forces in children's lives.

Violence as a Risk Factor

In most urban communities, poverty does not occur alone. Consequently in addition to enduring material hardship, children in poor communities are often exposed to high levels of violence. Children from poor communities tend to describe their communities as having more ambient hazards and dangers than do children from financially secure neighborhoods (Richters and Martinez 1993b). Such exposure to violence is strongly associated with an increased risk of several outcomes, the greatest impact being on behavior (i.e., aggression and opposition). Although poverty may affect development across more domains than violence, violence exposure may be more harmful to children and to society in the long run than the experience of material deprivation. In other words, the detrimental effects of violence are arguably greater in import than those stemming from the experience of material hardship and low levels of human capital.

An ethos of danger and violence in South Africa accelerates beliefs about aggression as an acceptable interpersonal tactic. Moreover the use of power-assertive strategies in managing interpersonal relationships is tolerated and becomes the norm. Like poverty, violence by itself does not dictate or completely determine child outcomes. As children growing up in poor and dangerous communities mature, their lives are more likely to be touched by substance abuse, teen pregnancy, juvenile crime, and premature termination of education than those of more advantaged children (Dryfoos 1990). Thus the sequelae of violence and poverty are hardly trivial or passing.

Violence contributed to both developmental regressions and to symptoms of post-traumatic stress disorder (PTSD). The specific impact of violence varied with its type. In general, proximal forms of violence such as family violence and direct victimization were related to developmental regressions and PTSD. For example, family violence was associated with behavior and speech problems at age four, feeding problems from age five to six, and somatic complaints and academic difficulties at age six. Political violence (a distal form of violence) was related to developmental regression. Political violence occurred in the first four years of life of the BTT cohort and was associated with fears at age two, feeding difficulties at age four, and bed-wetting at age five. By age six, children living in communities affected by political violence had higher rates of aggression, anxiety-depression, and somatic complaints. Ambient community danger was related to PTSD.

Growing up in dangerous communities with high rates of crime was also associated with increased risk of attention problems, anxiety-depression, oppositional behavior, and aggression at age six. Observations of children in violence-prone communities point to several sequelae of violence on children's social development: chronic anxiety, a low threshold for the startle response, hypervigilance, emotional withdrawal, and indifference in the face of loss.

For children, violence is aversively arousing, personally debilitating, and developmentally restrictive. This is very consistent with accounts from other parts of the world, where the effects of political conflict, ethnic strife, and criminal violence have taken their toll on children and adolescents (Cairns and Dawes 1996). Data collected around the world yield unmistakable evidence of disturbances of behavior, sleep, cognition, moral reasoning, and somatic functioning among children whose family lives and social environments are plagued by violence (Ladd and Cairns 1996). The perception of a community as threatening and dangerous is related to depression, anxiety, oppositional defiant disorder, and conduct disorder (Reinherz et al. 1993). Moreover youth who perceived their neighborhoods as more dangerous tended to have higher rates of disorders.

Varied Responses to Social Risks

Social risks such as poverty and violence have repeatedly arisen in our research as important sources of concern regarding the development of children in South Africa. They appear to have consistent relationships to the development of oppositional behavior, aggression, and conduct problems. Although these effects may be common, they are not guaranteed in every case. Moreover in reality, these effects almost always present in subtle ways. Although some effects result directly from the experience of violence or material deprivation, social risks are more likely to work their way into the lives of children in indirect ways. Perhaps poverty's effect on children's psychosocial development is indirect and due to poverty's effect on other factors such as malnutrition; exposure to environmental toxins; family stress and conflict; maternal depression; and residence in dangerous, unstable living situations in communities with substandard housing and inadequate schools (McLoyd 1998).

Social risks such as violence and poverty increase parental stress and depression, which in turn impair parental functioning. In this way, they compromise parents' capacity to guide, protect, and support their children. In addition, social risks may be associated with food insecurity and malnutrition, which can contribute to low birth weight, poor physical growth, compromised neurological development, and, ironically, obesity in late childhood and adolescence. These lead in turn to long-term deficits in physical health, motor coordination, problem-solving, attention, and academic achievement, as well as to shy, passive, and withdrawn behavior.

Children growing up in risky situations are more often exposed to traumatic events to which they have limited material and social resources to respond. This is the situation of Thandeka, one of the BTT children, and her mother, Maria, who represent examples of how combined social risks can impede healthy physical and socioemotional functioning.

Thandeka was born prematurely; she weighed a mere 1800 grams when her sixteen-year-old mother, Maria, gave birth to her in Zola Clinic. Maria became pregnant after being gang-raped on her way home from school—"jack rollered," as it is known in Soweto. Four boys had teased her for weeks that they wanted a date, and she understood the danger that posed for her. But her uncle and aunt, with whom she lived, couldn't have done much to protect her even if she had spoken to them. Neither could her teachers. Many of the Dusty Devils, the gang the boys belonged to, terrorized the school, including the principal and the teachers. Maria never told anyone about the rape. She did not want to burden her poor relatives with more troubles than they already had. She didn't realize she was pregnant until the baby began to move inside her. Her worries and sad thoughts kept her awake at night and she began to be afraid to go to school. Maria stopped eating properly and lost weight, making her pregnancy unnoticeable until the seventh month. Then her aunt noticed that Maria was ill and spoke kindly to her about the baby. But her worries didn't stop, and when the baby came she wasn't sure she wanted the child—who did it belong to? The baby, Thandeka, stayed in the hospital for three weeks, in an incubator and receiving oxygen. By the time Thandeka came home, Maria's milk had dried up and her depression had deepened. Her aunt had to see to the baby while Maria lay on her bed, deep in her own thoughts. Thandeka was a sickly child; she threw up her food and was allergic to bread and mielie meal, the family's staple foods. She grew and developed slowly, and at five months, she looked more like an old lady than a small baby. The aunt didn't like the baby much; with Maria sick, the baby became more and more of a burden. She was always sick, and visits to the hospital cost so much money; there was so little to spare. One day, Maria didn't come home. Her uncle and aunt searched frantically, asking all the neighbors if they had seen Maria. Two weeks later, they received a message that she had left home with a "sugar daddy," an older man who worked in the mine. Maria's aunt felt she couldn't go on looking after Thandeka and, when she was four years old, sent the small girl to live with her cousin on a farm outside Johannesburg. Under the circumstances, Thandeka did not endear herself to her family. She was a disobedient and difficult child. Her cousin beat her often, sometimes locking her outside the house for the night to punish her and get her to understand that she must help around the house and not be a burden. There seemed little point in sending Thandeka to school; she was small, sickly, and slow. Instead she was kept at home to clean, fetch the water, and tend the stove. After three years, the cousin's family had to move and they sent Thandeka to live with friends of theirs.

At that point, BTT lost contact with the child. We are left to speculate about how her life would unfold from here. Although the hope that her life will take a turn for the better is slim, there is a possibility that the family she was sent to live with might provide a more auspicious and supportive setting that will reverse the current course of her development.

In spite of poverty, violence, and other social risks, families can make important differences to children's outcomes. Family life has the potential for moderating the adverse consequences social risks often pose to development. Although we would predict that children growing up in circumstances of community violence and extreme poverty would likely exhibit impaired development, effectively functioning families with strong cohesive relationships and demonstrating effective task performance can alter the negative outcomes that we have otherwise come to expect.

Variations in Impairment Are a Source of Hope

The evidence presented here leaves little room for doubt that the consequences of social risks for South African children are real and deleterious. Poverty and violence indisputably exercise powerful influences in the lives of Mandela's children, which occur at practical, instrumental, and symbolic levels. Because of the incontrovertible impact of social risks on children, it may be tempting to conclude that all poor children or all children who are exposed to violence are destined for a life filled with emotional and conduct problems. To the contrary, development is very dynamic and fluid, and these effects are neither absolute nor inevitable. Wide variations continue to be found for both the magnitude of the risks and the effects they produce in the lives of children. Some children and families have been more negatively affected than others by violence and hardship. Moreover, the effects of social risks on development are small.

Distracted by an extensive documentation of the poor outcomes linked to social ills that seem ubiquitous in South Africa, it may be easy to miss the ray of hope about the future of South African children. Children exposed to great hardship and danger do not always go on to a life of impaired development and maladaptive functioning. Social risk factors do not account fully for what is happening to children over time. To the contrary, the wide variation in developmental outcomes hints that children are adaptive and susceptible to the influence of other more positive conditions and resources that may be at work in their families and communities, which help some children to exhibit no adverse consequences, and in many cases to thrive in spite of the risks. It is important to consider what else is going on to account for the different outcomes observed in the development of Mandela's children. "Like research conducted on child abuse, poverty, and other forms of adversity, dangerous and violent conditions offer important lessons about subjects such as risk and resilience and can teach us a great deal about psychological mechanisms such as stress, coping, and support" (Ladd and Cairns 1996:17).

Resilient Children

Differences in outcomes among children who encounter similar social risks may related to the individual, social, and emotional resources available to children and the ways that these resources are deployed. Moreover several qualities have been attributed to resilient children that also may account for the improved outlook enjoyed by some children. These personal characteristics or attributes include: optimism, humor, personal reflectiveness, self-efficacy, easy temperament, self-esteem, planfulness, affability, and a high level of cognitive skills (Garmezy 1991). These abilities equip many children to make adaptive, personal responses to challenges and to access the environmental resources that facilitate healthy and normal development (Masten 1989). Other attributes suggestive of resilience or that promote resilience include doing endearing things for others, a willingness to try new things, the ability to focus on a task and to stick with it even when it becomes difficult, and to derive pleasure from accomplishments.

Resilient Families

But children are rarely able to withstand the negative effects of social risks on their own. Resilience is not simply a function of the individual attributes and skills of children. Although much of the theoretical and empirical work on resilience has tended to view it as a quality of the individual, resilience is also a quality of the social context in which the child develops. Accordingly a combination of the child's individual or personal resilience and environmental protective factors in the family and community moderate the relationship between adversity and adjustment (Werner 1990; Zeitlin et al. 1990). Children's abilities to function under adverse conditions are related to a variety of social resources and experiences provided by their families. What aspects of families help children avoid problems, develop normally, make the most of their potential, and lead fulfilling lives? What are the qualities and attributes of resilience-promoting families? Observations made among Mandela's children confirm what researchers around the world report about children doing well in spite of adverse circumstances. Part of the answer to these questions is evident in one of the BTT families, who would definitely qualify as a prime example of a resilient family, as described below.

Hlengiwe was the sixth and last child born to this poor family. Essop and Mavis earned little but used what they had well. Although they had lost two children to illness in their early months, their other children were thriving. Sipho, the eldest, was good at school, and they were hopeful that he might go into the church. The Catholic priests were kind to him and he was a serious boy. The three girls (Nomsa, Pelele and Hlengiwe) were good children, and they all did what they could to assist their mother in the house.

Even the youngest, Hlengiwe, who was only four years old, helped her mother. She was affable, obedient, and helpful, and all the family loved her. Mavis took a long time to recover from the birth and bled for many months. Without her salary from domestic service, the family was hard pressed, and many a night they had nothing more than hot tea for supper. Essop took on weekend gardening to earn a little extra, so he was hardly ever at home. But sometimes Sipho went to work in the gardens with his father and tried to take on the heaviest work, knowing his father was getting old and that he was tired from having too little rest. Mavis's health deteriorated, and the doctors told them she had cancer of the womb. Her illness meant she was at home with Hlengiwe all through the child's early years. Mavis realized how much she had missed of the childhood of her other children, having gone back to work when they were barely three months old. Now she had Hlengiwe, and although she was tired and often in pain, the little girl brought her great joy. Mavis spent all her spare time with Hlengiwe, telling her stories and showing her pictures from the newspapers. The little girl was a loving companion to her mother. Mavis's health deteriorated and soon she was so ill that she became bedridden. The older girls took on the household responsibilities and Hlengiwe's care. Her oldest sister, Nomsa, left school even though she was only sixteen and took a job as a cleaner at the local café to help bring in some money to the household. Mavis died and the family mourned her passing. They revered her memory and missed her desperately every day. But Nomsa assumed Mavis's role and took Hlengiwe to her first day at school; she sat in the front row at the end of the year when Hlengiwe received a prize for good and consistent performance, and she watched with pride on Saturdays as Hlengiwe's team won the netball matches. There would be time for Nomsa to have her own children, but for now, she was happy to do her mother's duties and shepherd Hlengiwe through the important first few years of school.

Predicting the impact of social risks on children is not possible without understanding how families reorganize themselves, as well as the sources of resilience that enable many families to adapt successfully. Several attributes of resilience-promoting families are suggested by the systems model of family functioning presented earlier in this book (Richters and Martinez 1993a). Figure 13.1 specifically depicts how features of family life such as satisfying supportive relationships, low conflict, child socialization, and spiritual and cultural resources mediate the relationships between stress and developmental outcomes (Barbarin 1993, 1994). The model asserts that the direct effects of stresses such as urbanization, poverty, and violence on emotional, behavioral, and academic development are mediated by certain familial, cultural, social, and individual resources. The model proposes that the negative consequences of exposure to social risks such as violence can be moderated by family composition, effectiveness of task performance related to socialization, and care of children. This model is strongly consistent with the data from the BTT study.

Family Composition and Structure

The structure and composition of a family may help determine whether it is resilience-promoting. Family structure, its stability, and the effectiveness of its functioning mediate between risk and children's developmental outcomes. The central active feature of family composition in promoting resilience in children appears to be the number of adults per child who have a stable, long-term commitment to the child and who are involved directly or indirectly in contributing to the physical welfare and emotional nurturance of the children. This high ratio of nurturing adults to children seems to be particularly important in providing protection against the risk of behavior or conduct problems and the promotion of social competencies.

Children growing up in extended family structures are less likely to exhibit temper tantrums, particularly in comparison to children in single-adult households. Moreover the presence of a partner or spouse and a grandmother in the home is associated with better developmental outcomes for children and a lower risk of adverse social outcomes. When a mother has a partner living with her and assisting in

Figure 13.1: Family Model Adverse Environments and Psychosocial Development of South African Children

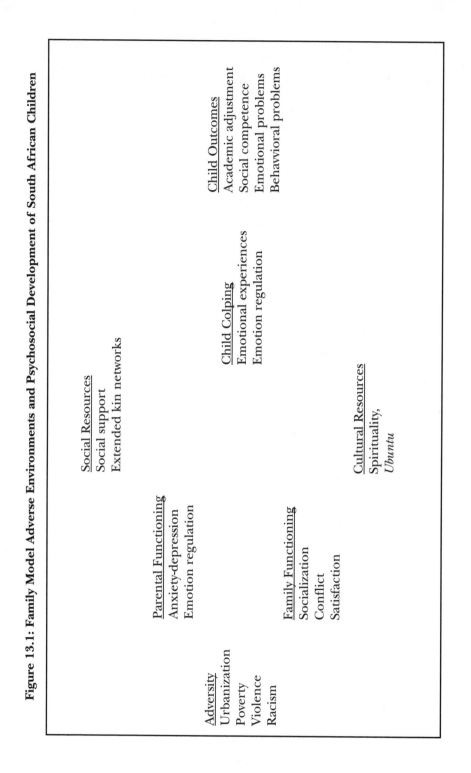

Social Resources
Social support
Extended kin networks

<u>Child Outcomes</u>
Academic adjustment
Social competence
Emotional problems
Behavioral problems

<u>Child Colping</u>
Emotional experiences
Emotion regulation

<u>Parental Functioning</u>
Anxiety-depression
Emotion regulation

<u>Cultural Resources</u>
Spirituality,
Ubuntu

<u>Family Functioning</u>
Socialization
Conflict
Satisfaction

<u>Adversity</u>
Urbanization
Poverty
Violence
Racism

raising a child, the child is less likely to have problems related to excessive crying, fighting, and clumsiness. When the mother is married to that partner, children are less likely to exhibit fears and oppositional behavior. The presence of a grandmother in the household seems to afford a degree of protection against the risk of aggression and language problems, and at the same time, promotes resilience in children. Clearly family structure and household composition contribute to child resilience.

Quality of Family Relationships

Resilience-promoting families have supportive processes and relationships in place that are especially important for young children, including interpersonal experiences with adults that build their self-esteem, reinforce their trust in others, and strengthen their hope and optimism about the future (Grotberg 1995). These outcomes are most likely achieved because the families express unconditional love, show appreciation and praise, and provide emotional support and role models. Resilience-promoting families also have at least one member to whom the child can talk about problems and feelings; they can be counted on when needed and they convey to the child a transcendental belief in a power greater than self.

Such supportive and satisfying family relationships are arguably the most important resource to children and serve as the principal guardian against the negative effects of adverse conditions, as well as the primary basis for the development of personal problem-solving, coping, and resilience. The importance of warmth, cohesion, and authoritative discipline have received consistent support in the research literature. Among BTT families, a strong, satisfying family life is associated with a decreased likelihood of behavioral and emotional problems and with higher levels of affability and resilience. For example, family satisfaction is inversely related to attention problems and somatic complaints, and directly associated with sound physical growth. High levels of cohesion within the family are related to enhanced social competence. In contrast, family conflict is a risk factor for behavior problems and is associated with lower levels of competence. Family violence is directly correlated with somatic complaints and inversely correlated with academic motivation.

A propitious family environment may be especially important in moderating the risk of negative sequelae in children's lives, but it is not the only source of protection. Because children live within a network of more salubrious environments such as home, extended family, the school, church, and peer groups, children may be insulated from the full impact of poverty, violence, and racism.

Good relationships outside of the family are also important to resilience-promoting families. Social support in the extended family, neighborhood, schools, and churches is reported to reduce emotional strain on parents and help to decrease parental reliance on punitive, coercive, and inconsistent parenting behaviors (Spencer 1996). These social networks have an indirect effect on the economically disadvantaged child's socioemotional development. Typically these networks involve mutual support in which a family is embedded in a network of social relationships with extended family and community. Within this network, members share and receive according to need and ability. When one member experiences significant need, hunger, sadness at the loss of a loved one, or economic loss, other members of the familial or community network come to their aid by sharing what they have or offering emotional comfort. These networks may be infused and strengthened by a set of cultural beliefs, values reflected in a strong ethnic identity, shared rituals, family traditions, religious ideologies and the spirit of *Ubuntu,* which may facilitate co-operation and mutual responsibility. Families can be poor materially and suffer great hardship, but this hardship may strengthen their resolve to support one another through the hard times. A family that learns to function effectively is able to deal with conflict in nonviolent means and to do the best it can with the resources available to it.

Sociocultural resources that contribute to minimizing adversity's impact on children include a strong ethnic group, clan, or family affiliation, spirituality, mutual support or *Ubuntu,* and emotionally strong family bonds. Effective functioning among families living in situations of high social stress takes the form of providing efficiently for the nutritional and educational needs of children and endowing them with a perspective on life that helps them to interpret the circumstances in ways that keep them from becoming self-blaming or from using their situation as an excuse for inaction. By working together cohesively, they derive strength from one another. Such conditions may contribute to children's efforts to cope successfully with hardship and distress. These resources contribute to individual and familial resilience and positive adjustment under adverse circumstances. They result in a more satisfying family life with low conflict and high emotional support. This favorable social climate may also extend outward to the community in which shared values and mutual obligation lead members to care for and protect one another. Access to such resources differs, and it is this differential access that is claimed here as the explanation for why aversive conditions associated with material hardship, violence, and urbanization lead to maladjustment in some but not in all children.

Family Socialization and Care of Children as a Source of Resilience

Some families develop an ability to cope with the stress of daily hassles by devising strategies for feeding children, keeping them safe, and making use of public resources and facilities. Community resources such as public facilities, recreation centers, and health clinics differ from community to community. Other families may have an increased socioemotional capacity to take setbacks in stride or maintain optimism, hope, determination, and a degree of self-efficacy, so that they avoid the negative sequelae of hardships and strain. These families are able to maintain the sense of equanimity and avoid the harshness and punitiveness that sometimes characterize the parent-child and spousal relationships of families that experience extreme economic hardship.

Other cultural factors may contribute, but we lack sufficient data on which to base speculations. It is conceivable that the retention in a modified form of more traditional family life, rituals, and clan/tribal identity afford protection to the developing child because they connect the child and family to a network of material, social, and psychological support. When families are able to handle the task of providing adequate nutrition, fewer emotional problems and higher levels of social competence develop in the children. In these families, children are more affable and resilient.

An important cultural resource in many families is spirituality. However its role in development is not a direct one. Specifically family religiosity and support can be construed as coping resources related to favorable adjustment in the forms of high academic motivation and low levels of attention problems. If spirituality has a favorable effect on child development, it is most likely an indirect rather than a direct effect. Religious involvement aids in the making of meaning. Individual spirituality, practices, rituals, and ceremonies surrounding birth, illness, and death give meaning to important transitions in life. Spirituality offers an ideology for dealing with loss and grief; belief about good and evil, sin and virtues; and one's relationship with God. It may affect child development through its influence on family functioning.

Spirituality is associated with high levels of cohesion and satisfaction in family life and low levels of conflict. In supporting this favorable climate within the family, spirituality contributes to the positive and healthy development of children. It is inversely related to problems of attention and opposition and positively correlated with academic motivation.

Socializing Values and Drawing upon Cultural Resources

The overarching goal of child socialization is to equip children with a set of values and skills to function well and cope with life challenges. For example, children living in poverty and surrounded by violence are challenged to master their fears, focus their attention, and marshal their cognitive resources to support academic achievement. For children growing up in poor and dangerous communities, effective emotional regulation is essential for handling difficult circumstances, to deal with fears, to manage frustration and nurture an achievement orientation. Parental socialization may also play a role in avoiding or slowing adversity's effects on children by providing a framework for understanding these pressures and helping children to cope.

Importance of Parents to the Promotion of Child Resilience

By considering the positive role of family and, to an extent, the community, we can conclude that the situation is far from hopeless even for children living in the most disadvantaged and dangerous of settings. The term "parents" is used very broadly here to refer to adults with primary responsibility for the care and socialization of young children for most or all of their days. It includes mothers, fathers, grandparents, relatives, and friends and caretakers of all kinds. It is clear that parents' ability, particularly mothers, to manage the distress related to violence and other life circumstances is critical to children's capacity to resist the negative effects of community violence. When parents cope well, they seem to provide an antidote to the effects of community violence on children.

Our data suggest that the role of the mother is particularly important. Within the family, biological mothers occupy the most significant role with respect to the protection of the child. Although mothers themselves are not immune to the strains that result from poverty and violence, they are able to lower the effects of these risks on their children to the extent that they successfully manage the stress themselves. When mothers reported low distress, the relationships of violence to child opposition and academic and attention problems were attenuated. Maternal coping contributes to children's ability to overcome the potentially adverse effects of violence. Parental optimism and perceptions of self as capable of coping successfully with life's problems are also important to outcomes such as children's social and academic functioning (Barbarin, Whitten, Bond, and Conner-Warren 1999). In addition, religiosity and a supportive family life may serve indirectly as protective factors for children insofar as they enhance maternal coping.

Parental emotional and motivational states are at the heart of responsive, developmentally sensitive behavior toward young children (Dix 1991; Bradley and Caldwell 1995; Richter 1993). According to this model, the level of interest, adaptability, and involvement required of an adult to make and maintain appropriate behavioral adjustments to young children's needs are driven by motivational and emotional factors based on beneficence and caring for the child, a desire to evoke positive responses from the child, and a long-term commitment to the child's well-being. Put simply, optimal adult-child interactions and relationships are based on the caregiver's love, care, and responsibility for the child, their desire to bring pleasure to the child, and their efforts to make things turn out well for the child in the future.

These regulating features of optimal caregiving have been shown to be particularly vulnerable to stress and hardship. Parental preoccupation, distress, emotional withdrawal, and depression affect children through a number of routes—inattentiveness to the child's state of mind and behavior, perception of the child in a negative light, passive and inappropriate responses to the child's initiatives, inconsistency, and punitiveness. A consciousness on the parents' parts of the importance of their behavior to children's development, as well as a belief in their capacity to fulfill their children's physical and emotional needs, has been found in several studies to be the point around which optimal child care takes place (Tinsley and Holtgrave 1989). These parental convictions entail a sense of pride in themselves and a belief in the meaningfulness of their lives and those of their children—sentiments that are, in turn, a reflection of the order and support of the wider social relationships in which caregivers are nested.

Good parenting is as much about what parents feel about themselves and their young children as about how much they know about child development. Interventions that improve support networks for caregivers, reduce their stresses, and endorse their importance in young children's lives are important to creating the necessary caring framework for effective parenting.

Maternal education is usually important to most forms of development, but it stands out as a crucial determinant of social competence, affability, and resilience in children, and it appears to have a stronger, more consistent influence than living standards. The provision of resources that involve the development of the talents all of caretakers, particularly mothers, will go long way in improving developmental outcomes for children. Accordingly interventions undertaken to support mothers in dealing with material hardship and violence will pay dividends in terms of increasing the child's capacity to stay the course of healthy development.

Given these findings, it is fortuitous that living in a family unit in which the mother was present was an almost universal experience for children enrolled in BTT. It was much less common for children to live with their biological fathers than with their mothers. When they were present, fathers contributed significantly to the healthy development of children. In addition to biological parents, the presence in the family of several other persons appears to impact the child's development. Cohabiting partners and grandmothers exert positive influences on children and may contribute to their success at coping and in this way tend to minimize the impact of the absence of the biological father.

Data from this study confirmed the relationship of violence to maternal adjustment and child development. Violence was related to higher levels of distress in mothers and greater impairment of emotional and behavioral regulation than for those living in neighborhoods considered safe and in households that exhibited no interpersonal violence. The data show clearly that the experience of violence does not have to be direct and proximal to have a negative effect on children's development.

The lessons to be drawn from this research are many. The principal one is that to live in an environment in which one is surrounded by violence is detrimental for everyone, but more so for children. The developing child has few devices with which to protect herself. However in the end, the level of distress and impairment exhibited by children in suboptimal environments is a function not only of the prevalence of hardship and risk but also of the availability to the child of family support and personal coping resources adequate to maintain a sense of equilibrium in the face of life disruption, personal loss, and physical harm.

The lesson about family adaptation to adversity is clear. Strong, effectively functioning families can make a big difference in the lives of children. Adaptive families produce resilient children. Obviously no family can totally ensure its children protection against hardship, but it can help them cope with difficulties through support and encouragement. It can guide them along a course toward healthy development by enhancing their capacity to deal effectively with hardship, by providing transcendental meaning to suffering, shaping prosocial values, and promoting self-acceptance and an active mastery-oriented and problem-solving stance toward life challenges. By what the family does and omits doing, by what it says and leaves unsaid, families can help children avoid the detrimental consequences of social adversity, particularly during the vulnerable period of their early development. Although the welfare of South African children is under threat from racism, poverty, and violence, most of Mandela's children are growing up in supportive family and community environments that can afford them some protection against these risks. By creating a climate of hope, caring, support, and encouragement, the family can blunt the sharp edges of racism, inequality, and community violence that can cut away and destroy the human spirit. It is no wonder that the family is widely regarded as the crucible of child development in South Africa.

A prominent New York psychiatrist once noted that when a list is made of the most heroic people of the twentieth century, at the top should come black mothers for their unrecognized courage, unseen selflessness, and underappreciated competence in raising children, often alone in the face of poverty and racism. Their accomplishments are all the more remarkable because they carry out this enormous responsibility with so few resources and so little support. At first glance this has been book about development, about children growing up in an era of promise who must still confront momentous odds of poverty, racism, and violence that imperil the promise of healthy development. But in a larger sense, this is more than a story about how children respond to social risks and the effects that accrue to them. In the background and in between the pages of the stories of children's lives and struggles are mothers, caretakers, and families, most of whom are heroic figures who carry out the important task of nurturing the development of their children, simply, generously, and with little notice. They do the many little things that make such a big difference over the long run in children's lives. Each day, many are called upon to make personal sacrifices for their children. Sometimes this takes the form of going hungry so that the children can fill themselves with the little food available in the home. In other cases, it may be walking while a child takes a bus from a clinic appointment because there is not enough money for two to ride. These are just small examples of many unseen acts of generosity that are commonplace for so many of the mothers about whose children we write in this book. They deserve much credit for their work and are the principal reason we can be hopeful for the future of their children. In the next and final chapter, we review the steps that South Africa has undertaken to support the efforts of families to care for and promote resilience in their children.

Chapter 14

Addressing the Needs of Children

Public Policy Innovations in South Africa

The development of Mandela's children has occurred within a miraculous period of sweeping political reform and social change. Urbanization, the modernization of family life, the demise of apartheid, and the transfer of political power to the black majority have coalesced in a stunning way within the brief life span of these young children. It is fair to say that these forces have altered the social landscape so fundamentally that it is impossible to predict fully at this time the consequences they will have in the lives of these children and of generations to come.

The broad social and political transformations under way in South Africa provide a reasonable, if uncertain, basis for optimism about the long-term prospects for South African children. Some of the changes will unquestionably have positive effects. For many children they will open up life aspirations and possibilities previously unimaginable. The lives not only of these children but also of most South Africans will be better in the future if they are not so already.

But the benefits of these social transformations have not reached all children, and the life prospects are not uniformly positive for all whose lives have been touched by these changes. Widespread unemployment, economic inequality, and pervasive material hardship remain as virulent as ever. In addition, the specter of the AIDS epidemic (which currently infects one of five adults and is projected to rise higher) dims the hopeful outlook for many families. The full force of the AIDS epidemic is going to be felt most keenly by Mandela's children through its erosion of the networks of care on which young children depend.

Social transformations have so profoundly altered family life that serious questions are raised about families' abilities to fulfill their socially mandated obligations to care for and socialize dependent children. The resulting strain on family life has been immense and has contributed to structural weaknesses and impaired relationships within families, and families' increased inability to function effectively. At no other time in recent history has the intentional abuse of children and their preventable neglect been so conspicuous.

Other ominous signs also give reason for alarm at a societal level. There have been numerous disappointments and setbacks in the implementation of social policies designed to create an environment more hospitable for children. The peace and tranquillity expected as an aftermath of political change have been elusive as political violence has given way to economically motivated violence and crime. Some fault Apartheid, with its distortions of law and consequent erosion of the moral order, for the prevalence of violence among South Africans. Others blame a longer-standing pattern of violence and ethnic conflict, its roots going back to the arrival of Europeans if not earlier.

No matter who is at fault, the consequences are detrimental for children. The natural creativity and spontaneity of children may be subdued and restrained by pervasive apprehension over personal safety in the community and even in the home. Although the level of violence may not be of the magnitude implied in media portrayals, it is still a credible threat generating a sense of uneasiness that can undermine the quality of life for many South African citizens.

In the wake of such consequential social transformation, questions arise about how best to minimize the adverse consequences of these social forces and create conditions that can foster healthy development. This is a matter of considerable debate and will undoubtedly give rise to a variety of proposals, some simplistic and some thoughtful. The answers to those questions must arise from a consideration of what children need for proper development and what they have a right to expect from society. It seems fitting to conclude with a discussion of efforts already undertaken by South Africa on behalf of its children, particularly those designed to address some of the troubling issues raised in this book. Has South Africa responded adequately in providing a suitable environment for the development of children and addressing the pressing needs of young children and their families?

Developmental Needs and the Rights of Children

Conclusions about the adequacy of a national response to children's needs must inevitably rest on some standards as a basis of judgment. The most widely accepted standard of a nation's responsibility for its children is codified within the United Nations Conventions on the Rights of the Child (UN General Assemply, Nov. 1989). These conventions articulate commonly agreed-upon developmental needs and rights that should be accorded to young children and adolescents. The conventions' fifty-two articles establish universal principles on which almost all of the world's nations join hands in agreement. These include freedom of expression, thought, conscience, assembly, religion, and, most fundamentally, the right to an identity which includes a name, culture, language, nationality, and life itself. The conventions also identify the social conditions essential to child health and development. Among these conditions are physical safety and a nurturing family that has resources to provide health care, proper nutrition, and adequate education for its children. Regarding family life, children have the right to know and be cared for by parents, protection against discrimination, and safety from environments that endanger their health and well-being.

In 1993 South Africa signed, and in 1995 it ratified the Conventions on the Rights of the Child. In 1996 it launched the National Programme of Action for Children in South Africa (NPA), which is overseen by a cabinet-appointed Interministerial Steering Committee, and gives priority to nutrition, child and maternal health, water and sanitation, early childhood development and basic education, social welfare development, leisure and cultural activities, and child protection measures. In the constitution, adopted in 1996, a bill of rights was included that guarantees children four unrestricted categorical rights: to survival, to development, to protection, and to participation. In many ways, the nation's ratifying of the UN Conventions on the Rights of the Child and adopting constitutional guarantees for children's rights spells out the ideals to which it aspires and the standards by which it agrees to judge its performance.

Policy Developments in South Africa

Much remains to be done by way of implementing policies and legislation to make the aspirations of the constitution and the UN conventions a reality in South Africa. Policy initiatives must take steps to minimize the risks of poverty, violence, and racism and to promote the familial, community, and cultural resources needed to give more children healthy life outcomes. Early development offers a window of opportunity to intervene to reduce, eliminate, or prevent the undesirable effects on development of children exposed to poverty and violence. While it is true that good outcomes can be guaranteed to no one, it is feasible to increase the odds by better understanding the conditions and factors that facilitate and promote the favorable development of children. Thoughtful and developmentally sensitive social policy and community-level intervention can improve the situation of children who are growing up under conditions that are not optimal for development.

Many initiatives are now under way in South Africa that promise significant progress toward building a society more responsive to the needs of children. Findings from the BTT research confirm what many have already suspected: There is no way to get around the importance of adequate material resources for the well-being of children. The improvement of living standards to provide what children need to sustain life and promote development must be assigned the highest priority if the downward trajectories noted in the development of the poorest children are to be reversed. The implications of these findings are quite clear. If we seek to improve the development of children, an investment must be made in increasing the living standards of children and their families, particularly with respect to nutrition and shelter.

New Welfare Policy to Moderate Child Poverty through Support to Families

Another important effort by the government relates to the reduction of childhood poverty by offering financial support to families to help them care for children. Strong families are essential for healthy children; social risks undermine family life. The government has a role in supporting families weakened by poverty and violence. When strong and supported, the family unit can be a powerful ally in the quest to reduce the effects of adversity on children. Social policy should first and foremost do what it can to strengthen families and channel through families its efforts to improve the conditions for children. These notions provide part of the underlying rationale for the new welfare policy that supports the families in providing the basic minimal needs of their children.

Providing direct monetary grants to families is the centerpiece of that policy. Until 1997, social welfare grants were provided to mothers with children who had special needs as a result of disability or lack of financial support (called the state maintenance grant). An enormous bureaucracy was required to administer this program, described even by its advocates as cumbersome. The grant recipients were mainly white and Colored urban families who could negotiate their way through the application requirements with the assistance of a social work service. Under the new policy of child support (called the Child Support Grant Program), all children under the age of seven years qualify for a flat-rate grant of R100 a month, regardless of the number of children in a household. This policy, introduced in April 1998, will be phased in over five years and should become fully operational by the year 2003.

Child Hunger

It is heartening to note that one of the very first initiatives taken by the newly elected African National Congress (ANC) government was directed at alleviating childhood hunger. A decision was taken to funnel this effort locally through schools. The reasoning behind the program was that children could not take the best advantage of educational opportunities if they came to school hungry. A school feeding program was introduced as a Lead Presidential Program in 1994 as part of the Reconstruction and Development Plan to counter hunger among children and to contribute to the culture of learning through improved educational outcomes and parent-school partnerships. Schools are identified for government-funded meals implemented through the provinces, based on socioeconomic indices of school districts. Districts with the highest levels of poverty were targeted to receive the program first. Although there is some flexibility by province and district, most schools have opted for a standard breakfast consisting of a peanut butter sandwich and a banana (or its equivalent), calculated at a standard caloric and protein rate that is about 30 percent of daily requirements. About three million children are reached by the program despite widespread corruption, which has occurred largely because provincial control has been retained over finances when the intention was to give this control and discretion to parent-teacher committees.

Health Care

Along with the school feeding program, a program for Free Maternal and Child Health was instituted as a Lead Presidential Program by Mandela in 1994 (Jacobs and McCoy 1997). This program was designed to increase access to medical services to the most vulnerable and needy population—young children and pregnant women. The emphasis was on primary health and preventive care. A system of publicly funded clinics already existed to serve the poor. Although the fees for services provided through these clinics were not high, they still constituted a barrier to services for the poorest of families. This program provides free antenatal services and follow-up care for mothers and children up to and including age five. Through these local clinics, mothers and children could receive basic primary health care without the worry of whether they have the money to pay for it. Unfortunately, insufficient attention is being given to the inclusion of mental health services along with physical health. This omission is not due to a lack of good models for mental health care but for lack of resources (Pillay and Lockhat 1997).

Education

The South African Schools Act (1996) makes schooling compulsory for all children. As a consequence of this new program, all children must attend school through at least the equivalent of Grade 7 in primary school. Publicly financed schools may charge a basic fee of R10 a year. However many schools do not have adequate facilities with electricity and running water, fully trained staff, or sufficient textbooks. For these basic needs, they rely on an education department whose budget is almost totally absorbed by staff costs, leaving few resources for capital improvements, repairs, equipment, or supplies. As a consequence, many publicly financed schools are adopting procedures of the old Model C schools and charging additional fees as set by parent-teacher committees. Currently public schools are charging additional fees between R20 and R500 a month. Some are charging more. With these funds, facilities are purchased, making some state schools as well-equipped as some private schools, but introducing an educational system that continues past inequities in which children of the very poor are disadvantaged.

In addition, policies have been adopted to reduce the number of children who enter and subsequently fail the first few years of school because they are not yet physically mature enough to withstand the rigors of a full day of school. From 2000, the Department of Education has passed legislation that no child will enter the formal education system in Grade 1 younger than seven years of age in the year in which they start school.

Data from BTT showed for the first time the surprisingly early age at which many children were starting school. For example, 1 percent of BTT children entered school in January several months before they turned four, and 11 percent entered the following year before they turned five. Mothers sent children to school early—sometimes because they were big, and sometimes by falsifying their birthdates—because child care is cheaper at school. Most of these early-entry children were so underage that they could not stay awake for the full school morning and fell asleep in the classroom. As part of the new policy, children will be eligible at age six for a preschool year much like kindergarten in U.S. school systems. Additional resources will also be provided for teacher training and to improve the physical facilities of schools.

Early Child Development

Much preventive work needs to be done to anticipate and minimize the impact of social risks on young children. The value of early childhood programs as effective prevention is now well established. The analyses done by the World Bank and reviews of early childhood intervention programs indicate that investments at the earliest ages in people's lives support a "human capital" approach to development (Dickens et al. 1997; McCall 1993; Myers 1995). In good programs, children grow better and improve cognitively; they become more alert, sociable, curious, and prepared for school; they get along better with their parents; and, in the longer term, they repeat grades less frequently, stay in school longer, and achieve more. "Early childhood programs have been shown to enhance school readiness, increase the efficacy of investments in primary schools and human capital formation, foster beneficial social behaviour and thereby lessen social welfare costs, and promote community development" (Young 1996:v). Many parents whose children are enrolled in high-quality programs cope better with their children at home and get more involved in their children's learning and academic activities. Providing safe child care also allows women the chance to continue their education, learn new skills, and enter and rise in the workforce, thereby addressing the intersecting needs of women and children.

The South African government's white paper on early child development is an important first step in the articulation of a national policy on early development. Fittingly South Africa has stepped up its own efforts in this arena and increased its expenditure. Publication of the Interim Policy for Early Childhood Development (ECD; 1997) has laid out the Department of Education's vision for ECD and its policy with respect to provision, funding, curriculum, accreditation, training, and employment. It is a well-thought-out document with sensible recommendations that should be implemented. The earliest implementation of this policy will take place through a project-based early childhood development program called the National ECD Pilot Project. This is the first step toward effecting the reception year for five-year-olds as part of the legislated ten years of compulsory schooling for all children.

Safer Environments for Children

The lingering question of violence and community danger poses the most vexing problem and the most serious long-term threat to the health and development of children. The necessity of reducing violence for child health and development is widely recognized in South Africa. The effects of family and community violence are well understood as damaging to developing children. They distort developmental processes, and influence character formation to the point that violence is normalized and becomes an inseparable feature of personal identity. In the earliest stages of development, the effects of violence are small and almost imperceptible. In fact, prior to age six, few can be detected. But with time, violence's effects on child development become more pronounced. This delay suggests that there may be a window of opportunity for early intervention. Postponing intervention past this critical period may mean that we miss the opportunity to make a difference. After age six, these effects may become ingrained and efforts to reverse them will require longer and more intensive intervention than might have been required earlier.

Programs at the community level to reduce exposure to violence are also welcomed (for example, see Greene 1993). Such programs could provide safe havens for children, as well as model alternative means to conflict resolution that do not involve the use of force and violence. By this modeling, children will learn to resolve difficulties in peaceful ways that preserve the physical and social integrity of the community. Living around family and community violence may have the same effect as intense radiation, which after sustained exposures alters DNA codes and in time begins to regenerate itself using the altered, faulty codes. Thereafter growth and regeneration become malignant as cancerous growth replaces and squeezes out healthy cells.

Government Task Force

The gravity of the problems of crime and violence is underscored by the steps the government is taking to combat them. In May 1995 several cabinet ministries (safety and security, justice, correctional services, home affairs, state expenditure, and intelligence) met to develop a National Crime Prevention Strategy that has been adopted for action. President Thabo Mbeke has attempted to mobilize public sentiment against violence by drawing attention to the seriousness of its consequences for the nation. In a stark analysis of the situation, he said:

> Ongoing political and criminal violence is destroying the socioeconomic as well as psychological life of many communities. The anguish over the loss of human life on such a scale is multiplied many times over if we consider the plight of relatives and communities concerned. The chaotic conditions in such

communities create fertile conditions for the spread of social ills such as the abuse of women and children and the spread of AIDS. The statistics [on violence] represent the scale of human suffering and wretchedness which by any standard is impermissible.

The sensibilities reflected in this underscore the critical importance of efforts to eradicate violence.

Recent Government Policies and Programs

Even now government attention to the problems of crime and violence have borne some fruit with respect to administrative and policy innovations. Through the National Crime Prevention Program (1996), several programs have been initiated to create secure facilities for youthful suspects awaiting trial, to empower and safeguard victims of crime and violence, to provide support services for children at police stations, and to educate children about crime prevention.

Related to these efforts is the National Strategy on Child Abuse and Neglect (1996), which bolsters child protection services by authorizing the creation and training of a special branch of the police to respond to and investigate child abuse and neglect. Neglect of children can have very detrimental consequences. Efforts to compel noncustodial parents to live up to their responsibility of providing for their children is a small but important component in a comprehensive program to protect children. One administrative step that will help in this effort is the integration of family advocates into the Family Court System so that issues of child support and custody can be dealt with in a nonadversarial environment in the best interests of the child.

Building Community to Combat Danger

If we are serious about increasing citizen safety, we must understand more about the conditions and cues that contribute to this sense of danger, and we must then address them. Such a strategy will fail if it relies exclusively on stepped-up law enforcement, more vigorous prosecution of criminals, harsher punishments, or longer prison sentences for convicted criminals. We should focus instead on things law-abiding citizens can do, as well as preventive and preemptive strategies. Government efforts must be combined with citizen initiatives to establish family support and community development programs aimed at strengthening ties within and among families and to draw on civic involvement to build communities. Providing safe, adult-supervised activities for children, as well as crime watches and other crime prevention programs, will broaden the range of alternative social control strategies that parents, teachers, and other adults have available so as to minimize reliance on physical punishment and coercion for discipline, socialization, and social influence.

We must also be aware that psychological processes related to expectations and hope for the future, as well as difficulties following the trauma of long-term conflict, also shape people's evaluation and response to social transformation after extended periods of conflict. These issues too should be factored into efforts to work with individuals and communities in the periods following violent conflict. The lessons learned may be helpful in several locations around the world, such as Northern Ireland, where extended periods of violence seem to be giving way to peace.

Vigorous discourse is under way about the need to rebuild support and reciprocal caring within community life. Some argue that relationships among South Africans must once again be governed by the traditional value of *Ubuntu*, the obligation to show mutual concern for and provide for the needs of others. Others call for rising above past suspicions and rebuilding police-community cooperation as a way to improve the effectiveness of law enforcement and reduce violent crime.

BTT lends credence to those who argue for family-level support programs. For example, supportive home visits by community health workers can be an effective means of early detection and problem intervention (Garbarino et al. 1998). Schools also have a role to play in the reduction of violence. These programs attempt to promote school environments in which children can feel safe, school staff are able reduce their reliance on power-assertive control strategies, and prosocial methods are used for resolving conflict. Such programs challenge extant norms about aggression as a principal means of dealing with problems (Taylor 1994). Because the economic inequality fostered by apartheid continues to be at the heart of the problems of violence in South Africa, any successful effort to reduce violence must attack the systemic and historical roots of the problem. As promising as these violence prevention programs are, they cannot be successful in the absence of significant economic transformation.

The South African Dilemma of Inequality

Emblematic of the ways crime, violence, poverty, and inequality flow together in South Africa is Busi, a young woman who was raped and stabbed late one Sunday and died a day later outside the front gates of a southern suburb hospital that had allegedly refused to admit her

(Woodgate 1996). Dev Groener and a group of his coworkers discovered the badly injured woman near the commuter train line on their way home from work. They called the police and asked them to send an ambulance. When neither had arrived after forty minutes, the men carried her piggy-back to the hospital a few blocks away. When they arrived, a security guard at the private hospital, after making a phone call to a supervisor, turned her away. The guard told them she could not be admitted because she lacked insurance that would cover the cost of her care and that she would have to wait for an ambulance. When the ambulance finally arrived, the medics pronounced her dead.

Some might read this and focus on the elements of this story that highlight all that is wrong in South Africa. On the surface, it does point to the unraveling of social fabric of the nation. However upon closer inspection, it also reveals something about the dilemmas of South Africans and the positive role to be played by civic-minded individuals who can respond sensitively to the needs of others. That the incident described in the preceding paragraph was the subject of a front-page story in the *Johannesburg Star* hints at its unusual nature. In tone it also gives a glimmer of the public outrage and indignation over the victimization of an innocent woman whose poverty made her life seem dispensable. This story is important not as a disclosure of the callous indifference of a for-profit medical institution with policies to protect it against unpaid medical expenses; it represents something more important about a current moral struggle in South Africa—the conflict between human empathy, concern for others, and human indifference. It captures the hope and peril that exist side by side in South Africa.

Within each South African is a Dev Groener who puts aside thoughts of fatigue and hunger to care for a stranger who is injured and dying. Within each individual is the hospital security guard who would prefer not to see and feel the obligation to help; who is overcome by a sense of helplessness, futility, inadequacy; and who finds it easier to turn away from the suffering and retreat back to the protection and isolation of the guard booth and the directive of a distant supervisor not to help, not to get involved, not to let anyone in. The problem is that the guard booth is small and confining. It provides no real protection against the moral dilemma of seeing and not responding to the needs of others. All South Africans are left with the dilemma of acting to make things better or watching them get worse. This is the core dilemma of South Africans as individuals and as a society. At stake is the survival of humanity, empathy, and caring about the life and suffering of other human beings.

Although many South Africans live in safety and have not experienced violence, and most have adequate resources to acquire the necessities of life, serious hardship still exists for a substantial number of South Africans in this land of plenty. The problems of crime and violence cannot be separated from the problems of poverty and hardship. The corrosive effect of such economic inequality on a sense of nationhood is indisputable. Consequently even with the benefit of wealth and a high material standard of living, those who have benefited from the inequities of apartheid cannot afford complacency in the face of such widespread hardship among blacks. The prospect for improvement in this situation lies in part in the capacity of those who were and still are privileged to recognize their self-interest in working toward a more equitable society. There is much wisdom in the saying, "As long as the poor cannot afford to eat, the wealthy cannot afford to sleep." This statement underscores the indissoluble link between those who suffer material deprivation and those who live in abundance. This interdependence can have dire repercussions when the needs of the poor are neglected by those who luxuriate in material comfort. Progress toward a stance of enlightened self-interest appears slow but steady as the people of South Africa push housing and jobs to the front of the national agenda.

Conclusion

For the majority of Mandela's children, life is happily routine and normal as they are off to a promising start in life. There is every reason to believe that they will mature into physically healthy, psychologically wholesome, and socially competent adults. For a minority, the story is quite different. They are beginning to show signs of difficulty with respect to behavioral, emotional, and academic adjustment that may impede their progress to a normal and well-adjusted adulthood.

But even for the children who are not faring well at this time, it is too early in their lives to draw the curtain and consign them to a life of difficulty. The script of their lives has not been completed. It is still unclear how indelible the imprints of poverty and violence will be on their character. There may still be time to act to resolve the social threat that may lead them to a life of impairment. With improvements in their physical and social conditions, it is possible that they may be restored to a path of sound health and development. We will track the changes to see whether hope prevails or the perils of social risks win out.

Risk factors, protective factors, family coping, and self-regulation represent important pieces needed to solve this puzzle. Our knowledge about the risks and protective factors associated with these outcomes is substantial, but there are still significant gaps in what is known about the actual processes involved. In our future studies, we will learn more about the validity of the propositions we have made here about the adverse effects of social risks; the value of human capital, family life, and cultural resources; and the ability of caring, supportive adults to attenuate the impact of negative social environments of children and how these factors contribute to their resilience in the face of distress.

By following children as they move from childhood to early adolescence, BTT will generate additional insights about the developmental sequence and its relation to long-term adjustment. We will also learn how well South Africa as a nation is able to take advantage of this new era of political equality to create a society that is also known for equality of opportunity. Hope lies in its ability to create a society in which all children are highly valued and cared for by a people who become as good, generous, and fair as its children deserve.

As Mandela's children look to the future, one that can be promising and hopeful, it is important that they and their families guide their lives with the wisdom shared with them by Nelson Mandela when he ascended to the presidency:

> Our deepest fear is not that we are inadequate.
> Our deepest fear is that we are powerful beyond measure!
> It is our light not our darkness, that most frightens us.
> We ask ourselves:
>   Who am I to be brilliant, gorgeous, talented and fabulous?
> Actually, who are you not to be! You are child of God.
> We were born to make manifest the glory of God that is within us.
> It is not just in some of us, it is in everyone.

> —Nelson Mandela,
> presidential inauguration
> speech, 1994

References

Aber, J. L. 1994. "Poverty, violence, and child development—Untangling family and community-level effects." *Threats to Optimal Development: Integrating Biological, Psychological, and Social Risk Factors*, vol. 27: 229–72.

Aber, J., N. Bennett, D. Conley, and L. Li. 1997. The effects of poverty on child health and development. *Annual Review of Public Health* 18; 463–83.

Achenbach, T. M. 1991. Manual for the Child Behavior Checklist/4-18 and 1991 profiles. Burlington, VT: University of Vermont Department of Psychiatry.

Achenbach, T. M., C. T. Howell, H. C. Quay, and C. K. Conners. 1991. National survey of problems and competencies among four- to sixteen-year-olds: Parents' reports for normative and clinical samples. *Monographs of the Society for Research in Child Development*, Serial No. 225, 56(3).

Ackerman, B., C. E. Izard, K. Schoff, E. A. Youngstrom, and J. Kogos. 1999. Contextual risk, caregiver emotionality and the problem behaviors of six- and seven- year old children from economically disadvantaged families. *Child Development* 70: 1415–27

Aderibigbe, Y. A., and A. K. Pandurangi. 1995. The neglect of culture in psychiatric nosology: The case of culture bound syndromes—Comment. *International Journal of Social Psychiatry* 41(4): 235–41.

Aneshensel, C. S., and C. A. Sucoff. 1996. The neighborhood context of adolescent mental health. *Journal of Health and Social Behavior* 37: 293–310.

Barbarin, O. 1983. Coping with ecological transitions by black families: A psycho-social model. *Journal of Community Psychology* 11: 308–22.

———. 1992. *Family Relations Scale: Manual.* Ann Arbor, MI: Assessment Psychometrika.

———. 1993a. Emotional and social development of African-American children. *Journal of Black Psychology* 19(4): 381–90.

———. 1993b. Social context, psychosocial resilience and psychopathology: Competing frameworks for understanding the emotional adjustment of African-American children. *Journal of Black Psychology* 19(3): 478–92.

Barbarin, O. A., and N. Khomo. 1997. Indicators of economic status and social capital in South African townships: What do they reveal about the material and social conditions in families of poor children? *Childhood: A Global Journal of Child Research* 4(2): 193–222.

Barbarin, O., L. Richter, T. de Wet, and A. Wachtel. 1998. Ironic trends in the transition to peace: Criminal violence supplants political violence in terrorizing South African blacks. *Peace and Conflict: Journal of Peace Psychology* 4 283–305.

Barbarin, O., J. Sargent, O. J. Sahler, K. Roghmann, R. Mulhern, P. Carpenter, D. Copeland, M. Dolgin, and L. Zeltzer. 1995. Sibling adaptation to childhood cancer: Collaborative research project: Parental views of pre- and post-diagnosis functioning of siblings of children with cancer. *Journal of Psychosocial Oncology* 13 (3): 1–20.

Barbarin, O., and R. Soler. 1993. Behavioral, emotional and academic adjustment in a national probability sample of African American children: Effects of age, gender and family structure. *Journal of Black Psychology* 19(4): 423–46.

Barbarin, O., C. F. Whitten, S. Bond, and R. Conner-Warren. 1999. The social and cultural context of coping with sickle cell disease: III. Stress, coping tasks, family functioning and children's adjustment. *Journal of Black Psychology* 356–77.

Basic Behavioral Science Task Force on the National Advisory Mental Health Council. 1996. Basic behavioral science research in mental health: Socio and environmental processes. *American Psychologist* 51: 722–31.

Berman, S. L., W. M. Kurtines, W. K. Silverman, and L. T. Serafini. 1996. The impact of exposure to crime and violence on urban youth. *American Journal of Orthopsychiatry* 66: 329–36.

Bomela, N. 2000. Demographic correlates of child malnutrition in South Africa. Paper presented at the Joint Human Sciences Research Council University of Michigan conference on Quantitive Analysis of Living Standards Survey Data. Durban, South Africa, February 4, 2000.

Boney-McCoy, S. & Finkelhor, D. (1996). Is youth victimization related to trauma symptoms and depression after controlling for prior symptoms and family relationships? A longitudinal, prospective study. *Journal of Consulting and Clinical Psychology*. 64. 1406–1416.

Bonner, P., and L. Segal. 1998. *Soweto: A History*. Cape Town: Maske Miller Longman.

Borge, A. 1996. Developmental pathways of behaviour problems in the young child: Factors associated with continuity and change. *Scandinavian Journal of Psychology* 37: 195–204.

Boult, B., and P. Cunningham. 1992. Black teenage pregnancy: An African perspective. *International Journal of Adolescence and Youth* 3: 303–9.

Bradley, R., and B. Caldwell. 1995. Caregiving and the regulation of child growth and development: Describing proximal aspects of caregiving systems. *Developmental Review* 15: 38–85.

Brooks-Gunn, J., and G. Duncan. 1997. The effects of poverty on children. *The Future of Children: Children and Poverty* 7: 55–71.

Cairns, R., and A. Dawes. 1996. Children: Ethnic and political violence—A commentary. *Child Development* 67: 129–39.

Cameron, N., T. de Wet , G. Ellison, and B. Bogin. 1998. Growth in height and weight of South African urban infants from birth to five years: The Birth to Ten study. *American Journal of Human Biology* 10: 495–504.

Campbell, C., and D. F. Schwarz. 1996. Prevalence and impact of exposure to interpersonal violence among suburban and urban middle school students. *Pediatrics* 98(3): 396-402.

Campbell, J. C., and L. A. Lewandowski. 1997. Mental and physical health effects of intimate partner violence on women and children. *Psychiatric Clinics of North America* 20: 353–77.

Campbell, S. 1995. Behaviour problems in preschool children: A review of recent research. *Journal of Child Psychology and Psychiatry* 36: 113–49.

Campbell, S. B., C. L. March, E. W. Pierce, L. J. Ewing, and E. K. Szumowski. 1991. Hard-to-manage preschool boys: Family context and the stability of externalizing behavior. *Journal of Abnormal Child Psychology* 19: 301–18.

Capaldi, D. M., and G. R. Patterson. 1994. Interrelated influences of contextual factors on antisocial behavior in childhood and adolescence for males. In D. C. Fowles, P. Sutker, and S. H. Goodman, eds., *Progress in experimental personality and psychopathology research* (pp. 165–98). New York: Springer.

Chesler, M., and O. Barbarin. 1987. *Childhood cancer and the family: Meeting the challenge of stress and social support.* New York: Bruner-Mazel.

Cicchetti, D., and M. Lynch. 1993. Toward an ecological transactional model of community violence and child maltreatment—Consequences for children's development. *Psychiatry—Interpersonal and Biological Processes* 56: 96–118.

Coleman, J. S. 1988. Social capital in the creation of human capital. *American Journal of Sociology* 94 (Supplement): S95–S120.

Cooleyquille, M. R., S. M. Turner, and D. C. Beidel. 1995. Emotional impact of children's exposure to community violence—A preliminary study. *Journal of the American Academy of Child and Adolescent Psychiatry* 34: 1362–68.

Corrigan, T. 1997. Crime: the news is mixed. *South African Institute of Race Relations: Fast Facts* 11: 1–5.

Costello, E. J., A. Angold, B. J. Burns, A. Erkanli, D. K. Stangl, and D. L. Tweed. 1996. The Great Smoky Mountains study of youth. Functional impairment and serious emotional disturbance. *Archives of General Psychiatry* 53 (12): 1137–43.

Coulton, C. J., J. E. Korbin, M. Su, and J. Chow. 1995. Community-level factors and child maltreatment rates. *Child Development* 66: 1262–76.

Daniels, E. 1996. Apartheid and its legacy lie at the root of the country's rampant crime. *Johannesburg Saturday Star*, August 24, 1996. Reprinted in *The Indicator.* Durban: University of Natal.

DeGranges, G., W. Porges, R. Sickel, and S. Greenspan. 1993. Four-year follow-up of a sample of regulatory disordered infants. *Infant Mental Health Journal* 14: 330–43.

Dryfoos, J. G. 1990. *Adolescents at risk: Prevalence and prevention.* New York: Oxford University Press.

Duncan, G., K. Brooks-Gunn, and P. K. Klebanov. 1994. Economic deprivation and early childhood development. *Child Development* 65(2): 296–318.

Durant, R. H., C. Cadenhead, R. A. Pendergrast, G. Slavens, and C. W. Linder. 1994. Factors associated with the use of violence among urban black adolescents. *American Journal of Public Health* 84: 612–17.

Durant, R. H., A. Getts, C. Cadenhead, S. J. Emans, and E. R. Woods. 1995. Exposure to violence and victimization and depression, hopelessness, and purpose in life among adolescents living in and around public housing. *Developmental and Behavioral Pediatrics* 16: 233–37.

Entwistle, D. R., and N. M. Astone. 1994. Some practical guidelines for measuring youth race/ethnicity and socio-economic status. *Child Development* 65: 1521–40.

Farrell, A. D., and S. E. Bruce. 1997. Impact of exposure to community violence on violent behavior and emotional distress among urban adolescents. *Journal of Clinical Child Psychology* 26: 2–14.

Felner, R. D., S. Brand, D. L. DuBois, A. M. Adan, P. F. Mulhall, and E. G. Evans. 1995. Socioeconomic disadvantage, proximal environmental experiences, and socioemotional and academic adjustment in early adolescence: Investigation of a mediated effects model. *Child Development* 66: 774–92.

Fitzpatrick, K. M. 1993. Exposure to violence and presence of depression among low-income, African-American youth. *Journal of Consulting and Clinical Psychology* 61: 528–31.

Freeman, L. N., H. Mokros, and E. O. Poznanski. 1993. Violent events reported by normal urban school-aged children—Characteristics and depression correlates. *Journal of the American Academy of Child and Adolescent Psychiatry* 32: 419–23.

Furstenburg F., J. Brooks-Gunn, and L. Chase-Lansdale. 1989. Teenaged pregnancy and childbearing. *American Psychologist* 44: 313–20.

Garbarino, J., and K. Kostelny. 1996. The effects of political violence on Palestinian children's behavior problems: A risk accumulation model. *Child Development* 67: 33–45.

Garbarino, J., K. Kostelny, and N. Dubrow. 1991. What children can tell us about living in danger. *American Psychologist* 46: 376–83.

Garmezy, N. 1991. Resilience in children's adaptation to negative life event and stressed environments. *Pediatric Annals* 20: (9)459–& SEP 1991.

Glanz, L., and A. D. Spiegel. 1996. *Violence and family life in contemporary South Africa: Research and policy issues.* Pretoria: Human Sciences Research Council Publishers.

Goduka, I. N., D. A. Poole, and L. Aotaki-Phenice. 1992. A comparative study of black South African children from three different contexts. *Child Development* 63: 509–25.

Gordon, A. 1986. Environmental constraints and their effect on the academic achievement of urban black children in South Africa. *South African Journal of Education* 6: 70–74.

Gore, S., R. H. Aseltine, and M. E. Coldon. 1993. Gender, social-relational involvement, and depression. *Journal of Research on Adolescence* 3: 101–25.

Gorman-Smith, D., and P. Tolan. 1998. The role of exposure to community violence and developmental problems among inner-city youth. *Development and Psychopathology* 10(1): 101–16.

Greene, J. 2000. Cell phone thief shot dead by victim. *Mercury* (Durban, South Africa), February 1, p. 1.

Greene, M. B. 1993. Chronic exposure to violence and poverty: Interventions that work for youth. *Crime and Delinquency* 39: 106–24.

Greenspan, S. I., and S. Wieder. 1993. Regulatory disorders. In C. Zeanah, ed., *Handbook of infant mental health* (pp. 280–90). New York: Guilford Press.

Grotberg, E. 1995. *A guide to promoting resilience in children: Strengthening the human spirit.* The Hague: The Bernard van Leer Foundation, Early Childhood Development: Practice and Reflections, No. 8.

Hamill P., T. Drizd, C. Johnson, R. Reed, A. Roche, and W. Moore. 1979. Physical growth: National Center for Health Statistics percentiles. *American Journal of Clinical Nutrition* 32: 607–29.

Hammen, C., and K. D. Rudolph. 1996. Childhood depression. In E. J. Mash and R. A. Barkley, eds., *Child psychopathology* (pp. 153–95). New York: Guilford Press.

Halpern, R. 1990. Poverty and early childhood parenting: Toward a framework for intervention. *American Journal of Orthopsychiatry* 60(1): 6–18.

Hauser, R. M. 1994. Measuring socioeconomic status in studies of child development. *Child Development* 65: 1541–45.

Hollingshead, A. B. 1975. Four-factor index of social status. Unpublished manuscript, Yale University, Department of Sociology, New Haven, CT.

Jacobs, M., and D. McCoy. 1997. Free care for pregnant women and for children under six. *Lancet* 349: 1541–2.

Jarrett, R. 1998. African American mothers and grandmothers in poverty: An adaptational perspective. *Journal of Comparative Family Studies* 29: 387–96.

Jersild, A. T., and F. B. Holmes. 1935. *Children's fears.* New York: Teachers College Press.

Keenan, K., and D. S. Shaw. 1994. The development of aggression in toddlers: A study of low-income families. *Journal of Abnormal Child Psychology* 22(1): 53–77.

Kellam, S.G., J. D. Branch, K. C. Agrawal, and M. E. Ensminger. 1975. *Mental health and going to school: The Woodlawn Program of Assessment, Early Intervention and Evaluation.* Chicago: University of Chicago Press.

Klasen, S. 1997. Poverty, inequality and deprivation in South Africa: An analysis of the 1993 SALDRU Survey. *Social Indicators Research* 41: 51–94

Kruger, J., and S. Motala. 1997. Welfare. In S. Robinson and L. Biersteker, eds., *First call: The South African children's budget* (pp. 65–114). Cape Town: IDASA.

Ladd, G. W., and E. Cairns. 1996. Children: Ethnic and political violence. *Child Development* 67: 14–18

Langner, T. S., J. H. Herson, E. L. Greene, J. D. Jameson, and J. A. Goff. 1970. Children of the city: Affluence, poverty, and mental health. In V. L. Allen, ed., *Psychological factors in poverty* (pp. 185–209). Chicago: Markham Publishing.

Lempers, J. D., D. Clark-Lempers, and R. Simons. 1989. Economic hardship, parenting, and distress in adolescence. *Child Development* 60: 25–39.

Liddell, C. 1998. Conceptualising childhood in developing countries. *Psychology and Developing Societies* 10: 35–53.

Liddell, C., J. Kvalsvig, A. Shabalala, and P. Qotyana. 1994. Defining the cultural context of children's everyday experiences in the year before school. In A. Dawes and D. Donald, eds., *Childhood and adversity: psychological Perspectives from South African research* (pp. 51–65). Cape Town: David Phillip.

Lobel, M. 1994. Conceptualizations, measurement and the effects of prenatal maternal stress on birth outcomes. *Journal of Behavioural Medicine* 17: 225–72.

Loening, W. E. K. 1981. Child abuse among the Zulus: A people in cultural transition. Pietermaritzburg: University of Natal.

Lund, F. 1996. Welfare. In D. Budlender, ed., *The women's budget.* Cape Town: IDASA.

Madywabe, L., 1997. Youth buried as senseless violence continues. *Johannesburg Star,* May 31, p. 5.

Magwaza, A. S., B. J. Killian, and I. Petersen. 1993. The effects of chronic violence on preschool children living in South African townships. *Child Abuse and Neglect* 17:795–803.

Mash, E. J., and R. A. Barkley, eds. 1996. *Treatment of childhood disorders.* New York: Guilford Press.

Mason, B. L., and B. L. Killian 1994. *The psychological effects of violence on children: The development of a trauma profile for black school children aged 8–12.* Pietermaritzburg, Kwa-Zulu-Natal: SAHSSO and Department of Psychology.

Masten, A. 1989. Resilience in development: Implications of the study of successful adaptation for developmental psychopathology. In D. Cicchetti, ed., *The emergence of a discipline: Rochester Symposium on Developmental Psychology* (pp. 261–94). Hillsdale, NJ: Lawrence Erlbaum.

McKendrick, G., and W. Senoamadi. 1996. Some effects of violence on squatter camp families and their children. In L. E. Glanz and A. D. Spiegel, eds., *Violence and family life in contemporary South Africa: Research and policy issues* (pp. 15–28). Pretoria: Human Sciences Research Council Publishers.

McLeod, J. D. and M. Shanahan. 1993. Poverty, parenting, and children's mental health. *American Sociological Review* 58: 351–66.

———. 1996. Trajectories of poverty and children's mental health. *Journal of Health and Social Behavior* 37 (September): 207–20.

McLoyd, V. 1990. The impact of economic hardship on black families and children: Psychological distress, parenting and socioemotional development. *Child Development* 61: 311–46.

———. 1998. Socioeconomic disadvantage and child development. *American Psychologist* 53: 185-204.

Meumann, C., and M. Peden. 1997. The Durban Metropolitan Pilot Study. *Trauma Review* 5(1): 3–8.

Molteno, C., M. Kibel and M. Roberts. 1986. Childhood health in South Africa. In S. Burman and P. Reynolds, eds., *Growing up in a divided society: The contexts of childhood in South Africa* (pp. 43–65). Johannesburg: Ravan Press.

Mtshali, M. O. 1988. Give us a break: Diaries of a group of Soweto children. Johannesburg: Skotaville Publishers.

Naidoo, P., and A. L. Pillay. 1995. Childhood psychopathology and nonintact family status in South Africa. *Psychological Reports* 77:734.

Nakao, K., and J. Treas. 1992. The 1989 socioeconomic index of occupations: Construction from the 1989 occupational prestige scores (General Social Survey Methodological Report No. 74). Chicago: University of Chicago, National Opinion Research Center.

Nelson, C. A. 1994. *Threats to optimal development: Integrating biological, psychological, and social risk factors.* The Minnesota Symposium on Child Psychology, Vol. 27. Hillsdale, NJ: Lawrence Erlbaum Associates.

Nsamenang, A., and A. Dawes. 1998. Developmental psychology as political psychology in sub-Saharan Africa: The challenge of Africanisation. *Applied Psychology: An International Review* 47: 73–87.

Offord, D., M. Boyle, and Y. Racine. 1989. Ontario Child Health Study: Correlates of disorder. *Journal of the American Academy of Child and Adolescent Psychiatry* 28: 856–60.

Ogbu, J. 1981. Origins of competence: A cultural-ecological perspective. *Child Development* 52: 413–29.

Open School. 1986. Two dogs and freedom: Children of the townships speak out. Johannesburg: Ravan Press/Open School.

Osofsky, J., S. Wewers, D. M. Hann, and A. C. Fick. 1993. Chronic community violence: What is happening to our children? *Psychiatry* 56(1): 36–45.

Paschall, M. J., and M. L. Hubbard. 1998. Effects of neighborhood and family stressors on African-American male adolescents' self-worth and propensity for violent behavior. *Journal of Consulting and Clinical Psychology* 66: 825–31.

Pillay, A. L., and M. R. Lockhat. 1997. Developing community mental health services for children in South Africa: Social Science & Medicine, uk, 45 no 10:1493–501 Nov '97.

Pitt, B. 1968. Atypical depression following childhood. *British Journal of Psychiatry* 114: 1325–35.

Pollitt, E., and K. Gorman. 1994. Nutritional deficiencies as developmental risk factors. In C. A.Nelson, ed., *Threats to optimal development: Integrating biological, psychological, and social risk factors.* The Minnesota Symposium on Child Psychology, Vol. 27. (pp. 121–144). Hillsdale, NJ: Lawrence Erlbaum Associates.

Pynoos, R. S., K. Nader, C. Frederick, L. Gonda, and M. Stuber. 1987. Grief reactions in school age children following a sniper attack at school. *Israel Journal of Psychiatry and Related Sciences* 24: 53–63.

Ramey, C., and Ramey, S. 1998. Early intervention and early experience. *American Psychologist* 53(2): 109–20.

Reid, M., S. Landesman, R. Treder, J. Jaccard. 1989. "My family and friends": Six- to twelve-year-old children's perceptions of social support. *Child Development* 60(4): 896–910.

Reynolds, C. R. 1982. Convergent and divergent validity of the Revised Children's Manifest Anxiety Scale. *Educational and Psychological Measurement,* 42(4) 1205–1212.

Reynolds, P. 1989. Childhood in crossroads: Cognition and society in South Africa. Cape Town: David Phillip.

Richman, N., and P. Graham. 1971. A behavioural screening questionnaire for use with three-year-old children: Preliminary findings. *Journal of Child Psychology and Psychiatry* 12: 5–33.

Richter, L. 1993. Many kinds of deprivation: Young children and their families in South Africa. In D. Eldering and P. Leseman, eds., *Early intervention and culture: Preparation for literacy—The interface between theory and practice* (pp. 95–113). The Hague: UNESCO.

Richter, L., ed. 1998. *In view of school: Preparation for and adjustment to school under rapidly changing social conditions.* Johannesburg: Goethe Institute.

Richter, L. and R. Griesel. 1994. Malnutrition, low birth weight and related influences on psychological development. In A. Dawes and D. Donald, eds., *Childhood and adversity: Psychological perspectives from South African research* (pp. 66–91). Cape Town: David Philip.

Richter, L., R. Griesel, and O. Barbarin. 1999. Behavioural problems among preschool children in South Africa: A longitudinal perspective from birth to age five. In N. Singh and F. Leung, eds., *International perspectives on child and adolescent mental health.* Amsterdam, Holland: Elsevier Publishers.

Richter, L. R. Griesel, and C. Rose. 1992. The Bayley Scales of Infant Development: A South African standardization. *South African Jounal of Occupational Therapy* 14–25.

Richters, J. E., and P. E. Martinez. 1993a. Violent communities, family choices, and children's changes: An algorithm for improving the odds. *Development and Psychopathology* 5: 5–29.

———. 1993b. The NIMH Community Violence Project: Children as victims of and witness to violence. *Psychiatry* 56(1): 7–21.

Robertson, B., and S. Berger. 1994. Child psychopathology in South Africa. In A. Dawes and D. Donald, eds., *Childhood and adversity: Psychological perspectives from South African research* (pp. 136–53). Cape Town: David Phillip Publishers.

Robertson, B. A., and A. Kottler. 1993. Cultural issues in the psychiatric assessment of Xhosa children and adolescents. *South African Medical Journal* 83: 207–8.

Ruth-Lyons, K. 1996. Attachment relationships among children with aggressive behavior problems: The role of disorganized early attachment patterns. *Journal of Consulting and Clinical Psychology* 64: 64–73.

Rutter, M. 1987. Psychological resilience and protective mechanisms. *American Journal of Orthopsychiatry* 53: 316–31.

———. 1990. Commentary: Some focus and process considerations regarding effects of parental depression on children. *Developmental Psychology* 26: 60–67.

Rutter, M., and N. Garmezy, eds. 1988. Stress, coping, and development in children. Baltimore: Johns Hopkins University Press.

Sahler, O. J., K. J. Roghmann, R. K. Mulhern, P. J. Carpenter, J. R. Sargent, D. R. Copeland, O. A. Barbarin, L. K. Zeltzer, and M. J. Dolgin. 1997. Sibling adaptation to childhood cancer collaborative study: The association of sibling adaptation with maternal well-being, physical health, and resource use. *Journal of Developmental and Behavioral Pediatrics,* 18(4): 233–43.

Sameroff, A., R. Seifer, A. Baldwin, and C. Baldwin. 1993. Stability of intelligence from preschool to adolescence: The influence of social and family risk factors. *Child Development* 64: 80–97.

Sampson, R., and Laub, J. H. (1994). Urban poverty and the family contest of delinquency: A new look at structure and process in a classic study. *Child Development* 65: 423–540.

Shaffer, D. 1999. *Developmental psychology: Children and adolescence.* Pacific Grove, CA: Brooks/Cole Publishing Co.

Shaw, M. 1995. *Partners in crime?: Crime, political transition and changing forms of policing control.* Center for Policy Studies: Research Report Number 39.

Skuy, M., M. Koeberg, and P. Fridjhon. 1997. Adjustment of children and interaction of parent and child among single mothers in a disadvantaged South African community. *Psychological Reports* 80: 1171–80.

Smith, C., and L. Holford. 1993. Post traumatic stress disorder, South Africa's children and adolescents. *South African Journal of Child and Adolescent Psychology.*

South African Department of National Health and Population Development. 1994.

South African Institute of Race Relations. 2000. South Africa Survey, 1999–2000. Millennium Edition. Johannesburg.

Spencer, M. S. 1996. Behavior problems in children of adolescent mothers: Exploring the role of attachment as a protective factor. Dissertation, University of Washington.

Steinmetz, S. K. 1977. *The cycle of violence: Assertive, aggressive, and abusive family interaction.* (pp. xv, 191). New York: Praeger.

Swarts, M. 1997. The family: Cradle of violence in South Africa. *HSRC: In Focus Forum* 5(4): 40–44.

Taylor, L., B. Zuckerman, V. Harik, and B. M. Groves. 1994. Witnessing violence by young children and their mothers. *Journal of Developmental and Behavioral Pediatrics* 15: 120–23.

Tinsley, B., and D. Holtgrave. 1989. Maternal health locus of control beliefs, utilization of childhood preventive health services, and infant health. *Journal of Developmental and Behavioral Pediatrics* 10: 236–41.

United Nations General Assembly. 1989. Adoption of a convention on the rights of the child. (U.N. Doc. A/Res/44/25). New York.

Valez, C. N., J. Johnson, and P. Cohen. 1989. A longitudinal analysis of selected risk factors for childhood psychopathology. *Journal of the American Academy of Child and Adolescent Psychiatry* 28: 861–64.

Wallen, J., and R. H. Rubin. 1997. The role of the family in mediating the effects of community violence on children. *Aggression and Violent Behavior* 2: 33–41.

Weissbourd, R. 1996. *The vulnerable child: What really hurts America's children and what we can do about it.* Reading, MA: Addison-Wesley.

Werner, E. 1990. Protective factors and individual resilience. In S. J. Meisels and J. P. Shonkoff, eds., *Handbook of early childhood intervention* (pp. 97–116). Cambridge: Cambridge University Press.

Werner, E. and R. Smith. 1989. *Vulnerable but invincible: A longitudinal study of resilient children and youth.* New York: Adams, Bannister and Cox.

———. 1992. Overcoming the odds: High risk children from birth to adulthood. Ithaca, NY: Cornell University Press.

Wigton, A., B. Makan, and D. McCoy. 1997. Health and nutrition. In S. Robinson and L. Biersteker, eds., *First call: The South African children's budget* (pp. 33–64). Cape Town: IDASA.

Wilson, F. 1994. *The Living Standards Survey.* Cape Town: South African Labor and Development Research Unit, University of Cape Town.

Wilson, F. and M. Ramphele. 1989. *Uprooting poverty: The South African challenge.* Cape Town: David Phillip.

World Bank. 1994. *South Africans rich and poor: Baseline household statistics.* Cape Town, South Africa: Saldru School of Economics.

———. 1996. *World Bank development report.* Washington, DC.

Yach, D. 1988. Infant mortality rates in urban areas of South Africa 1981–1985. *South African Medical Journal* 73: 232–34.

Yach, D., N. Cameron, G. N. Padayachee, L. Wagstaff, L. M. Richter, and S. Fonn. 1991. Birth-to-Ten: Child health in South Africa in the nineties; Rationale and methods of a birth cohort study. *Paediatric and Perinatal Epidemiology* 5: 211–33.

Yoshikawa, H. 1994. Prevention as cumulative protection: Effects of early family support and education on chronic delinquency and its risks. *Psychological Bulletin* 115: 28–54

Young, C., K. Savola, and E. Phelps. 1991. *Inventory of longitudinal studies in the social sciences.* Newbury Park, CA: Sage Publications.

Zeitlin, M., H. Ghassemi, and M. Mansour. 1990. *Positive deviance in child nutrition.* Tokyo: United Nations University Press.

Zill, N. 1985. *Behavior Problem Scales developed from the 1981 Child Health Supplement to the National Health Interview Survey.* Washington, DC: Child Trends, Inc.

Zille, H. 1986. Beginning life in an apartheid society. In S. Burman and P. Reynolds, eds., *Growing up in a divided society: The contexts of childhood in South Africa* (pp. 139–57). Johannesburg: Ravan Press.

South African Child Assessment Schedule

Suid-Afrikaanse Kinder-toetsing Skedule (SACAS)

Vandag se datum:_____ Kind se naam_____
Ondervraer_____ Wie het hierdie inligting verskaf?_____
Wat is persoon wat die inliging verskaf het se verhouding met die kind?_____

Ek het ín paar vrae oor die probleme en die vaardighede wat sommige
kinders het. Ek wil graag hí dat jy vir my moet vertel tot in watter mate dit is
dat jou kind hierdie het. Wanneer u reageer, sí vir my of dit
0=nie waar nie   1=partykeer waar 2=baie keer waar

1. Lyk _____ broos of huil hy/sy as ín volwassene net na haar kyk?
2. Luister en aanvaar _____ kritiek kalm?
3. Aanvaar _____ inperkinge wat volwassenens stel?
4. Tree _____ te jonk op vir sy/haar ouderdom?
5. Pas _____ goed aan by verandering in die klaskamer-roetine?
6. Is _____ liefdevol teenoor ander mense?
7. Is _____ ín driftige kind?
8. Benader _____ nuwe ondervindinge vol selfvertroue en sonder vrees?
9. Argumenteer _____?
10. Vermy _____ aktiwiteite waarin hy/sy nie goed is nie?
11. Spog of wys _____ af?
12. Knou _____ ander af of is hy/sy gemeen teenoor ander mense?
13. Sukkel _____ om te konsentreer vir ín lang tyd?
14. Sukkel _____ om sy/haar gedagtes van sekere onderwerpe af te kry?
15. Kan _____ nie stil sit nie?
16. Kan _____ dit aanvaar as dinge nie op sy/haar manier gebeur nie?
17. Voer _____ opdragte uit?
18. Klou _____ aan volwassenes, is _____ te afhanklik?
19. Gee _____ sy/haar samewerking?
20. Kla _____ van pyne in sy/haar arms of bene?

21. Kla _____ van lighoofdigheid?
22. Kla _____ oor hoofpyn?
23. Kla _____ oor eensaamheid?
24. Kla _____ oor naarheid?
25. Kla _____ oor maagpyn of maagkrampe?
26. Voltooi _____ sy/haar huiswerk?
27. Is _____ deurmekaar, het muisneste of hou nie by nie?
28. Huil _____ sonder enige rede?
29. Is _____ nuuskierig of entoesiasties oor nuwe aktiwiteite?
30. Dagdroom _____ baie of is versonke in sy/haar eie gedagtes?
31. Daag _____ outoriteit uit of breek reîls?
32. Breek _____ aspris goed wat aan ander behoort?
33. Eis _____ aandag?
34. Breek _____ sy/haar eie goed?
35. Is _____ ongehoorsaam tuis?
36. Is _____ ongehoorsaam by die skool?
37. Doen _____ ongewoon oorspronklike of kreatiewe werk?
38. Eet _____ sleg?
39. Is _____ maklik jaloers?
40. Druk _____ gepaste behoeftes en gevoelens uit?
41. Hanteer _____ die druk van kompetisie goed?
42. Het _____ spesifieke vrese?
43. Het _____ die vrees dat hy/sy iets slegs sal doen?
44. Voel _____ goed oor hom/haarself?
45. Voel _____ hy/sy moet perfek wees?
46. Voel _____ te skuldig?
47. Voel _____ waardeloos of minderwaardig?
48. Kla /voel _____ dat niemand hom/haar lief het nie?
49. Volg _____ reîls en instruksies?
50. Funksioneer _____ goed al is daar afleidings?
51. Is _____ oor die algemeen ontspanne?
52. Word _____ geterg deur ander kinders?
53. Is _____ goed met tel (wiskunde)?
54. Is _____ gelukkig?
55. Is dit moeilik om te verstaan wat _____ sî?
56. Het _____ 'n goeie sin vir humor, glimlag baie?
57. Het _____ baie vriende?
58. Het _____ vreemde idees? Indien, beskryf.
59. Hoor _____ dinge wat nie daar is nie: beskryf.
60. Huiwer _____ om nuwe dinge te toets?
61. Is _____ impulsief of tree op sonder om te dink?
62. Is _____ onafhanklik, hou ____ daarvan om dinge sonder hulp te doen?
63. Stel _____ belang in skoolwerk?
64. Is _____ geirriteerd?
65. Is _____ 'n goeie leser vir sy/haar graad?
66. Weet _____ wat sy/haar sterk punte en swak punte is?
67. Lyk _____ ongelukkig sonder rede?

68. Is _____ luidrugtig?

69. Is _____ liefdevol, en wys hy/sy dit aan ander?

70. Is _____ se gemoedstoestand stabiel en konstant?

71. Het _____ senutrekke of -bewegings?

72. Is _____ op sy/haar senuwees of gespanne?

73. Kan _____ beurte maak en deel?

74. Hou ander kinders nie van _____ nie?

75. Is _____ hiperaktief, rusteloos en kan nie stil sit nie?

76. Is _____ oormoeg, vaak deur die dag?

77. Is _____ oorgewig?

78. Val _____ mense fisies aan?

79. Speel _____ entoesiasties?

80. Is _____ bedagsaam?

81. Is _____ ___ sleg in sy/haar skoolwerk?

82. Is _____ se koˆrdinasie sleg of is _____ lomp?

83. Verkies _____ om met jonger kinders te speel?

84. Verkies _____ om alleen te wees?

85. Het _____ probleme met oÎ wat nie reggestel word deur 'n bril nie?

86. Het _____ inperkinge nodig om hom/haar te beheer?

87. Het _____ uitslag of ander velprobleme?

88. Weier _____ om in sekere situasies te praat?

89. Herhaal _____ sekere aksies oor en oor?

90. Los _____portuurprobleme op sy/haar eie op?

91. Is _____ hartseer of ongelukkig?

92. Skree _____?

93. Is _____ geheimsinnig, hou _____ dinge vir hom/haarself?

94. Lyk dit asof _____ dink ander mense probeer hom te na kom?

95. Sien _____ goed wat nie daar is nie?

96. Is _____ selfbewus of raak maklik verleÎ?

97. Begin _____ op sy/haar eie, sonder om vir 'n volwassene te wag?

98. Deel _____ goed met ander?

99. Toon _____ belangstelling in die mense rondom hom/haar?

100. Probeer _____ aandag trek deur narstreke of deur af te wys?

101. Is _____ skaam of beskimmeld?

102. Staar _____ in die niet?

103. Staar _____ in die niet of lyk afwesig?

104. Begin _____ gevegte?

105. Vertoon _____ vreemde gedrag beskryf.

106. Is _____ hardkoppig, nors of geÔrriteerd?

107. Verander _____ se buie of gevoelens skielik?

108. Trek _____ gesigte, broei of pruil?

109. Is _____ agterdogtig teenoor ander mense?

110. Praat _____ te veel?

111. Terg _____ ander kinders?

112. Het _____ woedeuitbarstings of is kort van draad?

113. Dreig _____ mense?

114. Is _____ bang of angstig?

115. Probeer _____ ander mense help?

116. Is _____ betroubaar?

117. Is _____ onderaktief, stadig van beweging of het te min energie?

118. Gooi _____ op?

119. Hou ander kinders in _____ se ouderdomsgroep van hom/haar?

120. Gedra _____ hom by die skool?

121. Is _____ teruggetrokke, raak nie betrokke by ander nie?

122. Doen _____ sy/haar werk volgens potensiaal?

123. Werk _____ goed sonder die hulp van volwassenes?

124. Suig _____ sy/haar duim?

125. Maak ____f seer (bv slaan sy/haar kop teen 'n muur)?

126. Bekommer _____hom/haarself?

B. Vergeleke met ander kinders sy/haar ouderdom, hoe goed kom _____
  _____ (kind se naam)....

127. oor die weg met ander kinders van sy/haar ouderdom?
1= slegter as ander kinders 2=omtrent dieselfde 3=beter as die ander

128. oor die weg met sy/haar broers & susters?
1=Slegter as ander kinders 2=omtrent dieselfde 3=beter as die ander

South African Child Schedule (SACAS) (Xhosa)

Inombolo yeBTT#_____Umhla_____Igama lomntwana
Obuzayo_____Ngubani ozise olulwazi?_____
Uhlobene njani lonmtu oze nolu lwazi nomntwana?_____

Ndinemibuzo endithanda ukukubuza yona malungana neenngxaki kanye
nobuchule abanye abantwana abanabo. Ndicela uphendule ngokuba undix-
elele into yokubana ingabe yinyaniso na ngomntwana wakho. Wena-ke uza-
wuphendula uthi......

0= Ayiyo nyani 1= Ngamanye amaxesha kuyenzeka 2=Ngexesha elininzi
kuyenzeka.

0   1   2   1. Ingabe u_____ubuthathaka futhi uyalila xa umntu omdala
            emjonga nje?

0   1   2   2. Ingabe u_____uyaphulaphula futhi azithathe izilumnkiso
            ngokuzola

0   1   2   3. Ingabe u_____uyamkela xa ekhuzwa ngabantu abadala.

0   1   2   4. Wenza izinto zabantwana abancikane kunaye.

0   1   2   5. Uyakwazi ukuthatha inxaxheba xa kukhona iingoqu
            egumbini lokufundela

0   1   2   6. Uyabathanda na abanye abantwana

0   1   2   7. Ngumntwana onomsindo

0   1   2   8. Izinto ezintsha uzenza ngononophelo engoyiki

0   1   2   9. Uthanda ukuphikisa

0   1   2   10. Akathandi ukwenza izinto aziyo into yokokubana akazazi

0   1   2   11. Uyazikhukhumeza xana ethetha ngaye siqu

0   1   2   12. Uyabahlupha abanye abantwana

0   1   2   13. Ukakwazi ukuhlala ephulaphule ngalo lonke ixesha

0   1   2   14. Akakwazi ukulibala zezinye zeengcingane zakhe

0   1   2   15. Akakwazi ukuhlala phansi azole

0   1   2   16. Uyakwazi ukuthi xa izinto zingahambi ngendlela ayifu-
                nayo yena ayamkele lonto.

0   1   2   17. Uyayenza into ayicelwayo nayixelelelwayo ngononophelo

0   1   2   18. Uxhomekeke kakhulu kubantu abadala.

0   1   2   19. Unobambiswano nokusebenzisana

0   1   2   20. Uhlala ukhalaza ngeenhlungu eengalweni nasemilenzeni

0   1   2   21. Ukhalaza ngesiyezi

0   1   2   22. Ukhalaza ngenhloko ebuhlungu

0   1   2   23. Unesizungu

0   1   2   24. Unobucaphuchaphu

0   1   2   25. Uphathwa sisisu neenhlungu

0   1   2   26. Uyawugqiba umsebenzi awunikwe esikolweni xa efika
                ekhaya

0   1   2   27. Ubonakala elahlekile ngengqondo

0   1   2   28. Uyalila kungenasizathu

0   1   2   29. Ubonisa intshisakalo yokufuna ukwazi izinto ezintsha

0   1   2   30. Ingqondo yakhe ihlala ingekho kule nto ayenzayo

0   1   2   31. Akaphulaphuli abantu abadala

0   1   2   32. Uyazophula izinto zabanye abantwana ngabom

0   1   2   33. Ufuna ukuhlala ejongwa ukuba wenza ntoni

0   1   2   34. Uyazophula izinto zakhe

0   1   2   35. Akalandeli into ayixelelwayo ekhayeni

0   1   2   36. Akaphulaphuli eskolweni

0	1	2	37. Uyakwazi ukwenza izinto aziqalele zona ngokwakhe ezifana nemizobo
0	1	2	38. Utya kakuhle
0	1	2	39. Uba nomona
0	1	2	40. Utsho into ayifunayo ngendlela evakalayo
0	1	2	41. Uyakwazi ukukhuphisana nabanye abantwana angabi namsindo
0	1	2	42. Zikhona izinto azoyikayo
0	1	2	43. Uhlala esoyika ukuba uzakwenza into embi
0	1	2	44. Uzibona engumntu ofanelekile
0	1	2	45. Uziva kufanele abe ngopheleleyo.
0	1	2	46. Uzibona enetyala
0	1	2	47. Uzibona eyinto engenamsebenzi
0	1	2	48. Ubona kungenamntu omthandayo
0	1	2	49. Uyayilandela imithetho
0	1	2	50. Usebenza kakuhle naxa kunezinto ezimthikamezayo
0	1	2	51. Ungumntu uzimameleyo
0	1	2	52. Abanye abantwana bahlekisa ngaye
0	1	2	53. Uyakwazi ukwenza izibalo kakuhle
0	1	2	54. Wonwabile
0	1	2	55. Ayivakali kakuhle into ayithethayo
0	1	2	56. Ukwazi ukuhlekisa abanye abantu
0	1	2	57. Unemihlobo emininzi
0	1	2	58. Uneembono ezingacacanga
0	1	2	59. Uva izinto ezingekhoyo
0	1	2	60. Akathandi ukuzama izinto ezintsha

0 1 2   61. Wenza izinto engacingisisanga

0 1 2   62. Wenza izinto engancediswanga mntu

0 1 2   63. Uyawukhathalela umsebenzi wakhe wesikolo

0 1 2   64. Ucaphuka msinyane

0 1 2   65. Ufunda kakuhle kweli zinga akulo

0 1 2   66. Uyazazi izinto akwazi ukuzenza nangakwaziyo ukuzenza

0 1 2   67. Uhlala engavuyanga kungenasizathu

0 1 2   68. Unengxolo

0 1 2   69.Uyabathanda abanye abantwana

0 1 2   70. Isimo sengqondo yakhe sihlala sisesiso

0 1 2   71. Uyaphakuzela

0 1 2   72. Akonwabanga

0 1 2   73. Uyabelana nabanye abantwana xa kudlalwa

0 1 2   74. Abanye abantwana abamthandi

0 1 2   75. Akakwazi ukuhlala azole

0 1 2   76. Uhlala ediniwe

0 1 2   77. Utyebile

0 1 2   78. Uthanda ukulwa nabanye abantwana

0 1 2   79. Uthanda ukudlala kakhulu

0 1 2   80. Uchubekile

0 1 2   81. Akasebenzi kakuhle esikolweni

0 1 2   82. Umpathalala

0 1 2   83. Uthanda ukudlala eyedwa

0 1 2   84. Uthanda ukuba yedwa

0	1	2	85. Unengxaki emehlweni engafuni izipeksi
0	1	2	86. Kufanele kubekwe imithetho ukuze angagangi
0	1	2	87. Unengxaki ngolusu lwakhe
0	1	2	88. Akafuni ukuthetha kwezinye iindawo
0	1	2	89. Uphindaphinda ezinye zezinto azenzayo
0	1	2	90. Uyazicombulula iingxabano zakhe nemihlobo
0	1	2	91. Ulusizi
0	1	2	92. Uyarhixiza
0	1	2	93. Uneenhlebo ezizezakhe yedwa
0	1	2	94. Ucinga ukuba abanye bafuna ukumdicilela phansi
0	1	2	95. Ubona izinto ezingekhoyo
0	1	2	96. Uhlala ezijonga futhi uneenhloni
0	1	2	97. Uyaziqalela izinto engancediswa mntu
0	1	2	98. Uyabelana nabanye
0	1	2	99. Uyabakhathalela abantu abamngqongile
0	1	2	100. Uyahlekisa futhi wenza abanye abantu bahleke
0	1	2	101. Uneenhloni
0	1	2	102. Ujonga ndawoni nye ixesha elide
0	1	2	103. Uhlala kungathi ikhona into ayicingayo
0	1	2	104. Uthanda ukuqala imilwo
0	1	2	105. Wenza izinto ezingaqhelekanga
0	1	2	106. Unenkani
0	1	2	107. Isimo sengqondo yakhe siyaguquguquka
0	1	2	108. Uhlala ekhathazekile edonse ubuso bungakhululekanga

0 1 2   109. Akabathembi abanye abantu

0 1 2   110. Uthetha gqithi

0 1 2   111. Uhlekisa ngabanye abantwana

0 1 2   112. Unomsindo ongalawulekiyo

0 1 2   113. Usongela abanye abantu

0 1 2   114. Unoloyiko kakhulu

0 1 2   115. Uyazama ukuncedisa abanye abantu

0 1 2   116. Ungumntwana othembekileyo

0 1 2   117. Wenza izinto ngokucothayo

0 1 2   118. Uyagabha

0 1 2   119. Abanye abantwana abalingana naye bayamthanda

0 1 2   120. Uziphatha kakuhle esikolweni

0 1 2   121. Uyarhoxa xa kwenziwa izinto

0 1 2   122. Usebenza ngamandla

0 1 2   123. Usebenza kakuhle engancediswa ngabantu abadala

0 1 2   124. Uncanca usithupha wakhe

0 1 2   125. Wenza izinto ezimlimaza yena siqu njengokuzibethisa odongeni ngenhloko

0 1 2   126. Uhlala ekhathazekile

B.   Xa kuthelekiswa nabanye abantwana abalingana naye, U_____(Igama lomntwana)

0 1 2   127. Uyavana na nabantwana abalingana naye

1=Unotshe 2=Ngokulinganayo nabanye 3=Kangcono kunabanye

0 1 2   128. Uyavana nobhuti nosisi bakhe

1=Nakanye 2=Ngokulinganayo nabanye 3=Kangcono kunabanye

Household Economic and Social Status Index (HESSI)

(Barbarin, et al, 1995)
Who provided the information below_____)

I. Family Structure/Household Composition(Score 1-10)
Ia. Marital Status of Mother
 1. Never married, not now living with a partner
 2. Married, but not living now with a partner(e.g. divorced, separated)
 3. Widowed
 4. Never married, but now living with partner
 8. Married and currently living with partner

Ib. Household Membership. How many people currently reside in the household?_____
 Number 18 and older_____
 Number 6–18 yrs old _____
 Number under 6 yrs old _____

Ic. Are there adult relative now residing in the household? 0. No   2. Yes.
If yes who are they in relationship to the child?_____

II. Social Status- (Education, Occupation,[2–18])
A. Mother's Education: What is the highest level of education attained by mother?
 1. Less than Standard 3
 2. Primary School (Standard 3–4)
 3. Junior Secondary (Standard 5–7)
 4. Senior Secondary (Standard 8–9)
 5 Matric/High School graduate/vocational training diploma
 6. 1–2 yr College, Technikon
 7. 3–4 yrs of University
 8. Ph.D., M.D., J.D., D.D.S., or other doctoral degree

B. Education of Mother's Partner: What is the highest level of education attained?
 1. Less than Standard 3
 2. Primary School (Standard 3–4)
 3. Junior Secondary (Standard 5–7)
 4. Senior Secondary (Standard 8–9)
 5. Matric/High School graduate/vocational training diploma
 6. 1–2yr College, Technikon
 7. 3–4 yrs of University
 8. Ph.D., M.D., J.D., D.D.S., or other doctoral degree

What are the names, occupation and industry of the primary wage earners in the house?

Name	Occupation	Industry
1.		
2.		
3.		

Access to Finances Who in the family earns money? Check all that apply.

___BTT mother
___Partner
___Parent
___Parent Pension
___Sibling/Aunt/Uncle

III. **Housing Accommodation**. In what type of housing do you live?
   0. None, homeless
   1. Shack
   2. Hostel
   3. Room, garage
   4. Flat, cottage
   5. Home shared with other family(ies).
   6. Home that is not shared with other families.

B. Does your home have
1) A **Separate Kitchen?**   0. No   1. Yes
2) A **Separate Bathroom?** 0. No   1. Yes

a) In your home how many separate rooms are there just for sleeping?
(circle one number)   **0**   **1**   **2**   **3**   **4** or more.

b) What type of toilet facilities does your home have:
   0. None
   1. Pit or Bucket
   2. Outside flush toilet
   3. Inside flush

c) Do you own or rent a home.
   0. Neither
   1. Rent
   2. Purchasing on Bond
   3. Own

d) How much do you pay monthly for rent or bond? R_____.
For Service Charges R____

e) For Electricity:
(highest in the last year) R_____
(the lowest) R_____

Does the place you live in have a . . . ?

a)	Refrigerator	0. No	1. Yes
b)	Television	0. No	1. Yes
c)	Telephone	0. No	1. Yes
d)	Car	0. No	1. Yes
e)	Video recorder	0. No	1. Yes
f)	Washing machine	0. No	1. Yes
g)	Microwave oven	0. No	1. Yes

h) In the past, have your children gone hungry because you did not have food?:
3. No, never
2. Rarely
1. Often
0. All the time

Factor VI. **Savings**: (Score 0-3)
a) Do you have <u>savings</u> or
participate in a savings plan?   0. No   1. Yes
b) Do you have <u>life insurance</u>   0. No   1. Yes
(version 1/25/96)

<u>Maternal Well-being</u>
Do you have any problems you might like to talk over with a doctor?
0. No
1. Yes (specify)

During the past 3 months have you had any physical or emotional condition for which you have been receiving treatment or taking medication?
0. No
1. Yes (specify)

During the past 3 months Have you been anxious, worried or upset?
Extremely so—to the point of being sick or almost sick
Very much so
Quite a bit
Some—enough to bother me
A little bit
Not at all

During the past 3 months, have you felt so sad, discouraged, hopeless or had so many problems that you wondered if anything was worthwhile?

Extremely so—to the point that I have just about given up
Very much so
Quite a bit
Some—enough to bother me
A little bit
Not at all

In **any one year** have you had at least 12 drinks of any kind of alcoholic beverage? Yes No

Have you ever had any serious physical handicap? 0. No 1. Yes
Have you ever been a patient (or outpatient) at a mental hospital, mental health ward of a hospital, or a mental health clinic for any personal emotional, behavior, or mental problem?:

Yes, during the past year
Yes, more than a year ago
No

Neighborhood Safety
A. In general how safe is the area in which you live?
1. Extremely dangerous
2. Dangerous
3. Safe
4. Extremely Safe

B. How much do you worry about your child getting hurt when s/he is outside of your home?
1. Never
2. Sometimes
3. Often
4. All the time

Satisfaction with Family Life (Support)
My family has a lot of problems:
1. Not True 2. Sometimes True 3. Often True 4. Always True

My family is always there for me when I need them.
1. Not True 2. Sometimes True 3. Often True 4. Always True

Index

abuse: child, 86, 151–52, 170, 224, 253, 266, 273; criminal, 84; of women, 273; physical, 84, 86, 204; sexual, 86, 151, 170; spousal, 151, 204–205, 224; substance (see substance abuse); underreporting of, 152

academic: achievement, 103, 134, 178, 194, 250, 260; adjustment, 10, 177, 183, 256; performance, 178–79, 195, 255; underachievement, 13, 175, 177, 179, 216, 249, 260

adolescence, 103, 119, 134, 179, 194, 197, 230, 250

adolescents, 10, 127, 168, 205, 213, 231, 249, 267; pregancy and, 13, 22, 101, 144, 179, 224, 249, 251; sexuality and, 13, 22

adulthood, 119, 134, 179, 197, 207, 275

adults, 147, 177, 255, 257

affability, 166–68, 172, 192, 253, 257–58, 261

Africa, 5, 21–22, 109, 121, 123, 147, 179, 202, 223

African: physicians, 39; societies, 138, 143

African Americans, 142, 221–42, 244–45; social context of, 223–25

Africans, 26, 33, 39, 44–45, 48–50, 52–55, 57, 58, 63, 81, 123, 240, 247;

homeless, 27; Natal region, 29; poor, 61, 62; urban, 8, 16, 33

Afrikaans, 8, 27, 28, 30, 87, 192, 240

Afrikaner resistance, 81

aggression, 10, 109, 115, 120, 121, 125–26, 127, 128, 134, 164–65, 168, 175, 177, 182, 189–90, 196, 209, 212–13, 216–17, 221–22, 244–46, 249–50, 257 (see also behavior, aggression; children, aggressive; fighting)

AIDS, 12, 142, 144, 265, 273; and family life, 21–22; children with, 21–22, 146

alcoholism, 170, 224 (see also drug use; substance abuse)

alienation, 17, 18, 94, 203, 216

ANC (African National Congress), 27, 29–30, 70–73, 85, 269; government, 93

ancestors, 137, 161; care of, 123

antenatal care, 6, 99, 269

anxiety, 120, 121, 123, 126, 131, 220, 256; in children, 131–32, 134, 166–67, 175, 182, 186, 187, 189–90, 191, 202, 209, 213–14, 216–17, 218, 232–33, 234–35, 238, 242, 247, 249; separation, 188

apartheid (see also racism, institutionalized), 1, 13, 16, 18, 23n. 1, 25–41, 48, 63, 66, 72–73, 85, 87, 93, 102, 163, 239–41, 266, 275; black

of, 123; early, 9, 13, 41, 59, 97–116, 118, 194–95, 217, 230, 244, 248, 267, 271; later, 134–35, 194, 250

children, 5, 12, 16–18, 21, 30, 32, 36, 37, 47, 50, 56, 63, 68–70, 83, 95, 98, 131–33, 137, 143, 156, 173, 183, 244; adult, 144–46; African, 5, 14, 106–108, 109–110, 115, 123, 145, 157–58, 189; African-American, 112, 221–42, 244–45; aggressive, 124, 125–26, 127, 131–32 (see also aggression; behavior, aggressive); American, 106, 109, 110, 112, 115, 125; and risks (see risk factors); and the effects of violence (see violence, children and the effects of); anxious (see anxiety, in children); black, 7, 14, 105, 150; Canadian, 112; death of, 201; dependent, 147; depressed (see depression, children's); disease and (see disease); disobedient, 124–25; European, 112; fearful, 109, 111, 115, 128–29, 134–35, 163–64, 178, 184, 186–88, 187, 221, 244 (see also behavior, fearful; fears); feeding, 47, 183–85, 187 (see also feeding problems); financial support for, 60, 108, 156–58, 273; homeless, 22, 156; immature, 124, 127, 128, 194, 232, 234, 238; Indian, 108; malnourished, 106–108, 110, 115, 123, 158 (see also malnutrition); of African descent, 222; perpetrators of violence, 203; poor, 3, 13, 101–102, 124, 176–77, 180, 182, 183, 187, 195, 196, 198, 234, 239, 248, 252, 260, 268–70; preschool, 112, 127; problem, 123–28, 134–35, 183–85, 197; protecting from harm, 159–60; refugee, 202–203; resilient, 243–64; rights of, 12, 18, 19, 139, 169, 266–67; rural, 3, 105; separation from, 19, 36, 47; South African, 3, 12–13, 14, 68, 99, 106–108, 112, 114, 172, 187, 210, 221–42, 243, 247–48, 250, 252, 256, 265; Soweto, 112; special needs, 268; stability of

disorders in, 130–31; traumatized, 212–15; Ugandan, 221–42, 245; urban, 3, 106, 210; weight and height ratios of, 106–107, 115, 192, 247; welfare of, 152; white, 7; with AIDS, 21–22, 146; withdrawn, 124, 126–27, 128, 131–32, 194 (see also behavior, withdrawn; isolation); without grandmothers in homes, 165–67; young, 130–31, 187, 198, 201, 204, 231, 247, 257, 261, 265, 267, 269

children's: behavior (see behavior; behavioral); growth (see physical growth); health, 4, 63, 66, 103–112, 182, 267, 271–72, 275; needs, 140, 148, 155, 156, 158, 169, 258, 261, 265–78; well-being, 180

Chris Hani-Baragwanath Hospital, 34, 38, 101, 124, 188

Ciskei, 29, 31

clans, 138, 241, 259

class. See SES; social, class

clumsiness, 165, 184, 186, 187, 247

cognitive: development. See development, cognitive; functioning, 209, 215; skills, 253

cohabitation, 141, 152, 157–58

Coleman, J. S., 56

colonization, 26, 44, 65, 223

Color Bar, 29

Coloreds (see also South Africans, colored), 5, 7, 26, 28, 29–30, 31, 33, 38, 44–45, 48, 50–53, 57, 81, 107, 124, 240, 247

communication. See language

Communist Party, 29

community(ies): black, 40–41, 69, 70, 73, 93; danger, 74–75, 83, 90, 195, 207–208, 230, 246, 249–50, 260, 271, 273–76 (see also danger, ambient; safety); development, 271, 273; environment, 9, 195, 197–98, 203, 271–76; formal housing, 177; intervention, 268, 271–72; life, 4, 12, 14, 78, 97, 195, 197–99, 239; members, 152; poor, 248–49; rural, 17; safety, 13, 224, 227, 229, 266, 271–76;

squatter, 15, 33–34, 177; traditional African, 18; urban, 49, 248; violence (see violence, community)

competence: maternal, 136; personal, 121; social (see social competence); socioemotional, 129

concentration. See attention

conduct (see also behavior), 245; disorders, 125, 131, 134, 168, 196, 250; problems, 10, 175, 178, 196–97, 239, 248, 255

conflict resolution, 148, 151–52, 168, 211, 239, 258, 272

Constables, Kit, 73

consumer goods, 49, 60–62, 182, 183, 185–86, 191, 192

consumption, 50, 54, 56, 181, 182, 184, 190, 227, 247; household, 48–52; material, 60, 182, 190

Conventions on the Rights of the Child, 267

coping strategies, 209, 219, 241, 253, 256, 257, 260–61, 275

crime, 14, 17, 65, 81–83, 86, 87–89, 93–95, 134, 191, 197–98, 203, 215, 224, 230, 249, 266, 272–73, 275 (see also murder; rape; robberies; victimization; violence); data, 88–89; juvenile, 179, 224, 249 (see also juvenile, problems); prevention, 272–76; property, 89; reported, 92; urban, 89; violent, 88–89, 92; vulnerability to, 93

Crime Information Management Centre (CIMC), 88–89

crying. See behavior, crying

cultural: mores and traditions, 12, 160–61, 258; resources, 14, 56, 155, 160–62, 259; values, 19, 137, 156, 161–62, 168, 258

cultural contexts, 98, 109, 121–22, 221; African, 121–28

danger: ambient, 206–209, 210, 216–17, 219, 249 (see also community, danger; safety)

daughters, 144–45, 169

death, 203, 208, 217

debt, 54–55, 58, 152, 173; and wealth, 53–54; repayment, 54

delinquency, 13, 127, 131, 175, 177 (see also juvenile, problems)

democracy (see also elections), 31, 63; black-majority-ruled, 240; multiracial, 14, 19, 29, 32, 40–41, 223

Denver Developmental Scales II, 10, 11

dependency ratio, 147–48, 167, 170, 229

depression, 120 (see also behavior, depressive); children's, 120, 121, 123, 131–32, 135, 166, 172, 175, 178, 182, 187, 189–90, 191, 209, 213–15, 217, 218, 232, 235, 238, 242, 249–51; maternal, 10, 101, 196, 220, 250, 256, 261

developing countries, 39, 108, 124, 241

development: behavioral, 112, 120, 181, 222, 232, 243, 247, 255; child (see child development); cognitive, 98, 174, 176, 177, 195; cross-national perspective on, 221–42; emotional, 98, 112, 118, 120, 177, 181, 194–95, 222, 232, 243, 247, 255; neurological, 133, 188, 194, 246, 250; neuromuscular, 109–112, 119, 244, 248 (see also motor skills); normal, 119, 135–36, 188, 201, 243–44; physical (see physical, development; physical growth); psychological, 9, 13, 59, 97–116, 181, 183–92, 193, 198, 231, 241; psychosocial, 9, 13, 59, 97–116, 183–92, 211, 221, 232, 234, 243, 250, 256; social, 98, 108, 112–13, 119–20, 177, 194, 219, 221–42, 245, 247, 249; socioeconomic, 162, 258; socioemotional, 117–21, 127, 155–72

developmental: delays, 98, 110, 113, 115, 127, 203; deviations, 132–33; milestones, 110, 115, 128, 136, 210; needs, 266–67; problems, 164, 183–85, 251; regressions, 209, 210–12, 216, 249; risk factors (see risk factors); stages, 18; tasks, 210

developmental outcomes, 4, 13, 57, 59, 117, 133–34, 167–68, 170, 176, 181–82, 189, 194, 218–19, 222, 231, 249, 251, 252, 255–56, 267; poor, 4, 175, 218, 221, 252

discipline, 196, 239, 257

disease, 14, 15, 35, 52, 99, 174, 178; infectious, 38, 107, 201, 243

disobedience, 124–25, 128, 221, 233, 244 (see also behavior)

divorce, 13, 139, 149

domestics, 16, 36, 101, 176, 254 (see also employment; mothers; women)

drug use, 87, 94, 230 (see also alcoholism; substance abuse)

DSM (Diagnostic and Statistical Manual of Mental Disorders), 125

Dube, Reverend John, 29

Duncan, G., K. Brooks-Gunn, and P. K. Klebanov, 175

Dutch East India Company, 26

economic: hardship, 94, 176, 191, 195 (see also material hardship); status, 53–54, 56, 58–59, 193–94, 199n. 16, 239 (see also SES)

economy: apartheid, 39–40; informal, 46, 57–58; South African, 30, 32–33, 39; wage-based cash, 46; whites-only, 29, 33

education, 10, 14–15, 18, 25–26, 39, 52, 56–58, 139, 147, 173, 182, 224, 231, 247–48, 267, 269–71; adult, 182; compulsory, 271; costs of, 173; early termination of, 179, 224, 230, 249; level of, 56–57, 62, 182, 183; maternal, 3, 59–60, 136, 184–86, 188, 190, 192, 193, 195, 225–26, 261; parents', 181–82

elderly, the, 143–44, 148, 170 (see also grandmothers; grandparents)

Elders, Joycelyn, 230

elections, 40–41, 223 (see also democracy)

emotional: development, 13, 59, 98, 118, 120, 156, 207, 243; disorders,

9–10, 113, 123, 133, 175, 183, 187–88, 192, 193; functioning, 150, 178, 208, 244; problems, 10, 136, 191, 198, 215, 221, 225, 229, 231–32, 238–39, 241, 244, 247, 256, 257, 259; regulation (see self-regulation, emotional); support, 219, 257

empathy, 178, 203, 206, 274

employment (see also labor), 14, 17, 18, 19, 25, 26, 37, 39, 52, 57, 58, 66, 85, 93, 144, 174, 183, 191, 247–48; adult, 62; men's, 142–43; women's, 21, 101, 141, 225 (see also domestics; mothers; women)

English, 147

Entwistle, D. R., and N. M. Astone, 56

environmental pollution, 15, 60, 174, 188, 224, 238, 250

equality, 94; social, 41, 275

ethnic: conflict (see interethnic conflict); culture, 136; diversity, 22; groups, 33, 72, 124, 223, 229, 231, 241, 259; identity, 56, 162, 229, 231, 241–42, 258, 259

ethnicity, 160

Europe, 109, 147, 202, 222, 266

expenditures, 56, 61, 63n. 4, 158–59

externalizing disorders, 10, 134, 175, 178, 198

families, 3–5, 7, 11, 12, 14, 15, 17–18, 21, 44, 49, 52, 54–55, 56, 58–59, 71, 86, 88, 117, 137–38, 152, 156, 171, 182, 191, 193, 198, 201, 220, 225, 243, 247, 252–55, 258, 265, 267–68; adaptive, 243–64; African, 22, 55, 141, 143, 147–48, 150–51, 158, 161; African-American, 229; and modernization, 18–19; apartheid and, 36–38; black, 17, 21, 40, 142, 143, 156, 158–59; dysfunctional, 137, 230; forced removal of, 26, 32, 93; men's roles in, 141–42; of workers, 36, 142; poor, 44, 53, 55, 62, 194, 269; resilient, 253–55, 257–58; South African, 17, 19, 54, 123, 147, 151–53, 169, 241; traditional struc-

ture of, 18, 22; urban, 22, 161, 268–69
Family: Court System, 273; Relations Scale, 156
family: advocates, 273; and social transformation, 17–22; cohesion, 150–51, 170, 224, 241, 257–58; composition, 13, 22, 38, 156, 163, 228, 231, 255–57; conflict resolution, 151–52, 257; effect on child development, 133, 162–63, 167; endangerment, 78, 217; extended, 22, 35, 37, 50, 137, 140–41, 142–43, 148–49, 156–57, 159, 160, 165, 170, 195, 240, 255, 257; functioning, 9, 12, 58, 113, 139, 148, 150, 156, 162, 166, 219, 255, 256, 259; influences on children, 155–72; life, 9, 14, 19–22, 65, 78, 84, 97, 100, 113, 136, 139, 140–41, 148–53, 156, 162–63, 167–69, 174, 176, 195, 202, 205, 221–22, 234–38, 239, 250–51, 257, 259, 261, 265–68; members, 56, 84, 137, 140, 151, 159, 202, 219; nuclear, 137–38, 148–49, 156–57, 165; privacy, 148, 152–53, 167–68; relations, 11, 14, 18, 21, 137–54, 156, 167, 241, 257–59; roles, 14, 19, 170; stability, 133, 224; structure, 12, 13, 32, 36–38, 56, 59, 139, 153, 170–71, 195, 202, 218, 231–32, 239, 255–57; task performance, 140–48, 155–57, 163, 167, 168–69, 197, 255; units, 139, 143, 146, 148; violence (see violence, family); well-being, 58; wife's, 140–41
famine, 106
fathers (see also husbands; male partners; men), 8, 60, 100, 119, 126, 143, 145–46, 157–58, 174, 191–92, 226–27, 229, 260; absent, 142, 143, 188; biological, 60, 141, 156, 157, 170, 225; involvement in child rearing, 142, 170; role of, 162; with AIDS, 21
fear(s), 206–207, 209, 212–15, 221, 257, 260 (see also behavior, fearful), fearful; children

fearful children. See children, fearful
feeding problems, 183–85, 187, 193, 208–209, 211–12, 216, 249 (see also children, feeding)
fighting, 128–29, 151, 163–66, 168, 188–89, 191, 257 (see also aggression; behavior, aggressive)
food, 50–51, 55, 56, 58–60, 106, 138, 146, 155–57, 167, 179, 180–81, 203; security, 158–59, 172, 199n. 16, 250, 259; shortages, 106, 194 (see also malnutrition)
Free Maternal and Child Health, 269
funerals, 55, 174, 198 (see also burials)
funnel of causality, 102

gangs, 65–67, 87, 94–95, 203, 207, 224, 230, 251
Gauteng province, 4, 88–89, 151
Gazankulu, 31
gender: and social development, 112–13, 239; differences, 112–13, 232–39; equality, 18; identity, 56; roles, 12, 19, 229
girls, 112–13, 231, 233–34, 238–39
Glen Gray Act, 26, 27
Government of National Unity, 30
grandchildren, 145–46, 170
grandmothers (see also elderly, the), 21, 138, 143, 149–50, 153, 161–63, 170, 173–74; as caregivers and surrogate parents, 144–47; in the home, 157–59, 159–50, 161, 165–67, 170, 226–27, 229, 255, 257
grandparents (see also elderly, the), 21–22, 38, 57, 148, 149–50, 153, 163, 170, 260; reliance on, 143–46
Groener, Dev, 274
Group Areas Act, 30, 31–33
growth. See development; physical growth
guerilla: attacks, 69; tactics, 87

Hammen, C., and K. D. Rudolph, 175
hardship: acute, 178–79, 243; chronic, 178–79; material (see also economic hardship), 14, 15, 18, 19,

maternal: age, 99, 101; competence, 136; coping, 216–17, 218–19, 260–61; depression (see depression, maternal); education (see education, maternal); emotional well-being, 99–100, 217–18; functioning, 216–17, 219; health, 267; mortality, 52; responsiveness, 10, 11; stress, 100; traditional roles, 22
maturation, 103, 178, 193, 244
Mbeke, President Thabo, 272
McKendrick, G., and W. Senoamadi, 216
McLoyd, V., 195
Medical Research Council of South Africa, 4
men (see also fathers; husbands; male partners), 60, 67, 92, 141, 142; attrition of, 142; employed, 142–43; role of in families, 141–42, 153; unemployed, 19, 142–43, 158, 170
mental health, 123, 128; problems, 123, 175; services, 270
migrant workers, 32, 33, 47, 141–42, 170
migration (see also rural-to-urban migration), 31, 94; of women, 100, 141–42
Mitchell, Brian Victor, 72
modernity, 12, 14, 18–19, 22, 143
modernization, 97, 139, 153, 163, 169–70, 265
Moletsane, 84
mood disturbances, 13, 177, 216
morbidity, 13, 47, 52, 108, 177, 224 (see also child, morbidity)
mortality, 13, 47, 52, 101, 102, 177, 224, 243 (see also child, mortality)
motherhood, 144, 166 (see also mothers)
mothers, 6, 7, 8, 10, 53–54, 56, 58–60, 68, 92, 101–102, 109, 119, 145, 151, 153, 156, 160, 161, 185, 188, 191–92, 208–209, 218–20, 260, 270 (see also motherhood); African, 150; African-American, 142; biological, 136, 158, 187, 225, 260; blaming, 218; death of, 202; divorced,

149–50, 152–53, 157, 161, 226; educational level of (see education, maternal); employed, 225–26 (see also domestics; employment; women); marital status of, 138, 149, 163–64, 225–26; married, 152, 157, 226; poor, 183; single, 59, 62, 110, 142–43, 145, 158, 163, 166–67, 173, 196, 231; teen, 101–102; unemployed, 110, 188; unmarried, 141, 149, 157, 159, 163–64, 169, 231; well-being of, 99–100, 217, 220, 248; widowed, 152, 157, 161; with AIDS, 21; with partners, 60, 62, 141, 149–50, 152, 156–58, 165, 231, 255; without partners, 60, 149–50, 152–53, 156–57, 159, 164, 169, 224, 226; young, 101, 144–45
motor skills, 13, 103, 109, 127, 182, 183–84, 186, 193, 194, 209, 211, 244, 248, 250 (see also development, neuromuscular)
Mtshali, Oswald: Give Us a Break, 68
murder, 78, 88–89, 95, 202, 230 (see also crime)
mutual obligation systems, 18, 137, 258
mutuality, 138, 258

Naledi, 84
Natal, 29, 76; Native Congress, 27
National: Center for Health Statistics, 225, 232; Crime Prevention Strategy, 272; ECD Pilot Project, 271; Party, 26, 27, 29–30; Programme of Action for Chidren in South Africa (NPA), 267; Strategy on Child Abuse and Neglect, 273
Native Land Act, 27, 29
neighborhoods. See community
newborns, 5, 101–102, 109 (see also infants)
NHIS-CHS, 225, 232
nonviolence, 66
nurturing, 163, 241, 255, 267
nutrition, 3, 46, 99, 105–107, 179, 259, 267–68

occupation, 56–58, 184; head of household, 59; status, 57, 61–62, 181, 182, 185–86, 188, 190, 191, 192, 193, 248

oppositional defiant behavior. See behavior, oppositional

oppression, 1, 95; black, 25; political, 66; racial, 87, 224

optimism, 253, 257, 259, 261

Orange Free State, 29

orphans, 22

PAGAD (People Against Gangs and Drugs), 87

parental roles, 145, 151, 229, 241

parenting, 101, 133, 146, 162, 195, 196–97, 250, 256, 258, 261

parents, 3, 8, 11, 19, 30, 38, 50, 57, 59, 67, 69, 78, 87, 108, 109, 115, 119, 124, 126, 128–29, 140–41, 142, 145–46, 150, 162, 168, 194–95, 197–98, 211, 213, 221, 223, 225, 241, 245, 258, 260–61, 267, 271, 273; -child attachment, 133, 150, 168, 196, 213, 259; -child separations, 150, 213; African, 242; African-American, 242; aging, 144; biological, 59, 137, 146, 150; death of, 68, 173, 202, 214, 217; distress and, 195; divorced, 149; poor, 177–78; single, 21, 139, 195, 231, 239; social status of, 133; South African, 14, 118, 123–24, 127, 230, 240, 242; surrogate, 144–47; violence and, 208, 214; well-being of, 198, 256, 261; widowed, 149; working, 37

Paschall, M. J., and M. L. Hubbard, 217

Patterson, Debaryshe, and Ramsey, 131

peace, 63, 65, 86, 266

Peterson, Hector, 28, 67

physical: abuse, 84, 86; development, 98, 176, 247; harm, 201, 204, 218–19; safety, 67, 90, 151, 198, 255, 267

physical growth, 9, 10, 13, 47, 59, 97–98, 103–108, 114, 190, 194, 225, 248, 250, 257; and social development, 97–116; catch-up, 108, 111; rates of, 105–106

Pitt Depression Inventory, 10, 101

police (see also South African Police), 67, 69, 70–74, 79, 87, 204, 273; black, 73

Police Riot Unit, 73

political: dissent, 65; empowerment, 14; reforms, 19, 40–41, 68, 265; transformation, 4, 12–14, 22, 97, 265–66; violence. See violence, political

poll tax, 27

poor, the, 41, 61, 86, 95, 152, 173, 180, 196, 234

population groups, 7, 44, 47, 53; black, 48, 52

Population Registration Act, 27

poverty, 1–2, 5, 12, 15, 16, 17, 39, 41, 54, 58, 63, 64, 97, 99, 101, 106, 108, 113, 133, 136, 144, 152, 155, 159, 170, 172, 179–82, 199, 210, 221–23, 224, 226, 228, 229, 231, 238–40, 242, 243, 246, 247–48, 249, 250–53, 255–56, 258, 260, 267, 268–69, 274, 275; acute, 178–79; among blacks, 58; and family life, 234–38; and social competence, 177–78; as food insecurity, 46–47; as restricted access to financial capital, 52–56; assessment of, 182, 183; child development and, 173–200, 239–40, 247–48, 250; chronic, 178–79; consequences of, 179, 181, 189, 193; defining, 43–47; extreme, 45–46; income-based, 43–46, 179, 193, 199n. 16; indicators, 47–56, 183; rates, 44–45, 49, 205, 224, 228; reduction programs, 180, 182; rural, 14, 15, 43; urban, 43–64

pregnancy and birth, 99–103, 225; teen, 13, 22, 101, 144, 179, 224, 249, 251 (see also juvenile, problems); unwanted, 100 premature: births, 100, 102, 114–15, 174; childbearing, 13, 22, 144; self-care and self-reliance, 177; sexuality, 13, 22, 177

prenatal care. See antenatal care

privacy, 148, 152–53

psychological: adjustment, 103, 113, 121, 127, 215, 238, 241, 247; development (see development, psychological); disorders, 123, 175, 177, 189–90, 191–92, 194; distress, 112, 205, 209; health, 123, 134

psychosocial: development (see development, psychosocial); functioning, 174, 231, 232–33

PTSD (post-traumatic stress disorder), 209–10, 212–15, 216, 249 (see also stress)

public: health, 30, 38; hospitals, 88; policy, 180, 265–66; safety, 67; transportation, 85; welfare, 92

Pynoos, R. S., 205

quality of life, 83, 181

Qwaqwa, 29, 31

race, 6, 53

racial: classification, 30; hegemony, 29; inequality, 13, 26, 32, 39, 97; segregation, 25–26, 30

racism, 3, 9, 11, 12, 14, 19, 26, 32, 38, 41, 99, 163, 169–70, 199, 221, 243, 246, 256, 258, 267; institutional, 25–41, 63, 224, 240 (see also apartheid)

Ramphele, Mamphela: A Bed Called Home, 142

rape, 88–89, 95, 251 (see also crime)

Reconstruction and Development Plan, 269

refugees, 202–203

regression analysis, 190

regulation. See self-regulation

relationships: family, 137–54; interpersonal, 249; intimate, 119, 204; quality of, 138–39, 148–53, 255, 258; social, 17, 37, 118, 206

relgious beliefs and practices, 161–62, 258, 261 (see also spirituality)

remittances, 50–51

resilience, 5, 136, 160, 162, 166–67, 170, 172, 189–90, 192, 241, 243–64

resistance. See apartheid, resistance against

resources, 49, 54, 56, 59, 98, 118, 168, 175, 199n. 16, 219, 253, 255, 259, 275; community, 259, 267; coping (see coping strategies); cultural, 14, 56, 155, 160–62, 242, 255–56, 258–59, 260, 267; economic, 49; family, 204, 218–20, 242, 255, 267; financial, 49, 56, 144–45, 152, 155, 158–59, 181, 193, 231; household, 158, 180; human, 182, 185; material, 48–49, 56, 59, 67, 138–39, 155, 180–81, 185–86, 250, 268; psychological, 56, 155; social, 56, 195, 204, 218–19, 250, 253, 256, 258

Reynolds, Pamela: Childhood in Crossroads, 139

Riebeek, Van, 26

rights: childrens', 12, 18, 19, 139, 169, 266–67; human, 31, 71–72, 76

Riotous Assemblies Act, 27

risk factors, 5, 41, 99, 133, 193, 195, 217, 238–39, 253, 260, 275; biological, 135; cross-national effects of, 231–32; developmental, 133; gender as a, 231, 239–40; in pregnancy, 101; poverty, 239–40, 247–48 (see also poverty); social, 4, 12–13, 132–33, 135–36, 163–64, 221–22, 229–32, 238, 250–52, 253, 255, 268, 271, 275; violence, 229–30, 248–50

robberies, 81–82, 86, 90, 95 (see also crime)

Robertson, B., 210

rural: -to-urban migration (see also migration), 14, 16–17, 19, 94; society, 37, 137; South Africa, 101–102

Rutter, M., and N. Garmezy, 212

SADF (South African Defense Force), 69
sadness, 128, 187, 212–14, 216, 232–33, 238, 242, 258
safety (see also security), 156, 167, 169, 172; citizens', 81, 273–76; community (see community, safety); of enviornment, 201; personal, 67, 92; physical, 67, 90, 159, 198, 214; public, 67, 94, 223; threats to, 206, 216
Samaroff, A., 136
savings, 55–56, 60, 173, 191, 227–28
school readiness, 189–90, 248, 271
schooling. See education
schools, 16, 29, 87, 193–94, 198, 203, 250, 258, 269–70; -parent partnerships, 269; compulsory education and, 271; private, 270; protests, 28, 67, 69, 87 (see also apartheid, resistance to); public, 270; urban, 198
security (see also safety): financial, 141; forces, 87; laws, 26
segregation (see also apartheid, social ppolicies of): laws, 32; territorial, 26, 224
self-confidence, 192
self-efficacy, 253, 259
self-esteem, 233–34, 257
self-regulation, 103, 113, 119–20, 128, 131, 160–61, 182, 186, 193, 195, 218, 238, 244, 275; and socioemotional development, 117–21; behavioral, 99, 112, 117–36, 174, 182, 221, 245, 248; biological, 210, 244; cross-cultural relevance of, 121–22; development of, 129, 134–35, 136, 209; difficulties in, 118, 123–24, 133–34, 164, 239; emotional, 13, 99, 117–36, 174, 182, 219, 241, 245, 256, 260; of attention, 112, 117–36
Senaoane, 84
SES (socioeconomic status), 9, 11, 53–54, 56, 58–62, 102, 133, 136, 175, 177, 181, 222, 228, 231–32, 239 (see also economic, class), status; social
Sesotho, 8

settlements: formal, 47, 215 (see also community, formal); informal, 15, 159, 210, 215; squatter, 15, 33–34, 176
sexual: abuse (see abuse, sexual); behavior (see behavior, sexual)
sexual activity, 18; teen, 22, 177
shantytowns. See settlements
shelter. See housing
siblings, 136, 142, 148, 231
Sithole, Oupa, 69
slums, 16–17
smoking, 10, 127
social: adaptation, 121, 178, 183; class, 7, 226, 228 (see also SES); context, 13, 121, 162, 253; control, 66, 143, 196, 273–74; development (see development, social); distance, 205–206; equality (see equality, social); functioning, 127, 208, 242; inequality (see inequality, social); maturity, 10, 103; networks, 100, 160, 162, 258; policies, 220, 223, 266, 267–71; relations, 17, 37, 118, 150, 177, 205, 206, 245; risks (see risk factors, social); status, 56–60, 199n. 16 (see also SES); stress, 22, 153; support, 9–10, 56–58, 112, 150, 162, 258–59; withdrawal, 152–53, 167–68, 206
social competence, 9, 10, 11, 99, 103, 118, 167–69, 178, 189–90, 192, 194–95, 206, 232–33, 234, 244, 248, 255–56, 257, 259, 261; and poverty, 177–88, 183
social development and physical growth, 97–116
social environment, 112, 137–38, 218, 242, 246, 250, 275; and child development, 3–4, 112, 133, 135, 247–48
social transformation, 1–24, 41, 93, 265–66; and the family, 17–22, 93, 171
social welfare, 224, 267–69, 271; system, 39
socialization, 13, 60, 66, 119, 121, 138, 140, 142, 145, 151, 153,

155–56, 160–62, 168, 196, 198, 202, 229, 238, 241, 255–56, 259–60

somatic complaints, 120, 121, 123, 131, 210, 249, 257

Sothos, 72, 124, 140

South Africa, 2, 7, 8, 12, 14, 18, 22, 28, 29, 33, 40–41, 44–47, 55, 57, 58–59, 67, 81, 93–95, 97, 100–102, 105–106, 108, 109, 120, 123, 143, 148, 150, 156, 201–202, 210, 222–23, 224, 229, 231, 241, 248–49, 252, 265–72, 274–75; child development in, 1–25; institutional racism in, 25–41; poverty in, 173–74, 180–82, 183–92, 221; rural, 101; social transformation in, 1–25; urban, 145, 156, 224; violence in, 65–80, 83, 204; white, 30

South African: black majority status, 58, 229, 231–32, 240, 265; citizenship, 31, 40; conceptions of child adjustment, 123–28; Department of Education, 270–71; gross national product, 32–33, 39; Institute of Race Relations (SAIRR), 79, 88–89; Police, 71–73, 89 (see also police); Schools Act, 270; society, 25, 41, 95, 133, 229, 247

South Africans, 1, 19, 26, 41, 43–44, 49, 52, 63, 65, 67, 78, 83, 91–92, 94, 106, 128, 147, 151, 221–42, 223, 243, 245, 265–66, 274–75; black, 29, 32, 92, 94, 107–108, 169, 178, 228, 232 (see also blacks); colored, 31, 92, 107–108 (see also coloreds); indian, 31, 107–108 (see also indians); whites, 92, 94, 107 (see also whites)

Soweto, 1, 4, 5, 6, 15, 23n. 3, 27, 28, 30, 34–36, 38, 67–68, 71, 74, 88–89, 100, 101, 102, 124, 125, 188, 201, 202, 206–208, 227, 245, 251; creation of, 33–34

spirituality, 156–57, 161–63, 167, 197, 218–19, 242, 255–56, 257, 258–59 (see also religious beliefs and practices)

spousal abuse. See abuse, spousal

standard of living, 9, 13, 15, 41, 47–56, 58–60, 63, 180–82, 190, 193–94, 199n. 16, 202, 228, 247, 268, 275; black, 39; importance of children's, 174–82, 183–92; poor, 58, 61, 174, 205

stokvels, 152

stress (see also PTSD), 9, 15, 177, 198, 211–12, 219, 253, 255, 259, 260–61; -related symptoms, 177; diathesis model, 194; environmental, 163; family, 217, 250; maternal, 100, 260; social, 22, 258

student protests, 28, 67, 69, 87 (see also apartheid, resistance to)

stunted growth, 11, 100, 108, 174

stunting, 106–107, 115, 243, 247

substance abuse, 13, 100–101, 127, 131, 134, 142, 174, 176, 179, 224, 249 (see also alcoholism; substance abuse)

suburbs, 79, 94

Suppression of Communism Act, 27, 28

Swaziland, 123

taxi: associations, 85; conflict, 85, 94

temper tantrums, 109, 111, 125–26, 127, 129, 165, 215, 233, 245–46, 255

temperament. See child, temperament of

Terreblanche, Captain, 72

toddlers, 111, 118, 129, 134–35, 155, 201

torture, 70, 73, 203

townships, 23n. 3, 66, 70, 87; black, 15, 33, 69, 89, 94, 138, 224; living conditions in, 15–16; South African, 158; urban, 14, 15

traditional values and practices, 22, 137, 197, 241, 259

Transkei, 28, 31; Constitution Act, 28

Transvaal, 29

trauma, 194, 201, 203, 207, 209–10, 212–15, 216–17, 218, 250

Truth and Reconciliation

Commission (TRC), 72–73, 78, 100
Tswanas, 124

Ubuntu, 256, 258
Uganda, 221–42; children in, 221–42, 245; Kampala, 223, 227, 229; social context in, 222–23
Ugandan Ministry of Education, 223
Ugandans, 221–42
underemployment, 13, 62
unemployment, 17, 46, 55, 62, 81–82, 86, 100–101, 144, 155, 156, 173, 179, 182, 188, 191; black, 32, 58, 87, 148, 224, 265; male, 19, 142–43, 158, 170
United Democratic Front, 72
United Nations: Coventions on the Rights of the Child, 169, 267
United States, 59, 101–102, 221, 229, 231; African Americans in the, 142, 221–42, 244–45; children in, 105–106, 109, 115, 174, 221–42, 244–46, 270; crime in, 89, 92; Department of Health and Human Services, 225; poverty in the, 179, 240; social contexts in the, 222–23; urban areas in, 94, 224, 230
University Education Act, 28
urban: centers, 15, 43, 87, 92, 94, 106, 201–202, 229; environments, 99, 198; legends, 81–82; life, 16, 18, 152; migration, 14, 16–17, 19; poverty, 43–64; society, 14, 47
Urban Influx Control Act, 27, 30
urbanization, 3, 12, 13, 14–18, 22, 32, 97, 103, 163, 169–70, 224, 255, 256, 259, 265; and family life, 19–203; stressors of, 153
Urbanization and Health Program, 4

values: cultural (see cultural, values); family, 157; socializing, 160–62, 260; spiritual, 156, 197; transmission of, 160
Venda, 29, 31
victimization, 17, 74–75, 81, 84, 90, 91–92, 198, 203, 206–209, 208–209, 211–12, 215, 216–17, 249 (see also crime; violence)
victims, 205, 273; blame of, 199, 218–20
vigilante groups, 71, 83, 87, 94
Viktor, J. J., 73
Vineland Social Maturity Scale, 10, 11
violence (see also crime; murder; rape; robbery; victimization), 9, 12, 13, 17, 41, 67, 76–77, 79, 83–85, 88–89, 92–94, 99, 136, 142, 151–52, 163–64, 172, 197, 216, 222–23, 224, 229–30, 239, 246, 248–52, 255–56, 258–59, 260, 266–67, 275; acts of, 81, 151, 230; against citizens, 76, 78; ambient, 81–84, 204, 206, 217, 218–20; and social distance, 205–206; children and the effects of, 67–68, 94, 95, 163, 198, 201–20, 261; chronic, 206–209, 215–16; community, 9, 11, 12, 14, 19, 74–75, 81–96, 97, 155, 174, 176, 204–206, 208, 211–12, 216–17, 218–20, 221, 251, 260, 272; criminal, 65, 86, 92, 101, 201, 204, 239, 249, 272; cross-ethnic, 67, 70–72; directly experienced, 78, 90, 204, 206, 208, 216, 249, 250; distal, 216, 249; exposure to, 198, 203–204, 206–209, 215, 248, 252, 271; family, 66–67, 74–75, 78, 81–96, 101, 151–52, 170, 204–206, 208, 211–12, 216–17, 224, 249, 257, 271–72; forms of, 13, 249; frequency of, 92–93; gang, 65–66; government, 66, 68, 70–73, 76; government task force on, 272–73; in South Africa, 65–80, 83; incidents of, 79, 84, 90, 206, 208; locus of, 204, 208; long-term effects of, 209–10; political, 14, 67, 68–79, 81, 84, 85, 86, 88, 90, 92, 94–95, 101, 159, 204–205, 208, 211–12, 214, 216, 249, 266, 272; proximal, 216–17, 249; psycholgical functioning and, 209–10; random acts of, 86, 142, 201, 230; reported by mothers, 78–79; stories about,

81–82; types of, 67, 78, 204, 209, 216–17; victims of, 205, 208–209, 211–12, 216–17, 249; witnessing of, 78, 90, 198, 202, 205, 206, 208, 213, 217; youth-related, 81, 87–88, 93

Vlakplaas, 73

wage earners: male, 48; primary, 57, 60–61, 188, 191, 248

war, 203, 206, 223

wealth, 54–55, 60, 181–82, 183, 188, 191, 227–28, 275; accumulation, 55; and debt, 53

weight and height ratios. See children, weight and height ratios of

welfare: grants, 268–69; policy, 268–69; social, 224, 267–69, 271; state, 39

Werner, E., and R. Smith, 179

West Junior Secondary School, 28

Western: concepts of psychological and social adaptation, 121–22, 127–28; societies, 137, 140, 221–22

whites (see also South Africans, white), 16, 26, 29–30, 31, 36, 38, 39, 44–46, 48–54, 56, 57, 58, 63, 68, 79, 82, 86, 88, 92, 94–95, 107, 158–59, 223, 224, 240; employers, 67; flight of, 16; hegemony, 26, 33, 65, 223; privilege, 25; retribution against, 95; suburbs, 16, 33, 37, 94; towns, 31; universities, 31

women, 21, 47, 60, 67, 86, 92, 99, 140–41, 197, 271; abuse of, 273; African, 115, 143; autonomy of, 141; black, 101–102; employed, 21, 141, 143 (see also domestics; employment; mothers); importance having children to, 143; married, 141, 152; migration of, 100; opportunities for, 19; rural, 101; single, 145; South African, 10; urban, 100; white, 102

World: Bank, 271; Health Organization, 106; War II, 106

Xhosas, 70, 72, 124

Yeoville, 16

Zulus, 70–72, 86, 124, 140, 147, 161–62